Thinking Queer

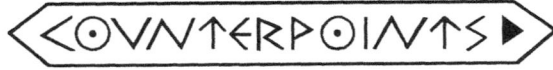

Studies in the
Postmodern Theory of Education

Joe L. Kincheloe and Shirley R. Steinberg
General Editors

Vol. 118

PETER LANG

New York • Washington, D.C./Baltimore • Boston • Bern
Frankfurt am Main • Berlin • Brussels • Vienna • Oxford

Thinking Queer

Sexuality, Culture, and Education

Edited by
Susan Talburt and
Shirley R. Steinberg

PETER LANG
New York • Washington, D.C./Baltimore • Boston • Bern
Frankfurt am Main • Berlin • Brussels • Vienna • Oxford

Library of Congress Cataloging-in-Publication Data

Thinking queer: sexuality, culture, and education /
edited by Susan Talburt and Shirley R. Steinberg.
p. cm. — (Counterpoints; vol. 118)
Includes bibliographical references and index.
1. Homosexuality and education. 2. Education—Social aspects.
3. Gays—Identity. 4. Lesbians—Identity. I. Talburt, Susan.
II. Steinberg, Shirley R. III. Counterpoints (New York, N.Y.); vol. 118.
LC192.6.T55   306.76'6—dc21   99-053017
ISBN 978-0-8204-4521-2
1058-1634

Bibliographic information published by **Die Deutsche Nationalbibliothek**.
Die Deutsche Nationalbibliothek lists this publication in the "Deutsche
Nationalbibliografie"; detailed bibliographic data are available
on the Internet at http://dnb.d-nb.de/.

Cover design by Lisa Dillon

© 2000, 2015 Peter Lang Publishing, Inc., New York
29 Broadway, 18th floor, New York, NY 10006
www.peterlang.com

Table of Contents

Preface: Getting Here

Shirley R. Steinberg

In this era of scholarly phrases, it is impossible to write a line without incanting the usual litany from border crossings to identity politics. As I am firmly ensconced in this era of scholarspeak, I will continue the tradition without too much of an apology. What a pleasure to write a preface for a collection of essays designed both to cross borders and to investigate identity. This collection was created to name, dename, and interrogate concepts of queerness and nonqueerness in pedagogy and cultural studies. Susan and I invited our authors to contribute to this volume as a voice in the evolving field of queer theory and as the continuation of a new voice in the field of education—teaching students to teach, teaching teachers to teach.

As we chose our authors, we looked for queer work by people queer, unqueer, or moderately queer who had something to say to these intersecting disciplines. What is queer theory? What is queerness? How do we name it, define it, find it? More important, how does this emerging discourse contribute to issues of pedagogy and social justice? The only answer I have thus far is that it is bigger than a breadbox.

In my local newspaper column I recently mentioned an incident of homophobia vis-à-vis one of my son's queer friends. An outraged reader objected to my use of the "offensive" word queer, and felt that his own homosexual ex-roommate ("some of my best friends" rhetoric reborn) would indeed be insulted if referred to as "a queer." As my dear brother Nelson Rodriguez always insists: "We're here, we're queer, get over it." I make no apologies for using queer or being queer. Queer is a noun and an adjective. It is a wonderful, expressive, multidimensional word. This book is here, its theory is queer, and we prepare you to be ready for it.

How do we situate ourselves as writers in this book? Are we all queer? Are our lovers or partners queer? Are we straight? What is straight? Is queer "bent" if straight is—well—straight? We situate ourselves as writers, teachers, and sexual beings who question whether one can ever be correctly "identified" as queer or straight. When Susan and I began we wanted to avoid what we felt was the triteness associated with questioning identity. At the completion of the book, I am now asking how identity can ever not be questioned. A fluid, tentative state, identity should expand and stretch as our lives and knowledges do. Queerness is a part of one's identity, one's ideology, and one's politics. Queerness is a part of all of us.

We enter a new century with words, parades, rainbow flags, and lavender triangles that demand a new era of respect and recognition. We also enter with increased gaybashing, homophobia, and state and city statutes designed to oppress a queer public. There can never be enough words written, explained, and articulated when one's life and style of life are questioned or silenced by violence and ignorance. The words in this book are part of the materials we need to work with as we assist our students and teachers to create not only classrooms of respect but a world that does not merely tolerate—a world that embraces queerness—all of it.

Foreword

William F. Pinar

There are several points to be made about this remarkable and strong collection of examples of "queer thinking." First, for those of us who identify with the lesbian and gay "community," there is in this volume an affirmation in being represented, in hearing our voices. For that, we all owe a debt of thanks to Susan Talburt and Shirley Steinberg and to the other contributors to this important book. The appearance of "queer thinking" in the field of education is recent, its formulation in an early stage, even as the political hour feels late. There is an urgency to this work—people are still dying, being bashed, being discriminated against, still suffering unnecessarily in a myriad of ways, public and private—that demands that we summon our courage, achieve some measure of solidarity, and press ahead. It feels as if there is momentum, however vague and fragile, and the appearance of this collection supports that.

But this book is not only about politics. In this early phase of conceptual development, it is of course important to think about everything. After all, it is "everything"—the straight world—that is our problem. That is evident here: from the opening of a gay and lesbian office on campus to film to television sitcoms, whatever occurs to us is legitimate subject matter for queer thinking. The point is to think about "whatever" queerly, not only to legitimate our own experience, but to teach others, both queer others who might feel isolated and intimidated and disempowered *and* straights, many of whom remain quite clueless, not only about us, but about themselves. In this regard the diversity of theme, of point of view, and of intellectual method are all strengths in this collection.

In terms of the broad field of education, there is an escalating movement into cultural studies, an umbrella term under which queer thinking, for many, for the moment, rests. Popular culture has become, it seems, a primary source of the scholarly study of education. In this collection films (*In & Out*) and television sitcoms (*Ellen*) are occasions for queer inquiry. Subjects perhaps more recognizable to our more conventional colleagues in education—school uniforms, adolescent literature (portraying lesbians and gay men), reading queerly (in this instance complexity theory), and a study of the opening of a gay and lesbian office on campus—are also explicated. The refocusing of scholarly attention away from the school toward the culture at large seems well underway among a number of straight as well as queer scholars.

Glorianne Leck needs no television to find evidence of commodification and standardization. Look no further than school uniforms, a policy proposed by a number of school boards (certainly the case here in south Louisiana), comprised of "representative members of the successful middle and professional class," whose "gender display and work costume . . . seems designed to reveal their performance of 'right' attitudes toward work, competition, gender, sexuality, nationalism, self-restraint, and religious conformity." Those school boards who have voted to endorse school uniforms evidently assume that by requiring students "to wear specific costumes of clothing," they "will reduce inappropriate displays of sexuality in the school setting and will reduce the often extreme social consequences of adolescent fashion competition." Leck is not persuaded: "Masking may appear to level the playing field, but those educators committed to working with social inequities are likely to find that the mask of a school uniform actually impedes their efforts." Why? Because "they do deny important socially interactive opportunities, and they do mask social cues." She quotes Georg Simmel: "At the same time it [fashion] satisfies in no less degree the need of differentiation, the tendency toward dissimilarity, the desire for change and contrast." As for herself, "clothes continue to do much to communicate the performance of my sexual, gender, and erotic orientation and my resistance to heteronormativity," and so she decries "the imposition of paper-doll clothes called school uniforms." In a wonderfully succinct summation of the state of contemporary U.S. culture, Leck notes that "prayer and the lottery appear to be the leading currencies of hope." In the bleak landscape that is the U.S. present, Leck concludes: "I wish to suggest, as one who claims voice as *a* feminist and *a* queer, that in the effort by school boards to neutralize the clothing displays of female children and to de-sex the clothing displays of nonheterosexually inclined and differently gendered children, there is a denial of the historical and individual conditions of each one of us."

Such "denial" is also evident on the big screen, as Shirley Steinberg points out. As she did with *To Wong Foo . . .* and other films in her earlier essay on "appropriating queerness" (Steinberg 1998), here Steinberg insightfully critiques Paul Rudnick's *In & Out* (1997), going, as usual, right to the heart of the matter. "Why then," she asks, "is Rudnick so careful to not allow his gay character to have sex?" She answers that the reason has to do with "crossing the heterosexual line of decency," a line that not only offers security to straight viewers, but in her view "defines what gayness might be." Queers in film (and she suggests the situation isn't much different on the small screen) function primarily to "accessorize and to get laughs." While many queer filmgoers may appreciate what appears to be a greater tolerance, Steinberg warns us that "we haven't come a long way, baby, and I am concerned that the public support and acknowledgement for a film such as *In & Out* perpetuates an intolerant tolerance that serves only to redefine in a palatable fashion what queerness *should be*."

Gee, is there no good news for those of us who think and live queerly? Certainly none in the widely celebrated "coming out" episode of comedian Ellen Degeneres, as evident in Nancy Lesko's smart analysis. Lesko begins by reiterating Arthur Korker's point that nothing happens in American culture unless it happens on television. Judged with this point in mind, Ellen's television coming out would seem to have been, she notes, "demonstrable progress, worthy of ecstatic celebration." But there the party ends, as Lesko points out that Ellen proclaimed her lesbian identity only in safe terms, ones that were "very familiar, non-sexual, personalized, and commodified." Lesko's argument is that in the commodification of Ellen, her lesbian identity was "contained within consumption, monogamous and invisible sexuality, and a middle-class emphasis on a therapeutized self." She recalls Robyn Wiegman and Lynda Zwinger's notion of "heterovisuality"—"the potential continuity between female homosociality and female homosexuality is disavowed through an intense insistence on a heterosexualized femininity, on the one hand, and through the cultivation of individual narratives of performance and personality on the other"—to underscore that Ellen's coming out "didn't take us very far." It "may have made us laugh, but questioned little else."

Nor is there much reason to celebrate when we consider lesbian and gay adolescent literature, as Rob Linné does. Linné points out that in adolescent lesbian and gay literature young queer characters are often punished with violence, even death, the message being that if you try gay sex something terrible will probably happen to you. Linné makes the sound suggestion that educators make sure they choose: "1) books that illustrate gay empowerment as well as gay victimization; 2) stories that openly explore gay sexuality rather than hiding it as something shameful; and 3) novels that include a multiplicity of character types," and concludes helpfully with a list of suggested readings.

So far, popular culture rules, but the queendom is not a happy place. The mood shifts a bit in Marla Morris's intriguing essay in which "high" culture makes an appearance, not that "high" culture is guaranteed to give us a rush. Morris summons Dante, no less, to assert that queer theorists/activists can be, quoting Mandelbaum, "zealously prophetic, politically messianic, indignant, nervous . . . theatrical." Although students of education have tended to regard theory and activism as separate spheres, Morris merges the two: "I read queer theory as a form of activism and queer activism as a form of theory." Agreeing with Derrida that identity is a "trap," she argues that queer representations are "prophetic" because "they announce the coming of an age in which sexualities are pluralities, genders are multitudinous, subjectivities are like tides of the ocean." That is a powerful image, suggestive of, among other things, the unconscious, a topic in which Deborah Britzman has considerable interest.

Britzman removes queer concerns from the surface of popular culture and the land of identity politics back to the ocean, to use Morris's image. That is, Britzman is interested in nothing less than the very character of sexuality and identity, suggesting that the two are not simply conjoined, and not only at the hip. We are, she suggests, not only estranged from ourselves in terms of consciousness or rationality, but even our semiconscious desires "slip between the fault lines of recognition and misrecognition, our urges divide in the strange calculus of ignorance and knowledge, and our passions contradict in aim and satisfaction." We know our straight friends are queer and don't get it, but have we considered that we too may misunderstand our desire? Psychoanalytically, Britzman points out, the very concept of sexuality implies excess; we desire "more than we consciously ask for or even want." Eros is, after Freud, "something between the wish and need." The three forms of resistance to sexuality that interest Britzman are structural, pedagogical, and psychical, this last form an indication that the self is divided from itself. "Can education be sexed?" she asks provocatively. There would seem to be a vague association between knowledge and sexuality, both of which threaten "to ruin innocent lives, or as . . . sacred object[s] that require protection, deferral, maturity, and social and legal sanction." Again she asks the provocative question: "Is there any difference between falling in love with ideas and falling in love with a person?" Is it possible to separate the idea from the embodied subjectivity who teaches it? Britzman would seem to answer no, because "without sexuality, the human would not desire to learn." More generally, "without sexuality there is no curiosity." "The question of sexuality," she writes (or is it the sublimation of sexuality?), "is central to the question of becoming a citizen, to crafting a self who can invent, over and over again, the courage to stand up for the self, to feel passionately for the conditions of others, to create a life from the experiments of learning to love and making from this learning to love, a love of learning." The fact that one loves, rather than the gender of the person one loves, may be paramount, as she concludes: "The question is not which policy to make on which sexuality but how the strange workings of sexuality can allow for the rethinking of education."

But it is the former that preoccupies many, as Susan Talburt knows. Her concern is policy in higher education, and specifically the complex, perhaps dialectical, relation between policy and identity politics. To study this problem she examines "the highly contentious" opening of a gay/lesbian/bisexual office at a public research university. Talburt is interested in how "institutionalized gay and lesbian identity politics can result in psychologizing gay men and lesbians" and in the process disguise the social and specifically institutional production of identities. In the campus rhetoric she studied, gays and lesbians tended to be represented as white, "women" were coded white and heterosexual, and all "raced" persons were assumed to be straight. In the opening of the office, identity politics was invoked to characterize gay men and lesbians as a preconstituted minority group, a set of citizens that pays taxes, is discriminated against, and merits its own office. There appeared, as an additional rationale, what Talburt terms a "pathology model" of gay and lesbian needs, needs produced by our suffering due to harassment. This displaced the first political rationale in arguments for the establishment of the office. In a third phase, identity politics, educational equity, and pathology merged as agreement was reached. As a sphere apart from the "real" world, the university was characterized as responsible for both leading and responding to social change. In terms of research on higher education, we might reframe questions of institutional stasis or transformation, Talburt suggests, in terms of the relations of institutional practices to identity-based movements, focusing our attention on how institutional practices both respond to and construct identity.

Clearly, queer thinking may be focused on extant fields of study, such as higher education in Talburt's essay or on social research, as when Darleen Opfer sets out to disprove Lipset and Raab's (1970) and Hofstadter's (1965) thesis that "extremism" and "paranoid politics" result when corporate status displacement becomes anomic status displacement. In other words, when individuals suffer social displacement, particularly of an economic nature, Lipset, Raab, and Hofstadter argued that they then refocus their frustration on a target population, which then gets the blame for their change in social status. Sound familiar? Opfer doesn't think so. She suggests that if this theory were true for the contemporary religious right, the incidence of anti-gay action should be declining because its power seems steady or ascendent. But this is not the case. Opfer argues that the typical fundamentalist engages in anti-queer activism due to specific religious beliefs (something that is accepted in this study but might well be challenged). For this reason, she concludes that the religious right cannot be dismissed as paranoid or extremist. Not only is the status displacement theory mistaken, but using it now, Opfer worries, provokes more fundamentalists to anti-gay action and limits pro-gay action—and is therefore ill-advised.

Others who think queerly seem unconcerned about the right, or is that because they live in Toronto? For Brent Davis and Dennis Sumara, queer theory involves reconceptualizing an extant area "queerly." Davis and Sumara reframe "complexity theory" as another queer theory and, in particular, use it to question taken-for-granted ideas of development, education, research, and identity. They aim to render "strange" (an echo perhaps of Maxine Greene's 1973 book) and "queer" those academic discourses, including "complexity theory," that, in their words, "have banished the mark of the troublesome biological body to support an idealized epistemic body." They define complexity theory as a field of inquiry that "examines those phenomena that are self-organizing, adaptive, and dynamic," or, to put the matter another way, "phenomena that are alive or, at least, that we tend to describe with metaphors drawn from vibrant bodies, evolving organisms, and life processes."

Vibrant bodies? Davis and Sumara come to the conclusion that any study of "queer" identities must not begin with "the lived experiences of those who explicitly identify as queer," but with the contentious process of emptying the "heterosexual closet." That closet, while marked "straight," is not. This relational understanding of queer identity mirrors a queer refusal of other binaries, including "mind/body . . . theory/practice." Such an understanding of "queer" and of "complexity theory" persuades

Davis and Sumara "to find the resources to meet with students, parents, and teachers; to participate in teaching projects; to become involved in community events." This involvement avoids the "critic/criticized" binary, which, "like the others . . . dissolves in complicity." Their refusal to be complicit in the status quo prompts them "to reconsider the unformulated ground, striving to afford less privilege to the formulated figure," which they take to be "nothing short of an ethical imperative as it transforms and conflates the projects of research and education, pushing them both toward a hermeneutic attitude. We are admonished to understand—and to refuse to allow curriculum events to hang uninterpreted. This matter goes beyond how we approach our research: It is a statement of how we should live our lives." Indeed.

Eric Rofes is interested in vibrant bodies as well. An unrepentant sexual "revolutionary," Rofes continues—despite what he calls the "excuse" and reality of AIDS—to "immerse myself in communities that value sex." He describes his own sexual practices as "nonmonogamous," "promiscuous," or, thinking of Walt Whitman, very much "democratic" in spirit. "Each day when I wake up, two people move in me: the teacher and the lover. I hunger for a community of educators who live out our class, gender, race and sex politics, not simply in our teaching or our academic publishing, but in our *everyday* lives." And so he seeks to "learn from other gay male educators who may face similar barriers, fears, and points of controversy as I." This won't be easy, as Rofes understands, because "teachers—including queer teachers—[are] a notoriously conservative lot." More than a few, he acknowledges, would pronounce his preferences "disgusting." Rofes cites Bourdieu to suggest that such disgust should be "unpacked." He points out that some have argued that public sex functions in radical and liberating ways, that promiscuity and casual sex may be regarded "as life-affirming practices of bonding and exchanges of pleasure, intimacy, and affection." Nor does he want his sexed body kept out of the classroom: "I've had . . . encounters with my undergraduates that have challenged my commitment to including sex and the body in my teaching as something more than distanced, depersonalized intellectual exercise." He ends with a call for dialogue regarding the sacrifices queers have suffered and the implications these sacrifices have for democratic education and social change.

Townsand Price-Spratlen is well aware of sacrifices, gendered and racial. His "autoethnography" focuses on where he lives, at least part of the time: his faculty office, "a political space of multiple dialectics." In particular he focuses on the images he has chosen to decorate the office, photographs that provide visitors "with a visual language of various representations of the occupant's identity." Such "workplace images" become moments in the process of "negotiating legacies," or "learning the lessons of history by seeking to understand the contemporary and historical contexts and contributions of [one's] ancestors." As a gay scholar of African descent, he negotiates his legacies by exhibiting on his office walls a set of ancestral images he values most. In so doing Price-Spratlen makes use of Baldwin's three gifts of language, courage, and tenderness (which are also appreciated by Toni Morrison in a passage he quotes to open the piece). There are three photographs displayed on the walls: 1) "Pre-Kindergarten Kisses," a shot of "two young males of African descent embracing each other . . . as they smile lovingly, looking into the other's eyes," reminding one of Marlon Riggs's declaration at the conclusion of *Tongues Untied* that "black men loving black men is *the* revolutionary act" (quoted in Simmons 1991, 193); 2) a photo of Audre Lorde; and 3) a photo of Marlon Riggs. Price-Spratlen rests daily within "the gaze cast by this very special pair of eyes." When he looks at the shot of Audre Lorde, he hears a powerful sentence from her 1989 lecture at UCLA: "My poetry calls for an answer from each of you in your lives." The images of Lorde and Riggs affirm for him "a fictive friendship and a lived intimacy" he enjoys with both, inspiring him to "justice-doing," a notion of "liberating activity that challenges human oppression," grounded in, quoting Robert Goss, "the resistance narrative of Jesus, His struggles, death and God's liberative practice." Such "gifts of legacy" inspire him to "move forward, acting on the ever-present duty that my many blessings warmly, kindly impose."

That is a lovely phrase—"the ever-present duty that my many blessings warmly, kindly impose"—is it not? Yes, we have sacrificed, we have suffered (and suffer still), and it behooves us to remember that being alive—as many of our comrades are not—is a duty to remember our blessings, to "move forward" (to borrow Price-Spratlen's language again), in friendship (fictive, sexual, and familial, however unconventionally that last adjective is defined), unafraid, unembittered, willing to hope, determined to have fun. As queer teachers and scholars, it is both our duty and pleasure to think queerly, blessed by those who have gone before, aroused by those around us now, and in fidelity to those who are yet to come.

Works Cited

Simmons, Ron. 1991. Tongues untied: An interview with Marlon Riggs. In *Brother to brother: Collected writings by black gay men*, edited by Essex Hemphill. [Conceived by Joseph Beam. Project managed by Dorothy Beam.] Los Angeles: Alyson Books.

Steinberg, Shirley R. 1998. Appropriating queerness. In *Queer theory in education*, edited by William F. Pinar. Mahwah, N.J.: Lawrence Erlbaum.

PART ONE

THINKING THEORY

Chapter 1

Introduction: Some Contradictions and Possibilities of *Thinking Queer*

Susan Talburt

Like any project that invokes the term "queer," this book is bound to contain contradictions. As presently constituted, queer seeks to disrupt the discrete, fixed locations of identity by understanding sexuality and its meanings not as a priori or given but as constructed, contingent, fashioned and refashioned, and relational. Eve Sedgwick (1993) has written: "On the scene of national gay/lesbian activism, in the *Village Voice*, in the 'zines, on the streets and even in some classrooms, I suppose this must be called the moment of Queer" (xi–xii). She says, "something about *queer* is inextinguishable. Queer is a continuing moment, movement, motive—recurrent, eddying, *troublant*. The word 'queer' itself means *across*—it comes from the Indo-European root –*twerkw*, which also yields the German *quer* (transverse), Latin *torquere* (to twist), English *athwart*" (xii). Consonant with poststructural, postmodern, and feminist theories that challenge binary constructions of identities, the unitary nature of subjectivity, liberal ideas of the autonomous individual, and community as predicated on sameness, and consonant also with the political practices of such groups as Queer Nation, ACT UP, and the Lesbian Avengers, the language of queer turns from being and identity to doing, performing, and enacting. Queer has been said not to be a noun, for nouns stabilize in time and space, but an adjective or a verb that cuts across identities, subjectivities, and communities. However, although queer would challenge heteronormative orders, the notion of identity, and gay and lesbian identity politics, queer continues to depend on identity at this particular historical juncture. Symptomatic of this intertwining of queer and identity is what might be called a "return of the repressed," in which gay and lesbian identity haunts "queer," throughout many of the essays in this volume. The "terms of identity," to borrow Nancy Lesko's phrase in this volume, such as "visibility," "voice," "representation," and "community," surface throughout this text, even as its authors would upset the assumptions underlying their logic.

Judith Butler (1993) has written of the temporality of "queer." Whereas my interest in its historicity lies in the haunting of queer by identity, Butler theorizes the appropriation of queer's negative meanings for new, affirming uses. Queer's resignification, she argues, depends on convention, in which the reiteration of queer does not copy past uses but draws on them for the creation of new meanings in contemporary contexts. Because neither convention nor the present is stable or unitary, invoking queer mobilizes a multiplicity of meanings whose possibilities are out of actors' control. "To recast queer agency in this chain of historicity," Butler says, "is thus to avow a set of constraints on the past and the future that mark at once the *limits* of agency and its most *enabling conditions*" (228). Although constrained, new iterations are essential to projects for change. Queer can never be fully owned, but "only redeployed, twisted, queered from a prior usage" (228). Because this twisting necessarily draws from a history that has constructed queer as an identity, efforts to shift queer's meanings from noun to verb, from identity to practice, from modality of being to modality of doing will be neither linear nor complete but contextual and partial.

I would like to suggest that this tension, in which identity is sedimented in queer thought and practice—even as queer would disrupt identity claims—is productive. In her essay in this volume, Marla Morris unites queer theory and activism as an "acting out" against the stasis and normalization that the naming of identities can impose. The tension underlying her discussion, in which queer efforts for change depend on queer visibility, is marked by her doubly meaningful use of the term "challenging identities": queer becomes an identity (however temporary, unfixed, and unfixable) at the same time that it would challenge the idea of identity. Even as queer disrupts the "naturalness" of continuities of sex-gender-desire that dominant discourses would construct by announcing and enacting alternatives, queer depends for intelligibility on a "something" to reject (a "something else" to be). Morris tell us that "Queering up the subject means outing the subject" whereas the "in" of passing is complicit with maintaining the present order. But what if we turn her formulation upside down to say that outing is complicit with a political economy of visibility, the construction of categories, and the very structure of the closet? What if we were to say that passing refuses the terms of identity, the terms of visibility, the terms of the closet? Such an upside-down is certainly facile and dichotomous and needs contextualization, particularly in light of the idea that the haunting of queer by identity, as part of the present moment, allows for queer's legibility. Although the legible isn't always desirable, it may in certain locations enable dialogue and action that press at the limits of often seemingly intractable social, institutional, and educational structures. In other words, this tension is productive precisely because queer engages the identity discourses that structure the terms of educational policy and practice while at the same time pushing beyond them. In fact, Brent Davis and Dennis Sumara's essay turns us from the simplicity of identity to the complexity of queer subjectivity, in which "A complex system is more than the sum of its parts," and represents an "unfixing" of what they call "*the space of the possible*." Recognizing our implications in what surrounds us, they describe complicity as "focused on the contingencies of the immediate situation, acknowledging that the future depends on the present but is not determined by it." Their identification of "*complicitous research*" and education as responsible and responsive to the contexts that structure the conditions of their possibilities emphasizes the constraints and possibilities, as well as the moral and ethical dimensions, involved in the performative rearrangement of identities and knowledges that space would contain.

This problem of knowledge is a central challenge that queer brings to educational research, theory, and practice. For example, the frequent "liberatory" response to the canonized curricular question What knowledge is of most worth? has been to demand that gay and lesbian subjects be represented. Consistent with the logic of identity politics, anti-homophobia projects have worked to include affirmative representations in curricula as well as to create campus offices, school organizations, and activities. The codification of identity works toward the codification of knowledge; questions turn to what kind of representation, how much, in what locations, for whom? Although such projects have been enabling in numerous ways, they are also constrained by the very fact that they constitute objects of knowledge. Jonathan Silin (1995) has pointed out that "The demand for certainty—for a safe, agreed-upon body of knowledge—has worked against the inclusion of controversial issues in the curriculum" (12)—a difficulty dramatically underscored by the demise of the Rainbow Curriculum in New York City. Yet there is more at stake than representation. If one takes the stance that sexuality is central to the ego's curiosity, and thus its capacity to learn, as Deborah Britzman argues, sexuality can't be contained or bracketed off as a domain of knowledge. Britzman's questions about how pedagogy can enable the ego to touch and be touched refuse the terms of identity, the creation of proper subjects, and attendant concerns with representation and recognition. Rather, she asks us to consider that when sexuality and education meet, a problem emerges that "has to do with how the curriculum structures modes of behaviour and orientations to knowledge that are repetitions of the underlying structure and dynamics of education: compliance, conformity, and the myth that knowledge cures." To extend Foucault's unveiling of the falsity of the "repressive hypothesis" that liberation lies in speaking the "truth" of sex, we must rethink the "knowledge hypothesis" that liberation (or correction) lies in making sexuality a topic of knowledge in schools. Given an educational zeitgeist that would cure by representing and providing knowledge and another educational zeitgeist that would ignore the ways in which subjects live their lives creatively and relationally, we must ask how knowledge, both determinate and indeterminate, queer and not, can be put to new uses. Despite the limitations of identity, even the creation of proper subjects may open possibilities. For example, while Britzman points to the dangers of creating proper subjects and knowledges for purposes of subjection and control, she also gestures toward the ways such disciplinary practices become sites for human creativity: "But also, given the productive possibilities of power and resistance, new identities are made."

Rob Linné's essay, "Choosing Alternatives to *The Well of Loneliness*," in which identity is indeed at stake, may appear to be no more than a call for greater variety and "better representations" of gay and lesbian subjects in young adult literature. Yet attention to the need for multiple representations of sexuality and subjectivity has implications for those seeking to insert into educational practices a range of subject positions that enable multiple identifications. Despite the reification inherent in creating "fictional role models," literature surfaces repeatedly in gay and lesbian coming-out narratives as productive of the movement of subjects from isolation to feelings of participation in a community of "like" persons, what Kath Weston calls "the gay *imaginary*" (34). However, as Weston points out, participation in identity-based communities often brings about a sort of "anti-identification," in which gay or lesbian identity does not provide the common bonds it appears to promise. What if pedagogy took into account the relations and identifications students form with the representations they encounter? What if community and relationality were placed at the center of curricular process and content? Walcott (1998) reminds us that "the concept of community as singular means that only two positions are possible—in or out" (162). He explains that understanding community as predicated not on common experiences but on identifications "gesture[s] to community as a process that is never complete or finished. Such claims have profound effects for a pedagogy of social justice invested in singular social identities and disuniting identities into single categories as either victim or victimizer" (169). A queer educational project might ask itself: Where do identities live? In individual subjects? In communities? In practices? In relations? Identifications and relation play a central role in Townsand Price-Spratlen's reflection on his placement of affirming, oppositional images on the walls of his university office. These images are less role models than a representational "process of 'negotiating legacies,'" which Price-Spratlen and his visitors interpret and put to new uses in the present. Like de Certeau's renter, who "transforms another person's property into a space borrowed for a moment by a transient . . . [and] make[s] comparable changes in an apartment they furnish with their acts and memories" (xxi), Price-Spratlen transforms institutional public/private space into a "social space" to enable the creation of new meanings. Not strictly "the terms of identity," Price-Spratlen's legacies embed past in present to suggest the expansion of the "space of the possible" by enlarging it visually. He leaves it to the reader to surmise the responses of visitors to his office, how they grapple with their own knowledges and ignorances in reading the murmurings of the images he offers.

How do these tensions between seemingly tangible and codifiable knowledges and resignification through more fluid terms frame the bodies of teachers and students, particularly given the cultural creation of identities through the curricula of everyday life? As Nancy Lesko's analysis of Ellen's "coming out" and Shirley Steinberg's reflection on *In & Out* attest, "better representations" may signify "better (more efficient) containment." Lesko points out that contemporary political identities are increasingly grounded in doing rather than being. Structured by duties and obligations, these identities set the terms for the actions of subjects and their strategies for creating alliances in the public sphere. The "terms of identity," as it turns out for Ellen, are not so liberating as they might first appear. Rather, they enable her mainstream incorporation and normalization as shopper rather than sexual subject, as commodified object rather than activist, leaving Ellen contained within "the picket fence around her Beverly Hills home." Similarly, in what Steinberg calls the "pedagogy gone awry" of *In & Out*, "teaching tolerance" depends on the use of gendered, homophobic stereotypes and the desexualization of the homosexual, resulting in the normalizing and "coraling [of] queerness into a fenced arena." In both cases, audiences "don't want *too much informa-tion*," as Steinberg says, because knowledge of "what they do," however titillating, might disrupt the façade of tolerance, the pleasure of the gay spectacle. The social frames of inclusion, like educational frames, meet their limits at "controversial" knowledge.

A problem becomes how to disrupt the normalization—through knowl-edge, social relations, pedagogical practices, and cultural mediation—of both hetero- and homosexuality. Projects that teach tolerance (to straights) and offer role models (to queers) create necessarily distorted knowledges through partial, normalized images and depend on intact identities that can be rationally seen and received. Anti-homophobia projects, for ex-ample, have created an idealized image of "the gay male teacher," who is no more threatening than Ellen Degeneres or Howard of *In & Out*. In this context, Eric Rofes' reflection on what it means to bring together two seemingly discrete categories, the lover and the teacher, explores the meanings of transgression in the context of his interactions with stu-dents, whose social knowledges play a part in defining his potential to disrupt normalization. What knowledges do his students already hold? Have they seen *In & Out?* What are the effects of his performance of masculinity and sexuality within and against the knowledges of students? How willing are they to rearrange their knowledges? Is it possible that in order to expand a category while living under its sign one becomes en-trapped in the role-model discourse that characterizes liberal politics, even if one is something of an anti-heroic role model? How does the "gay male teacher drag" he enacts expand the space of the possible, or is it contin-gent on multiple, unknowable circumstances? Related to Rofes' (and my) questions, Glorianne Leck's interrogation of the standardization of stu-dent bodies through uniforms questions how masking masks the creation of knowledges and subjectivities that may exceed the realm of the "so-cially acceptable." Just as "curriculum drag" is the masquerading of knowl-edge as neutral and value free, students are asked to don drag that sup-presses the knowledges and values they hold. Uniformity becomes a means of masking material and cultural differences, of visually suppressing the ways individuals and groups are implicated in social and institutional prac-tices. If clothing represents a means by which youth represent their gendered, raced, classed, and sexual positionings and stake out the terms of their identities and communities, who benefits from regulating their access to such signifying practices?

If neither curriculum nor student nor teacher bodies can be fixed by identities or standards, what would it mean to unfix knowledges in a

pedagogy that does not assume its subjects beforehand? Could we shift
from the known and identifiable to the ineffable and complicit? Deborah
Britzman writes:

> When students begin to speak back to the curriculum, to interpret the curriculum,
> educators can begin to listen differently, to receive differently, what students make.
> For this to occur, both educators and students have to learn to see knowledge as
> something that is made in and altered by relationships. In this view the curricu-
> lum becomes an opportunity to explore the significance knowledge has to the
> lives of others and to one's own life. In conversations then, the teacher's work
> begins with three kinds of interpretations: the teacher interprets the curriculum
> and as the teacher interprets the student's interpretation, the teacher can also
> consider how her or his own fears and desires are shaping the response. In this
> unfinished and uncertain exchange of ideas, pedagogical content comes closer to
> the pedagogical relation.

The radicalism of this seemingly simple proposition lies in its refusal to
reify knowledge, students, teachers, or curriculum as static objects and in
its insistence on their open-ended relationality. In her discussion of queer
pedagogy, Susanne Luhmann (1998) argues:

> Subversiveness, rather than being an easily identifiable counter-knowledge, lies
> in the very moment of unintelligibility, or in the absence of knowledge. If subver-
> siveness is not a new form of knowledge but lies in the capacity to raise questions
> about the detours of coming to know and make sense, then what does this mean
> for a pedagogy that imagines itself as queer? Can a queer pedagogy resist the
> desire for authority and stable knowledge; can it resist disseminating new knowl-
> edge and new forms of subjection? What if a queer pedagogy puts into crisis what
> is known and how we come to know? (147)

She tells us that her own inquiry into queer pedagogy "is not very heroic.
It does not position itself as a bulwark against oppression, it does not
claim the high grounds of subversion but hopefully it encourages an ethical practice by studying the risks of normalization, the limits of its own
practices, and the im/possibilities of (subversive) teaching and learning"
(154). Elsewhere (Talburt, 2000) I have suggested that queer theory and
research are not about allowing us to see how sexuality "fits in" with our
work as teachers or researchers but rather they are about helping us to
understand how queer things happen in our work and our relations to
others. In this sense, Elizabeth Grosz's (1995) caution against naming
and overtheorizing queer subjectivity and sexuality may apply to curricular and pedagogical processes as well: "To submit one's pleasures and
desires to enumeration and definitive articulation is to submit processes

and becomings to entities, locations, and boundaries, to become welded to an organizing nucleus of fantasy whose goal is not simply pleasure and expansion but control, the production of endless repetition, endless variations of the same—in short, the forces of reaction" (226). To codify queer, like codifying curricular knowledge, is to doom ourselves to repeating the terms of our identities, to keeping "the space of the possible" small and contained.

What must be emphasized is that the haunting of queer by identity can make it appear that queer offers knowledge of some sort—about acts, identities, communities. But that knowledge, partly because it is relational and social, is a contingent knowledge whose meanings must be constantly reevaluated and reinterpreted. To my mind, the most provocative aspects of queer lie in its uncertainty, its strangely relational and contextual nature, and its inability or refusal to offer final or complete knowledges. Diana Fuss (1991) has remarked,

> Questions of epistemology ("how do we know?") enjoy a privileged status in theorizations of gay and lesbian identity. How does one know when one is on the inside and when one is not? How does one know when and if one is out of the closet? How, indeed, does one know if one is gay? The very insistence of the epistemological frame of reference in theories of homosexuality may suggest that we cannot know—surely or definitively. Sexual identity may be less a function of knowledge than performance, or, in Foucauldian terms, less a matter of final discovery than perpetual reinvention. (6–7)

The instability of the knowledge queer offers suggests that we never quite know what to do with what we seem to have at hand. Sedgwick (1993) has commented, "Anti-intellectuals today, at any rate, are happy to dispense with the interpretive process and depend instead on appeals to the supposedly self-evident" (17). But what happens when the self-evident disappears? We must think. As a figurative embodiment of epistemological uncertainty and noncorrespondence to a "real," queer demands thought. It may then be the task of educators to disrupt the self-evidence of identities.

In a moment in which "thinking" as a term is increasingly being evacuated of meaning, "critical thinking" means as many things as there are speakers who utter its refrain, and thinking is becoming increasingly divorced from our technology-enhanced desire to "access information," it may be necessary to dwell on the political dimension of what it means to think. Sedgwick (1993) has characterized the U.S. intellectual right's defense of a fixed heritage of knowledge to be dispensed to future generations as an effort "to revoke every available cognitive and institutional affordance for reflection, speculation, experimentation, contradiction, embroidery, daring, textual aggression, textual delight, double entendre, close reading, free association, wit—the family of creative activities that might, for purposes of brevity, more simply be called *thought*" (18). However, even these "fixed" knowledges demand that something be done with them. Bill Readings (1996) has commented that "no knowledge can save us the task of thinking" (154).

In his consideration of the educational implications of the decentered subject and the decentered, or posthistorical, university, Readings (1996) turns to the idea of thought, which has "no proper identity" (191). With the demise of education's mission of producing autonomous, reasoning subjects "who are supposedly made free by the information they learn," he argues, "the scene of teaching can be better understood as a network of obligations" (19). Thought highlights the impossibility of the autonomy of students, teachers, and bodies of knowledge:

> [T]o listen to Thought, to think beside each other and beside ourselves, is to explore an open network of obligations that keeps the question of meaning open as a locus of debate. Doing justice to Thought, listening to our interlocutors, means trying to hear that which cannot be said but that which tries to make itself heard. And this is a process incompatible with the production of (even relatively) stable and exchangeable knowledge. (165)

The complicity of subjects in knowledge suggests that fixity, being put in place, is impossible. Thinking and queer, like communities and identities, are temporal rather than spatial, related rather than autonomous.

Placement as gay or lesbian has had its political efficacy, but it is a strange placement that suggests a neat alignment of personal identity and group identity and the ability of policies to respond to these neatly placed and aligned identities. If all subjects are the sites of converging sets of relations, Judith Butler (1993) argues, "It is in this sense that the temporary totalization performed by identity categories is a necessary error. And if identity is a necessary error, then the assertion of 'queer' will be necessary as a term of affiliation, but it will not fully describe those it purports to represent" (230). Affiliations will always be lived differently, will always implicate different persons in different ways, and will always change in their terms and meanings. In the conclusion of her provocative book *Outside Belongings*, Elspeth Probyn (1996) says,

> If I have argued against the idea of identity, it is because it can only describe the specificities of categories of belonging; it cannot reach the desire to belong and the ways in which individuals, groups, and nations render and live out their speci-

ficity as singular: as that which is now, in this way, with this affect. In turn, any singularity of belonging must continually be freed and encouraged in its movement to constantly become other. (152–153)

It is the project of enabling *queer* and *thinking* to become other in which the essays in this volume take part.

Works Cited

Butler, Judith. 1993. *Bodies that matter: On the discursive limits of "sex."* New York: Routledge.

de Certeau, Michel. 1984. *The practice of everyday life.* Translated by Steven F. Rendall. Berkeley: University of California Press.

Fuss, Diana. 1991. Inside/out. In *Inside/out: Lesbian theories, gay theories*, edited by Diana Fuss. New York: Routledge.

Grosz, Elizabeth. 1995. Bodies and pleasures in queer theory. In *Who can speak? Authority and critical identity*, edited by Judith Roof and Robyn Wiegman. Urbana: University of Illinois Press.

Luhmann, Susanne. 1998. Queering/querying pedagogy? Or, pedagogy is a pretty queer thing. In *Queer theory in education*, edited by William F. Pinar. Mahwah, N.J.: Lawrence Erlbaum.

Probyn, Elspeth. 1996. *Outside belongings.* New York: Routledge.

Readings, Bill. 1996. *The university in ruins.* Cambridge, Mass.: Harvard University Press.

Sedgwick, Eve Kosofsky. 1993. *Tendencies.* Durham, N.C.: Duke University Press.

Silin, Jonathan G. 1995. *Sex, death, and the education of children: Our passion for ignorance in the age of AIDS.* New York: Teachers College Press.

Talburt, Susan. 2000. *Subject to identity: Knowledge, sexuality, and academic practices in higher education.* Albany: SUNY Press.

Walcott, Rinaldo. 1998. Queer texts and performativity: Zora, rap, and community. In *Queer theory in education*, edited by William F. Pinar. Mahwah, N.J.: Lawrence Erlbaum.

Weston, Kath. 1998. *Long slow burn: Sexuality and social science.* New York: Routledge.

Chapter 2

Dante's Left Foot Kicks Queer Theory into Gear

Marla Morris

Dante is an exiled, aggressive . . . salvation-bent intellectual, humbled to rise assured and ardent, zealously prophetic, politically messianic, indignant, nervous, muscular, theatrical, energetic.   —Mandelbaum, 1982, 8

Mandelbaum's description of Dante sounds "queer." Dante's critiques of the Church in the *Divine Comedy* are aggressive, ardent, zealously prophetic. He critiques, in a rude-positive way, or in an in-your-face way, the scandals of the medieval papacy: This is called "queer" politics. He also subverts notions of identity: Witness Tiresias "who changed his mein . . . from a man . . . into a woman" ([1307] 1982, 181). Sexuality as a shifting, changing way of being in the world is "queer." A queer sensibility attempts to subvert the apparent neat and tidy relation between sex and gender. Queer politics, thus, serves to undermine rigid categories of identity. The birthing of queer identity means grappling with ambiguity and complexity around the notion of what it might mean to be a person. Personhood, for queer theory, is a contradictory and complex phenomenon. Witness the diviner Amphiaraus: "He's made a chest out of his shoulders and since he wanted so to see ahead he looks behind and walks a backward path" ([1307] 1982, 181). Discontinuous, jagged, backward ways of walking through the world are also "queer."

Like Dante, queer theorists/activists are "zealously prophetic, politically messianic, indignant, nervous . . . theatrical" (Mandelbaum 1982, 8). Although theory and activism might be interpreted as two distinct things, I collapse the two. I read queer theory as a form of activism and queer activism as a form of theory. I find the bifurcation between theory and activism a difficult one to maintain. Exposing and critiquing the violence of language and categories, queer theorists/activists struggle, in ludic ways, creating spaces for queerer representations of identities and politics. Ludic ways of being may embrace play, humor, and jokes. And the joke, although it might seem to be merely silly, can serve to interrupt the status quo; humor can serve to undermine the taken for granted. For me, then, ludic sensibilities can become political. Subverting notions of identity and sexuality, queer theorists/activists turn taken-for-granted categories upside down and backward. Discontinuous, jagged, backward ways of talking about identity are queer. Queer workers also fight against heteronormativity, homophobia, and hate crimes.

Queer theory emerged in around 1990, when Teresa de Lauretis coined the term. Foucault's *History of Sexuality* (1978) and the writings of other poststructuralists, such as Jacques Derrida, have become crucial for queer analyses of identity and politics. Many queer theorists, then, draw on poststructuralism. Judith Butler's *Gender Trouble: Feminism and the Subversion of Identity* (1990), Michael Warner's *Fear of a Queer Planet: Queer Politics and Social Theory* (1993), Eve Sedgwick's *Epistemology of the Closet* (1990), and her later work *Tendencies* (1993), helped set the stage for a new academic discipline.

Initially, queer theory was a response to the AIDS crisis. David Bell and Gill Valentine explain that queer theorists' "resistance to the dominant mythologies of the AIDS epidemic and to the state's inactivity and feeble responses to the current health crisis has been activated through an embodied geography of raging activism" (1995, 153). Due to homophobia, during the early days of AIDS, the deaths of gays/lesbians and other marginalized people went without much notice from health agencies or the government. Many members of the Christian right were saying that homosexuals "deserved" to die. And right-wing politicians like Jesse Helms advocated quarantining AIDS patients (read concentration camps for queers). As Berlant and Warner say of this context, "It is no accident that queer commentary has emerged" (1995, 345). Indeed, queer theory emerged as a reaction and resistance to this cold eye of do-nothing, see-nothing, hear-nothing. Queer theory/activism takes the form of angry protest, resisting insidious discursive practices that do violence to the marginalized. Queers act up/act out against homophobic, or what I call queer-a-phobic, practices, through in-your-face, rude, ludic performances. Challenging identities, such as queer identities, disrupt mainstream American culture. This paper will analyze the emergence of queer subjectivities. I will suggest that queer subjectivities are politically radical. Finally, I will draw some implications that these challenging identities might have for education.

Deconstructing the Subject:
Undoing Normalizing Philosophic Discourses

Derrida (1978; 1995a; 1995b) and Foucault (1978) teach that categories such as "the subject" are produced historically, culturally, discursively. Subjects are always already inscribed by culture even before they are born. The philosophically conceived subject has done violence to humankind by its constricting, objectifying, reifying effects. Derrida (1995a) remarks that identity is a "trap." Unlike traditional philosophical discourse, queer theory attempts to re-construct the subject in ways that avoid the trappings of identity. Queer theory teaches that identity is a cultural construction. Students and teachers construct their identities in complex ways since they are always already immersed in culture. For young people especially, TV has much to do with how their identities might be constructed. Kids might tend to imitate people on TV with whom they identify. But it is nearly impossible to determine just how identities are formed because their very formation is highly ambiguous.

In order to understand, historically, how it has become possible for queer subjects to have emerged, a genealogy of the subject is necessary. Western philosophy has had a stranglehold on the subject. From Aristotle to Dewey, philosophers have managed to colonize the subject, box the subject in, desexualize and normalize the subject. In *The Metaphysics*, Aristotle ([335–323 b.c.e.] 1968) discussed the notion of "substance." Aristotle said, "So, too, then, are many senses in which a thing is said to be, but all refer to one starting point; some things are said to be because they are substances" (314). The subject, I contend, was born out of the notion of substance. A substance is a thing that can stand alone; a self can stand alone. "I" can stand independent of this computer or that pen or that chair. The self as substance is a thing. And this thing is "self-maintaining" (Bohm 1978, 93–94) and separate from other things. Identity, then, is produced in isolation. Aristotle managed to turn selves into isolated things. Thing-i-fication, according to religious scholar Lee Bailey (1996), has had devastating effects on Western culture. Selves conceptualized as things justify treating selves as objects. Treating human beings like objects, as Marcel (1988) points out, is completely unethical.

Like Aristotle, Thomas Aquinas ([1273] 1989) suggested that selves are unified and thinglike because they have core qualities that center subjectivities. In the *Summa Theologica* ([1273] 1989), Aquinas said that certain "essential" qualities or "innate" qualities (core qualities) make us human. Aquinas stressed that sexuality is an innate, core quality. He said that it is "natural" to be "inclined" to "do good things." One of these good things is engaging in sexual intercourse. But sexual intercourse must be "natural," he wrote. "Unisexual lust" (65–66), or homosexual sex, is against nature. If human beings "act against nature" they act against God. Thus the natural self is one that acts in accordance with God's laws. This essentialized self, then, must be essentially heterosexual.

Aquinas managed to codify "natural sex." Long before Aquinas, though, the Roman Church had already been punishing Catholics for engaging in "illicit sex" (McNeill and Garner 1979). As late as 1350, public penance served to humiliate and shame sex offenders (Mansfield 1995). Tertullian ([220 c.e.] 1959) warned that if you did not perform the discipline of "exomologesis" (public penance) then you must "meditate in your heart on hell" (35). Penitents, most of whom were sex offenders, wore sackcloth and ashes; some were imprisoned (Poschmann 1964), some were "flogged or pilloried" (Mansfield 1995, 104), and some were wrapped in pig intestines while set in a pillory (Mansfield 1995). The Roman Church demonized and tortured those who "deviated" from "natural" sexual activities.

As witches burned outside the window of Descartes, he wrote his meditations on the self. Like Aristotle and Aquinas, Descartes suggested that selves as substancelike things are detached from the world and others. From Descartes to Dewey the notion of the subject as substance changed little.

However, the face of the subject began to change with the advent of process philosophy (Dewey, Bergson, Whitehead) and modern physics. Whitehead ([1929] 1978) suggests that the subject is composed of "actual occasions" that are interrelated in a process of becoming and perishing. Actual entities or occasions are an "adventure" in the becoming of what Whitehead calls the "creative advance" (32). For Whitehead, the subject is in flux, is changeable and interrelated to nature. Whitehead's position is clearly ecological since the subject is no longer isolated but connected to her/his world. Whitehead says that "there is no possibility of a detached, self-contained, local existence. The environment enters into the Nature of each thing" ([1938] 1951). Like Whitehead, many pragmatists (James, Royce, Dewey) resituated the subject back into nature and began to talk of subjectivity as a stream. But the subject continued to appear desexualized (with the exception of Aquinas).

The scientific demolition of substance occurred with the advent of modern physics. Einstein was able to demonstrate that the idea of substances as eternal, unchanging, independent things was inaccurate scientifically. Tom Driver says "Einstein was able to show that objects (masses) are energy. The devastating truth of $E=mc^2$ became a fact of modern life that in 1945 . . . the absolute character of any 'substance' . . . has been demolished" (1981, 70). Fields of energy, interrelations of waves and particles, make up the universe, and because we are part of the universe, we must be, in some ways, made up of that same energy. Thus, selves are wavelike, fluid energy.

Physicist David Bohm (1978) says that particles are in a process of becoming and perishing; particles are capable of being created and destroyed, are transformed and interrelate in a "holomovement." Bohm suggests that the universe is much like a hologram, whereby particles interconnect, move, and create complex pictures that admit of ambiguity and constant change. For Bohm, subjects are holomovements.

Poststructuralists such as Derrida and Foucault re-sound some themes of modern physics in their descriptions of subjectivities. Derrida says that we are made up of a "vibrating or resonating system of relations" (1995b, 137). Thus, the "dream" of unitary subjectivity is over. The self is shattered and splits apart, drifts as image, appearance, ghost. Unlike process philosophers, Derrida is interested in showing how subjects have been produced through culture and language. Derrida claims that identity is always already "inscribed in a determined textual system" (1978, 160). Therefore, I am not radically free. I "carry the detour, the contour, and the memory inscribed in the culture of [my] body . . . these reading grids, these folds, zigzags, references and transferences are, as it were, in [my] skin" (1995a, 353).

Understanding that the self is a cultural product is a first step toward change and reinvention. Reinvention, however, is not a transgressive movement. Transgression presupposes that the self can step outside of its culture and history and completely change. On the contrary, only slight change, slight movement is possible because the self is trapped in language, culture, history. Still, teachers might encourage students to do self-work, that is, to work on reinventing and recreating themselves. After all, creative lives are the ones worth living.

But it is schooling, so often, that does not encourage continual self-creation. Schooling tends to produce squashed selves because many teachers and school administrators already have preconceived notions about who kids are, or who they should become when they grow up. American schools are like mini-corporations or mini-factories where students must learn to be obedient to the bosses and factory owners. Corporate America does not, for the most part, like difference or ambiguity. Just look around at the way businessmen dress: same suits, same ties, same haircuts.

When one is subverting the culture of conformity, Derrida (1995a) tells us, reinvention of self becomes crucial. Creative self-identity is resistance to cultural forms, and school (as the mini-corporation) is one of these cultural forms that demands interruption. American schools want kids to be robots who can spit back the same things on exams (and this is called knowledge?), and score the same numbers on standardized tests (and this is called wisdom?). This would be a tragedy of education. Educators might begin to understand the profound wisdom of queer theory as it asks all of us to reinvent who we are and what we know in creative ways. Standardized knowings will never allow for creative becomings.

Foucault's work has helped many understand the complexities of taken-for-granted knowings. He also wonders about how it is that we take for granted, unknowingly perhaps for some, our own becoming, our own self-identities. Foucault claims that subjectivities are produced by discursive and nondiscursive practices. Prisons, schools, the Church, language, culture, and history all play a part in producing selves. More than anyone else, Foucault has shown how subjects have been normalized by complex webs of discursive practices, beginning with the confession. In *The History of Sexuality* (1978), Foucault examines "the effects of power generated" (11) by confession. Confession generated a "polymorphous incitement to discourse" (11) which unleashed talk of sex and sexuality.

Incessant talk of sex, however, did not lead to salvation, as the Church Fathers had hoped, but led rather to categorization, normalization, and oppression. "Through the various discourses, legal sanctions against minor perversions were multiplied, sexual irregularity was annexed to mental illness" (11). Like the Church, the psychiatric community punishes what they consider to be unnatural sexual activities. Homosexuals were labeled mentally ill until recently. But still the American Psychological Association (APA) labels those who "suffer" from "a persistent discomfort with . . . sex or sense of inappropriateness in the gender role of that sex [as having] gender identity disorder" (1994, 246–47). More insidiously, the APA's *Diagnostic and Statistical Manual IV* says that children who insist on participating "in the stereotypical games . . . of the other sex" (246–47) suffer gender identity disorder. The psychiatric community is not alone in its attempt to normalize gender identity. Deborah Britzman points out that "the work of the apparatuses of education, law, and medicine becomes preoccupied with normalizing sexuality to the confines of proper object choice" (1996, 6). Normalization practices are everywhere.

Queering Up the Subject

Queer subjects were born out of the work of the poststructuralists. David Halperin (1995) even calls Foucault "Saint" in his work *Saint Foucault: Toward a Gay Hagiography*. Both Foucault and Derrida have pointed out that subjects have always already been produced through language and culture. We arrive on the scene already invented. And those of us who do not fit into prescriptive categories are demonized, medicalized. Queer theorists, continuing Foucault's work, attempt to call these demonizations, normalizations, and medicalizations into question. Overturning normalization practices is key to queer activism.

Queer subjects have appropriated the term "queer," which signals several things. Historically, the term "queer" has been negative; it has typically been used to refer to effeminate men (fags) or masculine women (dykes) or wierdos. The reappropriation of this negative word has upset some members of the gay/lesbian community. But others feel that queer now means pride. Witness this queer slogan: We're queer, we're here, we're everywhere, get used to it. Queer now takes on a rude-positive connotation announcing the coming of a prophetic age (Morris 1997).

Queer announces more than "lesbian," "gay," or "bisexual." Queer refers to anyone who feels marginalized by mainstream visions of sexuality. Straight queers are welcome in the queer parade, too. Ultimately, queer identities are performances (Bell and Valentine 1995; Blessing 1997; Meyer 1994; Tyler 1994). And these performances are radically unstable since the queer self is not bound by any particular label or desire. Queer desire is unstabled. Some gay and lesbian theorists are unhappy with queer theory because, for queer theorists, desire seems to move around too freely. Some gay/lesbian theorists believe that selves are determined by specific objects of desire. Queer theorists, on the other hand, explode these constricting notions. Halperin says queer connotes a "wrenching sense of recontextualization" (1995, 61–62).

Gender performances are changeable, shifting, dynamic, fluid. Queer theorists insist that there is no such thing as a core gender because gender is socially constructed. There is nothing "natural" about gender, as Aquinas would have us believe. Biddy Martin tells us that the sex equals gender paradigm is also problematic because "what we come to experience as our relation to sexual difference, our most deeply felt sense of gender is, in part, the consequence of reducing a complex set of relations to a false unity of gender under the sign of sex" (1994, 103). This complex set of relations we call gender/sexuality is produced through language, TV, schooling, medicine, law, and religion. And these discourses serve to normalize and stabilize.

Queer theory attempts to disconnect sex and gender by suggesting that the two are not necessarily related. Jennifer Blessing's description of a Man Ray photograph of Marcel Duchamp as Prose Selavy is a pertinent example that disconnects sex and gender and shows how both categories are socially constructed. Blessing says, "Man Ray photographed Marcel Duchamp in drag as Prose . . . Prose is not beautiful, she is not Helen, and she is not a she. Like the phantom Helen in Euripides' account, this Helen is not the "real" Helen, but rather an imposter" (1997, 19). Duchamp's performance demonstrates that he is not who he appears, he is a she, but not a she after all. The phantom Prose Selavy became a spokesperson for Belle Halein perfume but all the while, he/she was fooling her/his audiences, masking her/his identity. Certainly, I would call this performance queer. Queer performances confuse notions of sex/gender and identity.

Donna Haraway (1991) suggests that we might enter what she calls a "post-gendered" age whereby we can transgress the notion of gender altogether. But I think this is impossible, because we are always already inscribed in a culture that insists upon talking about gender. The best we can do, then, is resist notions of gender that become oppressive. Jennifer Blessing tells us that "in some languages no distinction between the words [sex/gender] presently exists, and the connotations of these and related terms are constantly shifting" (1997, 112). But in our language there is a long, complex history concerning the distinction between sex and gender, and this history has served oppressive ends.

Deborah Britzman (1996) says sexuality is movement. Queer sexualites are like waves moving gently along the sandy beach, colors multitudinous, moods changeable, textures drifting. The fluidity of queer subjectivities offers relief from the fixity of normalized gender/sex identities. Some worry, however, that fluid subjectivities, queer subjectivities, become so dreamlike, so disjointed that they are really nonidentities (Martin 1994). Carole-Anne Tyler (1997) tells us that Elizabeth Grosz and Leo Bersani complain that unless queer theorists "work with a concept of sexual difference, queers cannot do justice to homosexual specificity" (130). But queers do not want to talk about homosexual specificity, or specifixity. Fixing desire traps. Names trap, labels like lesbian, gay, and transsexual trap. Naming kills. At any moment identity can trap, block, freeze. And this is my worry. Queer sensibilities continually deconstruct the trappings of identity, continually problematize arrested psyches. Queer theory works to undo these dangerous practices. Troubling, challenging identities work to disrupt discourses that enclose selves, pin down desires. Queer sexualities are movements, movements away from self-enclosures.

Movements in queer spaces are not, however, progressive or linear. They are jagged, backward, upside down, discontinuous. Queer representations are prophetic (Morris, 1997). They are prophetic because they announce the coming of an age in which sexualities are pluralities, genders are multitudinous, subjectivities are like tides of the ocean.

Internalized Shame and Queer-a-phobia

As Kermit the Frog reminds us, it's not easy being green. It's not easy being queer either. Internalized shame and queer-a-phobia are difficult to avoid. Othering practices such as homophobia, hate crimes, heteronormativity are pervasive in American culture. In fact, consumer capitalism itself thrives on othering practices. David Sibley (1995) explains that consumer capitalism "depends on . . . expel[ling]" (8) the other. TV advertisements reproduce heteronormativity while expelling queers. Who buys life insurance? Straight, white, middle-class couples. Who buys cars? Straight, white, middle-class couples. Who buys flooring, tiles, stocks, shoes, burgers, cereal? Not queers.

There are very few queer representations on TV. This absence of things queer for young people who happen to be queer can be very hard to deal with. I recall my own experience growing up in suburban America watching shows on TV like *The Brady Bunch*. Why didn't the Bradys have a queer sister or brother like me? I couldn't relate to any of the Brady kids. This absence of queer folks, even in my beloved cartoons (I especially loved *Bullwinkle*), made me feel like an alien. I didn't even have words to describe why I could not relate to people on TV. I just intuited that I was different and that my difference was bad. I grew up feeling like the character Rhoda in the film *The Bad Seed.* And I knew that I could never reveal my queerness until I left the burbs and the Bradys behind.

Like TV, the academy is still, for the most part, guilty of othering queers. As Waldrep suggests, "The academy's approach to those who do queer work is often predictably homophobic" (in Bredbeck, Gonzalez, and Waldrep 1996, 88). Some of my graduate school friends choose to play the game of "passing" for straight because they are terrified that coming out would jeopardize their careers. "Passing" is a troubling notion that demands some interrogation, for it may suggest a strict binary relation between being (in) the closet (passing as straight is a way of being in the closet) as opposed to being (out) of the closet. Being out of the closet is a way of being that admits of queerness. On the contrary, passing is a way of *hiding* in the closet.

But is lived experience *ever* cut up neatly into these two places: *in* the closet or *out* of the closet? Perhaps life is much more complex than this bifurcation allows. Perhaps these categories of *in* and *out* do not reflect the world as we experience it. So one might argue that the term passing is problematic, on one level, because it suggests that there are only two places to be in the world, two possible ways of being in the world. Either one can pass and stay in the closet or come out of the closet and get real. A variation on this theme might read this way: One can be in the closet *sometimes* and out of the closet at *other times.* But even if the dichotomy is qualified in this way, the problem still remains that life is lived in many places at once, ontologically speaking. Dwelling in the world is a complex thing. The reduction to closet space is much too simplistic to capture the ways in which one experiences life.

The more pressing problem, though, has to do with hiding. This question, for me, does not turn on ontology but on ethics. I argue that although lived experience, ontologically, is streamlike and fluid, and that, in actuality, there is no inside and outside of the closet, and although queer identities admit of ambiguities, honesty about one's ambiguous, queer desires becomes an ethical responsibility, at least for me. To me, passing is most fundamentally being dishonest and is ultimately unethical. Of course there will always be circumstances when one must lie, or when one must hide in order to survive, especially during times of political unrest and war. But Americans today are living during a time of political stability and peace, and thus being honest about one's queerness becomes a possibility and a choice. And the choice to be honest or to lie affects us all. I argue that hiding one's queerness is, in the long term, not a good thing. Thus, "passing" is not what I would call queer. As Carole-Anne Tyler points out, "Passing has become the sign of the victim, the practice of one already complicit with the order of things, prey to its oppressive hierarchies" (1994, 212).

Queering up the subject means outing the subject. It has "passed" through my mind whether or not I should *erase* from my curriculum vita publications on queer theory for fear that future employers would not hire me. But I refuse to closet my vita. I refuse to *erase myself.* I can certainly understand, however, why many choose to live closeted lives. Queer-a-phobia is everywhere, hate crimes persist, and queers have little protec-

tion against discrimination. Gonzalez tells us that "while judicial prece-
dent is on the side of women and ethnic minorities, sexuality still is not a
protected class within the whole academy or the country" (in Bredbeck,
Gonzalez, and Waldrep 1996, 86).

It is difficult for queers, then, not, in some way, to internalize queer-a-
phobia. Because queer-a-phobia exists on most every level of American
culture, many suffer from a sense of shame and humiliation from admit-
ting queer identities. The feeling of shame may be just as scarring as
physical abuse. Silvan Thompkins says that "while terror and distress
hurt, they are wounds inflicted from outside which penetrate the smooth
surface of the ego, but shame is felt as an inner torment of the soul" (in
Sedgwick and Frank 1995, 133). Internalized shame quickly turns to self-
hatred. Self-hatred can destroy a life. Self-hatred can also be psychologically projected onto others and become manifest as hatred of the other.
Within queer spaces this negative projection exists. For example, many
drag queens imitate women but simultaneously project hatred onto women
as well. Many butch queers who are women, although imitating men, also
project hatred onto men. Straight queers, too, get trapped in some kind
of internalized homophobic responses. For instance, Peter/Petra, a co-
worker with me at the Columns Hotel in New Orleans, exhibited much
homophobia but dressed in drag at night, did construction during the day
and marched his girlfriend (who really was a woman) around in between.
And straight straights can't resist homophobia either, at least on some
level. Just check out any heterosexual bar and I'm sure you'll hear the
word fag used to describe a man who is not quite macho enough.

Diana Fuss claims that internalized homophobia (or queer-a-phobia)
may begin with what deconstructionists call the logic of the supplement.
According to Fuss, an outsider's [queer] subject position is "formulated as
a consequence of a lack internal to the system it supplements" (1991,
14). The queer's subject position, in other words, is produced in conjunc-
tion to/with the heterosexual's. Insiders (heterosexuals) understand outsiders (queers) as a "contaminated" lack (1991, 14). The heterosexual
man/woman may project negative images, the images of filth, dirt, onto
queers. And these images, in turn, become internalized by queers. These
internalized images, then, may become possible sites of humiliation and
shame. Queer subjectivities are produced in response and reaction to
nonqueers.

Nonqueers are also produced within the context of queer spaces. Queer-
a-phobia is born out of what Derrida (1978) calls "absolute alterity." Self
and other are seen as completely exterior, completely separate, completely

other. And when subjects are positioned as absolutely exterior, phobias
are born. Derrida (1978) tells us that we must be "deaf" to the idea of
absolute alterity. Subjectivities are not completely separate and exterior
to each other. We are born in intertextual ways. The other is in us and we
are in the other. Identities are co-implicating and co-complicating. Thus,
someone who is queer-a-phobic cannot negotiate queerness within herself, himself. Similarly, someone who is heterophobic cannot negotiate
heterosexuality within himself or herself either. Queer and nonqueer identities are co-produced.

Queer Subjects Are Politically Radical

Queer identities are politically radical. To be queer is to be rude-positive,
in-your-face, out. Queer politics are oppositional. "The aim of oppositional politics is . . . not liberation but resistance" (Halperin 1995, 18).
And resistances against policing discourses occur at the local level. The
fight against othering practices begins by outing oneself. It is not easy to
publicly confess queerness. I have felt a sense of humiliation when I've
engaged in these public confessions. But I know that silence = death.
Lynn Miller says, "silence denies the existence of difference and allows
the dominant culture to believe it is the only culture" (1994, 214). Like
Miller, Eve Sedgwick declares that "queer survival" turns on making "invisible possibilities and desires visible; to make tacit things explicit; to
smuggle queer representation in where it must be smuggled" (1993, 3).
Outing is performance and some prefer more out-rageous performance
than others. Abelove (1993) tells us that members of Queer Nation, which
has had chapters all over the United States and Canada, have staged
same-sex kiss-ins in suburban shopping malls and heterosexual bars. Other
out-rageous outings occur during Mardi Gras in New Orleans.

The Mardi Gras "fashion show" is fashioned on imitating fashion shows.
This is queer theatre extraordinaire! Queers imitate heterosexual fashion
shows, turn heterosexual fashion on its head by subverting attires. Last
year, for instance, the presidents' wives lined up on stage: "Pat Nixon,"
"Betty Ford," "Hilary Clinton," and many others strutted about in their
latest dresses and hairdos. But all the presidents' wives were really men;
all the presidents' men were men. Queer fashion shows are fun but they
are also political. If anything, they demonstrate how gender is fashioned
on imitation. Judith Butler (1990) was one of the first to point this out.

Carnival in New Orleans is not unlike the early days of Carnival in
medieval Europe. Carnival was sanctioned by the Church during the middle

ages, but for many, Carnival served as a site of resistance against the Church. Bakhtin's dissertation on Rabelais (1459–1553), called *Rabelais and His World*, illustrates this point. Bakhtin suggests that, for Rabelais, Carnival was a counterpolitic that parodied Church doctrine. During Carnival, people undermined "ready-made and completed ideas on eternity, hell, salvation" (Morris 1994, 200). The absolutes of eternity, hell, salvation were turned upside down, backward, made silly and annoying. Bakhtin says that Carnival was a "boundless world of humorous forms and manifestations [that] opposed the official and serious tone of medieval ecclesiastical and feudal culture" (Morris 1994, 196). And like Carnival of old, current Carnivals serve, for some, counterpolitical ends. The queer fashion show certainly attempts to undermine the status quo.

Queer politics is more than advocating tolerance (Garber 1994; Morton 1996). Queer politics is more than changing beliefs and attitudes that perpetuate oppression. Queer politics must work toward dismantling institutionalized queer-a-phobia. Michael Warner explains: "Because the logic of the sexual order is so deeply embedded by now in an indescribably wide range of social institutions, and is embedded in the most standard accounts of the world, queer struggles aim not just at toleration or equal status but at challenging those institutions and accounts" (1993, 13). Dismantling institutional homophobia/queer-a-phobia is a difficult task because these insidious practices are so deeply interwoven into the very culture and language of American life. But queer workers cannot sink into nihilism. The struggle goes on. Hope might be the only thing keeping us alive, but still, hope helps.

What's Queer Theory Got to Do with It? Implications for Educators

Queer theory might seem completely irrelevant to education, but it isn't. Consciousness-raising about this new field might help teachers better educate their students about the complexities of identities. Perhaps queer theorists might help foster understanding and even empathy toward those who have been labeled in damaging, violent ways. Queer theory teaches that all identities are performances and these performances are interrelated and complicit in many ways, queer and nonqueer. The damaging effects of labels are still felt by many in the queer community. If anything, queer theory teaches that naming kills. Perhaps one day educators will queer up the field and "tilt the tower" (Garber 1994) by joining the fight against the violence of naming, heteronormativity, hate crimes.

This hellish hurricane, which never rests, drives on the spirits with its violence: wheeling and pounding, it harasses them. When they come up against the ruined slope, then there are cries and wailing and lament . . . I learned that those who undergo this torment are damned because they sinned with flesh, subjecting reason to the rule of lust. (Dante [1300] 1982, 43)

Dante draws on Christian doctrine and was probably familiar with the punishments of exomolgesis or public penance. Those who sinned with flesh are placed in eternal damnation behind the gates of hell. "Abandon every hope, who enter here" (Dante [1300] 1982, 21). These famous words that describe the chilling details of *The Inferno* are meant as a warning. The warning is not unlike Tertullian's as he told Catholics to meditate on hell if they did not submit to confession, submit to the reasoning of Church law. Dante was probably familiar with the writings of Tertullian as well.

Queer theorists hope that warnings such as these have become laughable. But these fears haunt many who engage in literal readings of the Judeo-Christian scriptures. Perhaps Dante put so-called sex offenders in hell to point out how silly that punishment would be. Queer theorists say that disciplining the body is immoral, unethical, and just plain wrong. When will a queer exodus from hell take place? How will we abandon the gates of hell? Is the journey a "lost path" (Dante [1300] 1982, 13)? Queer journeys are struggles but in all the lostness we move as a stream toward better days where the gates of hell have vanished from our paths forever. Dante's left foot kicks queer theory into gear.

Works Cited

American Psychological Association (APA). 1994. *The American Psychological Association diagnostic criteria for DSM IV desk reference.* Washington D.C.: APA.

Aquinas, T. [1273] 1989. Summa theologica. In *Ethical theory and social issues: Historical texts and contemporary readings,* edited by David Theo Goldberg. New York: Holt Reinhart.

Aristotle. [335–323 b. c. e.] 1968. The metaphysics. In *Philosophic classics: From Thales to Ockham,* edited by Walter Kaufmann. Translated by W. D. Ross. Paramus, N.J.: Prentice Hall.

Bailey, L. W. 1996. The no-thing-ness of near-death experiences. In *The near-death experience: A reader,* edited by Lee W. Bailey and Jenny Yattes. New York: Routledge.

Bell, D. and G. Valentine. 1995. The sexed self: Strategies of performance, sites of resistance. In *Mapping the subject: Geographies of cultural transformation,* edited by Steve Pile and Nigel Thrift. New York: Routledge.

Berlant, L. and M. Warner. 1995. What does queer theory teach us about x? *PMLA* 110, no. 3: 343–49.

Blessing, J. 1997. Prose is a prose is a prose: Gender performance in photography. In *Prose is a prose is a prose: Gender performance in photography,* edited by Jennifer Blessing. New York: Guggenheim Museum Publications.

Bohm, D. 1978. The implicate order. *Process Studies* 8, no. 2: 73–99.

Bredbeck, W., M. Gonzalez, and S. Waldrep. 1996. Queer studies and the job market: Three perspectives. *Profession 1996*: 82-90.

Britzman, D. 1996. "On becoming a little sex researcher": Some comments on a polymorphously perverse curriculum. *JCT: An Interdisciplinary Journal of Curriculum Studies* 12, no. 2: 4–11.

Butler, J. 1990. *Gender trouble: Feminism and the subversion of identity.* New York: Routledge.

Dante, A. [1307] 1982. *The divine comedy of Dante Alighieri: Inferno.* Translated by Allen Mandelbaum. New York: Bantam Books.

Derrida, J. 1978. *Writing and difference.* Translated by Alan Bass. Chicago: University of Chicago Press.

———— 1995a. A madness must watch over thinking. In *Points . . . Interviews, 1974–1994 Jacques Derrida*, edited by Elisabeth Weber. Translated by Peggy Kamuf. Stanford, Calif.: Stanford University Press.

———— 1995b. Dialanguages. In *Points . . . Interviews, 1974–1994 Jacques Derrida*, edited by Elisabeth Weber. Translated by Peggy Kamuf. Stanford, Calif.: Stanford University Press.

Driver, T. 1981. *Christ in a changing world: Toward an ethical christology.* New York: Crossroad.

Foucault, M. 1978. *The history of sexuality. Volume one: An introduction.* Translated by Robert Hurley. New York: Vintage.

Fuss, D., ed. 1991. Introduction. In *Inside/out: Lesbian theories, gay theories*, edited by Diana Fuss. New York: Routledge.

Garber, L., ed. 1994. *Tilting the tower.* New York: Routledge.

Halperin, D. 1995. *Saint Foucault: Toward a gay hagiography.* New York: Oxford University Press.

Haraway, D. 1991. *Simians, cyborgs and women: The reinvention of nature.* New York: Routledge.

Mandelbaum, A., trans. 1982. Introduction. In *The Divine Comedy of Dante Alighieri.* New York: Bantam Books.

Mansfield, M. 1995. *The humiliation of sinners: Public penance in thirteenth-century France.* Ithaca: Cornell University Press.

Marcel, A. J. 1988. Phenomenal experience and functionalism. In *Consciousness in contemporary science*, edited by Anthony J. Marcel and Edoardo Bisiach. Oxford: Clarendon Press.

Martin, B. 1994. Extraordinary homosexuals and the fear of being ordinary. *differences: A Journal of Feminist Cultural Studies* 6, nos. 2 and 3: 100–25.

McNeill, J. T. and H. Garner. 1979. *Medieval handbooks of penance: A translation of the principal libri poenitentials and selections from related documents.* New York: Routledge.

Meyer, M. 1994. *The politics of camp.* New York: Routledge.

Miller, L. 1994. The politics of self and other. In *Queer words, queer images: Communication and the construction of homosexuality,* edited by Jeffrey R. Ringer. New York: New York University Press.

Morris, M. 1997. Ezekiel's call: Toward a queer pedagogy. *Taboo: The Journal of Culture and Education* 1: 153–66.

Morris, P., ed. 1994. *The Bakhtin reader: Selected writings of Bakhtin, Medvedev, Voloshinov.* New York: Edward Arnold/Hodder Headline Group.

Morton, D. 1996. Review: The class politics of queer theory. *College English* 58, no. 4: 471–82.

Poschmann, B. 1964. *Penance and the annointing of the sick.* Translated by Frank Courtney. New York: Herder and Herder.

Sedgwick, E. K. 1990. *Epistemology of the closet.* Berkeley, Calif.: University of California Press.

———— 1993. *Tendencies.* Durham: Duke University Press.

Sedgwick, E. K. and A. Frank, eds. 1995. *Shame and its sisters: A Silvan Thomkins reader.* Durham: Duke University Press.

Sibley, D. 1995. *Geographies of exclusion: Society and difference in the West.* New York: Routledge.

Tertullian. [200 c. e.] 1959. *Treatises on penance: On penitence and purity.* Translated by William P. Le Saint. Maryland: The Newman Press.

Tyler, C. A. 1994. Narcissism, identity and difference. *differences: A Journal of Feminist Cultural Studies* 6, nos. 2 and 3: 212–48.

———— 1997. Death masks. In *Prose is a prose is a prose: Gender performance in photography,* edited by Jennifer Blessing. New York: Guggenheim Museum Publications.

Warner, M. 1993. Introduction. In *Fear of a queer planet: Queer politics and social theory,* edited by Michael Warner. Minneapolis: University of Minnesota Press.

Whitehead, A. N. [1938] 1951. Nature and life. In *Classic American philosophers,* edited by Max Fisch. Paramus, N.J.: Prentice Hall.

———[1929] 1978. *Process and reality.* The corrected edition by David R. Griffin and Donald Shernbourne. New York: The Free Press.

Chapter 3

Precocious Education[1]

Deborah P. Britzman

While it may be rather unpopular to begin with Sigmund Freud's views on sexuality–and here, I leave it up to the reader to supply the more commonplace remittances against Freud–there remains something quite radical in Freud's theories that should cause educators to rethink our resistance to the associations of sexuality, to the intractableness of Eros and its labile design, and to the startling and often off-putting questions made from this original urge. When Freud divided the human subject with his notion of the unconscious, and suggested that there is a part of each of us that cannot be tamed or known; that resists rationality, time, and negation; that tolerates without judgement the coexistence of contradiction; and that obeys the continuum of pleasure and unpleasure as opposed to the fragile laws of reality-testing, he also suggested a stunning breach in sexuality. We are not just alienated from knowing ourselves in terms of consciousness, rationality, and intention: Even our desires slip between the fault lines of recognition and misrecognition, our urges divide in the strange calculus of ignorance and knowledge, and our passions contradict in aim and satisfaction. The wanderings of sexuality signify excess, more than we may consciously ask for or even want. Freud named this otherness the instinct of Eros, where instinct suggests a "frontier concept," something between the wish and the need.[2]

Freud conceptualized instinct as sheer urge, the push that comes before representation and in its search for satisfaction, the instinct's aim, object, drive, and source work against each other, may momentarily meet but only to divide again, and then, in the strange trajectory of desire, instinct loosens its bearings, falls away, only to begin again. The instinct searches before it knows its wants. As a demand to work, the workings of instinct are precocious, arriving before knowledge and understanding. It is difficult, then, to determine once and for all the place, destination, choices, and reasons of sexuality. This mix-up, something beyond the view that sexuality is on the side of utility or can somehow be explained in the logic of academic discipline, marks the very question of sexuality as perverse, as subject to reversals, condensation, substitutions, and misconstrual. What actually happens when the desire for the other's desire meets and perhaps trips our own play of curiosity?

These unruly views on sexuality, of trying to decide what has to do with sexuality and what seems to escape the relation Freud called Eros, raise significant questions for and resistance in the field of education. There are three forms of resistance to sexuality relevant to our inquiry: structural, pedagogical, and psychical. Structural resistance, the very design or organization of education, raises significant questions as to how education defines its subject: where knowledge is rendered as legitimate through its disciplinary structure; where intellection and affect are viewed as somehow capable of separation and then, agreement; where the public and private are in strict opposition and strangely entangled; and, where the figure of the teacher and her or his authority is tied to a capacity to occupy the role of subject-presumed-to-know, the representative of a stable knowledge.[3] In this view any admission of anxiety somehow signifies individual ignorance, incorrect ideas, and perhaps incompetence. That structure itself might induce anxiety is also resisted. A second resistance to sexuality works in the nature of pedagogical relations. One direction worries about Eros between students and teachers.[4] Another direction considers sexuality as the secret of an individual's nature. When discussions of sexuality move quickly into affirming identities, criticizing social structures, and doing away with stereotypes, or when unexpected questions seem to disrupt and test the failure of the teacher's knowledge, sexuality is often responded to as a threat in need of containment. Curiosity, itself a sign of our sexuality, is diminished. A third resistance concerns psychical resistance or the conflict within, itself a symptom of a self divided from itself. In Freud's view, sexuality is other to education, to cure, and to the confines of authoritative knowledge, even as sexuality is the condition of and cause for our capacity to learn, to seek pleasure in both the making and unmaking of knowledge, and to craft erotic relations from the strangest places. Freud extends this intimate paradox to everyone, which then allows psychical resistance to sexuality to take the form of ambivalence. If we can make anything from the stunning reach of our sexuality, or better, if sexuality can make anything of us, then how is it possible to "know" our sexuality? These forms of resistance and the possibility of working through them raise rather serious questions on the nature of education and on the uses of educational anxiety. Can sexuality with its wild qualities be educated? And, can education be sexed?

Such strange questions are foreclosed when discussions of sexuality in education tend to be viewed as relevant only in the small space of the curriculum of sex education and then, reduced to instruction on the prevention of sexual disease transmission and teenage pregnancy, and to the importance of abstinence and heterosexual marriage. Mainly, sexuality is then supposed as either a problem that will violently erupt to ruin innocent lives, or as a sacred object that requires protection, deferral, maturity, and social and legal sanction. But there is also another trouble that emerges when sexuality is inserted into the school curriculum. This has to do with how the curriculum structures modes of behaviour and orientations to knowledge that are repetitions of the underlying structure and dynamics of education: compliance, conformity, and the myth that knowledge cures. This conflict, when the will of the curriculum meets the will of the students, is best illustrated in research on HIV/AIDS education. During the 1998 Geneva World AIDS conference, for example, Montreal researcher Robert Bastin, who studied approaches to AIDS education in secondary schools, reported that AIDS education is too tied to the dynamics of authority and evaluation of traditional pedagogy and that "rationally [students] have no choice but to give the right answers rather than engage in honest dialogue" (cited in Picard). Discussion is impossible when the pedagogical relations are aligned by the imperatives of school structure. Just as significantly, the capacity to grapple ethically with the very instability of knowledge, particularly in the question of HIV/AIDS, is foreclosed. While studies of HIV/AIDS education may well provide us with the limits of any sex education, the insights offered also suggest something intractable about our subject.[5]

In this chapter, drawing from psychoanalytic insight and the methodological claims of queer theory,[6] I suggest some of the ethical imperatives that can be made when transgressing this limit, and argue for the importance of developing a much wider and more generous understanding of the stunning and surprising reach of anyone's sexuality. This argument suggests a graver consideration: that education's present structure and modes of thought resist ethical actions and can be viewed as criminally negligent in its censorship of safer sex education, in its eschewal of difficult ideas, and in its incapacity to notice its own harm. While a certain impatience marks my discussion, particularly in the second part of this chapter, my purpose is to provoke the conceptual work necessary to understand sexuality as a lifelong project or what Michel Foucault (1988) called, in one of his last studies, "care of the self."[7] We will explore why any educator should consider the dynamics of sexuality as central to the capacity for human curiosity, for living a vital intellectual and social life, and for our capacity to attach passionately to knowledge, other people, and life projects. We will consider what theories of love and hate mean for theories of sexuality. And, finally, this chapter will sketch the significance of these claims to the rethinking of pedagogical relationships and curriculum reconceptualization. What is sexuality that it can be considered as learning to live a life? Is there any difference between falling in love with ideas and falling in love with a person? How might we begin to address our own anxieties, our own uncertainties, our own symptoms of the inadequacy of knowledge when we attempt to have conversations about sexuality in educational settings?

The sorts of questions that structure this chapter follow an insightful approach Eve Sedgwick (1990) developed in *Epistemology of the Closet*, her stunning study of homosexuality as relation and as "open secret." Rather than discuss sexuality in terms of the now familiar constructivist/ essentialist debates, on, for instance, whether sexuality is learned and organized in discursive structures, cultural representations, and historical discourses, or whether it is a natural or ontological event and hence implicitly biological and thus immune from, at some level, the re-workings of representation and social interventions, Sedgwick offers different terms: minoritizing and universalizing discourses. These allow for the question of implication and seem more adequate to the accidental sociality educational conceptualizations attempt to address. A minoritizing view secures the meaning of sexuality to the confines of identity and to its choice of object. In this way only certain knowledge is relevant to certain folks and then, for instance, heterosexual sex has nothing to learn from homosexual sex.[8] A universalizing view attempts something polymorphous and attends to the dynamic expressed in content. It assumes that anyone thinks from sexuality and finds ideas in the most unusual places, that sexuality is central and difficult for anyone, and that knowledge of sexuality is always somehow insufficient to its object, aim, pressure, and source. When Sedgwick writes, "People are different from each other" (22), she eschews the content and meaning of difference, focusing instead upon obviousness, interminablity, and surprise, and upon the conditions that make categories thinkable, how they perform, and what sort of relations they put into place. But there is also another dimension opened when sexuality is conceptualized through a universalizing gesture—it can become unhinged, or conceptually set loose from its commonplace binaries of homosexuality and heterosexuality, from nature and culture, from boy and girl, from satisfaction and dissatisfaction, and from active and passive, for instance. And this has to do with the question of opening a conception of sexuality that is capable of reading the symptoms of sexuality, of addressing the anxieties anyone has, of questioning the curious combinations made from psychical and symbolic apparatuses, and of encountering the uncertainty, the curiosity, the alterity, and the strange relations sexuality also presses into form. To conceptualize sexuality as a universal and to resist filling in that universal with laws, rules, content, manners, cultural imperatives, and so on, is only to claim that anyone begins in sexuality and that this beginning allows us the desire to enter into, use, and re-find symbolic structures and objects necessary to sexuality.[9]

Most generally, then, sexuality is a force that allows the human its capacity for passion, interests, explorations, disappointment, and drama. Its centrality can also be the basis of the argument that sexuality is a human right of free association. Of course to think about sexuality as a human right requires that we consider not just the obstacles to its elaboration but also how sexuality is made in specific cultural contexts and within the conflict of needs, desires, drives, and everyday wishes. But because the material of sexuality is so diverse, multiple, and surprising, because sexuality is both private and public—something from inside of bodies and something made between bodies—we must focus on sexuality in terms of its contradictory, discontinuous, and ambiguous workings. And this suggests that any working definition of sexuality must be generous and expansive. This is because there is something about sexuality itself that is more than the sum of cultural rules, upbringing, and specific laws. There is something about sexuality that opens questions about the psychical calculus of what Drucilla Cornell (1995) calls "the imaginary domain."[10] The imaginary domain, for Cornell, is tied to a renewal of the imagination and to our sense of freedom. In the most general terms, I offer a thought of sexuality as passion within and between people and as passionate living and ask readers to think what sexuality has to do with freedom, liberty, and the right to craft an interesting, relevant, and vital society.

Defining "sexuality" without closing it down is difficult. And perhaps the methodological rule most relevant is that of free association, allowing whatever to come to mind, fooling censorship by acknowledging the things furthest from the mind. Words, however, are different from feeling and making pleasure, even though words can excite passion, arouse anxiety, provoke breakdowns, urge misconstrual. The words *Eros, urge, life force, drive, pressure,* and *desire* come to mind, along with words like *freedom, creativity,* and *social bonds.* The Greek prefix *ur* may also be of use, for this term refers to something original, innate, the beginning. *Ur-Sexuality,* is, of course, an awkward term. But from our sexuality, we reach into language, making ourselves as we attempt to touch and be touched by others. This awkward term, *ur-Sexuality,* may allow us to explore the idea that sexuality begins at the beginning of life, and because it begins when the human infant is learning to live and learning to love during its most extreme experience of dependency and helplessness, sexuality begins too early to count on understanding. We might view this early or original sexuality as precocious, for at least in the beginning, sexuality knows only one kind of knowledge: the urge that wants satisfaction and the desire for pleasure. In this view, sexuality is the first condition for human curiosity and hence the first condition or force of learning. Simply put, without sexuality, the human would not desire to learn. The urge of sexuality, then, is made from the desire to touch and to be touched by people, by ideas, and by living. The urge that is sexuality also makes us vulnerable to times when satisfaction cannot be made, when meaning becomes lost, and when misunderstanding abounds.

Our original Eros is elaborated over the course of a lifetime. The materials for this elaboration are ideas, engagement with other people, the capacity to explore and make pleasure, and the time to think and get lost in fantasy. In the beginning of our lives, sexuality is not tied to thought, only to aim, to re-finding satisfaction, the lost object. These early ties and infantile strategies for re-finding love do not go away and instead continue, albeit unconsciously, to influence the aim, object, and source of sexuality. Education, however, begins in an opposing direction, with its insistence that finding satisfaction is made from delaying satisfaction and with confronting the immediacy of urges and desires with the tensions of sublimation and the demand to renounce instinct. In psychoanalytic views, education is both a place of precarious libidinality and a frustrating obstacle to its realization.[11] Analyst Siegfried Bernfeld (1973) captured the constitutional ambivalence of education in his definition: "the reaction of society to the fact of development" (90) and his idea that education is antimony. Educators must learn to notice and respond differently to the constitutive conflict that is education's design when they work with reconceptualizing sexuality. For while relations of loving to learning seem to be the idealized sublimation of sexuality, we must also note that loving has the labile capacity to reverse its content and become a hatred for learning and for the teacher's efforts.

Still, our sexuality gives us the instability of curiosity, the desire to learn, and the passion to ignore all that stands in the way of learning. Without sexuality there is no curiosity. The question of sexuality is central to the question of becoming a citizen, to crafting a self who can invent, over and over again, the courage to stand up for the self, to feel passionately for the conditions of others, to create a life from the experiments of learning to love and making from this learning to love a love of learning. This right to make sexuality is composed of tiny and daily movements: the right to craft the self, the right to make pleasure, the right to adequate information, the right to ask questions that cannot be settled in answers, the right to attach to the social, the right to make curiosity, the right to love. Foundationally speaking, sexuality requires basic bodily conditions: food, shelter, and clothing; experiences of the love of others; experiences of pleasure and satisfaction.

Now in noting some of the conditions of the care of the self, we must also note that which impinges upon or woefully disregards the self. Sexuality is also the place where injustices, anxieties, and modes of aggression attach and become enacted. But this notation must not overtake and diminish the persistent question of intimacy, the imaginary domain, even if the focus on intimacy may seem, at first glance, to be a retreat from the social or the political, overtly psychological, and even a luxury that only a few of us can exercise. Indeed, we might notice that in tracing the small history of the subject, we have, as well, an epic history of the social.

Many scholars of sexuality have suggested that sexuality has a history and is not a timeless and unchanging nature.[12] Rather the history of sexuality is a history of ideas, of social practices, and a study of population control. Many have studied how sexuality is an invention or effect of larger institutions that link knowledge, power, and pleasure to people's everyday practices and offer the view that sexuality is a question of how knowledge made in institutions works to organize the thinking and action of what is both permissible and prohibited. These institutions that attempt to organize sexuality include medical establishments, police, governments, schools, and religion. Academic knowledge is also put into this service. This work reminds us that when sexuality becomes an object of knowledge that becomes applied to populations, new forms of human subjection, inequality, and population control become put into place.[13] But also, given the productive possibilities of power and resistance, new identities are made.

Problems of subjection, the workings of power/knowledge/pleasure upon inscriptions of identities, however, are not the end of the story of sexuality, particularly if the story has the capacity to speak to the desire for the pedagogical relation. While we must consider how sexuality is organized outside the body, loosening these conceptual controls allows us to focus on everyday dynamics of human attachment, passion, and our susceptibility to making pleasure from ideas. These dynamics are central to our capacity to attach to education. In a small way, educators want their students to experience a passion for learning, a love of reading, a passion for life. My guess is that while there are many roads to becoming an educator, one essential quality that good educators craft is a belief in the illusion that knowledge can make a difference in how one lives, in the choices one can imagine, and in the capacity we also use to disillusion knowledge from its idealized promises.[14] Knowledge does not, indeed, cannot, solve much, but engagement with ideas might allow one to live better, more vitally, more thoughtfully. We know that for the imagination to be a place of inspiration, it must also be inspired by questions of fiction such as art, music, and the capacity to notice their dynamics in the world. And, perhaps we want our students to have the experiences of falling in and out of love with ideas, with respecting and exploring the vulnerabilities of living, and with learning to stand up for one's self by using language well, by persuading others of the importance of their views, and by listening to what others offer before one makes up one's own mind. As I shall try to show, thinking about these affective bonds and attachments means we must think differently about the reach of sexuality.

What follows are some general considerations for thinking about education and sexuality. I hope these ideas will be useful in making a view of sexuality that is relevant to invoking conditions for citizens who take pleasure in having ideas, in imagining new forms of sociality, new kinds of social bonds, new responsibilities, and new pleasures in caring for the self and making a life. These areas suggest problems in conceptualization and in creating new discourses: 1) sexuality and culture and politics; 2) sexuality and knowledge; 3) sexuality and information; 4) sexuality and creative living; and, 5) sexuality, citizenship, and the curriculum. Of course, these areas are not exhaustive but have been chosen because such dynamics are already structuring the question of education.

Sexuality and Culture and Politics

When sexuality, culture, and politics are brought together we can explore the right to free expression, to free association, and to choices and so ask: What comes to mind when sexuality comes to mind and where does the mind live in sexuality? Do our meanings make sexuality a big space or a small space? When adults think about sexuality, they may think about what adults do with each other. Logically, this thinking is anchored in a view that sexuality culminates and reaches its expression in sexual object choice. Illogically, the view is also a symptom of the adult's forgetting of his or her own infantile sexuality. Sexual object choice usually refers to whom one loves and is often spoken about in terms of heterosexuality, homosexuality, and bisexuality. Some may decide that who one loves, *as opposed to that one loves*, matters most. And, at some level, who one loves does matter, if there are social limits that link sexuality to the question of what is normal and what is abnormal, what is acceptable and what is unacceptable. Object choice matters most in times of intolerance. The problem is not which choice or sexual orientation one is after, but how object choice has become tied to only one legitimated form: heterosexuality through marriage. If, however, the time of sexuality is longer than the erotic relations between people, we might also consider how the regulation of sexuality inhibits our capacity to tolerate human rights. If the State does not recognize certain forms of practice and these practices are still performed, what happens to those who are seen as outlaws? This too is a question of citizenship, for the space of sexuality must be made as large as possible for people to participate in intimate relationships and in political projects.

And yet, in linking sexuality to cultural and political questions, our definition of culture and politics must also be enlarged. Michel de Certeau is helpful in this regard. Culture, for Certeau, "consists not in receiving, but in positing the act by which each individual *marks* what others furnish for the needs of living and thinking" (68). In making a mark upon what others have offered, culture is a creative and vital experience. Certeau offers this definition at the end of a talk titled "Culture and the Schools." He argues for a plurality of languages in education, for multiple and open talk, a mixing of different ways of thinking and saying. Certeau also asks a basic question we must continually answer: What is "the connection between the content of teaching and the pedagogical relation" (56)? What conditions allow us to think about knowledge as a social relation? How are the ideas pedagogy offers related to the ways we encounter one another? Many educators have pointed out that significant obstacles to learning emerge when knowledge and social relations are viewed as a problem of compliance and conformity to outside experts. Essentially, education becomes a place where culture cannot be made, where teachers are reduced to the only authority, and where students are reduced to a holding place, a depository, a passive and dependent object. When the capacity to think and imagine is foreclosed, teachers and students become more rigid. We also lose the chance to experience making relationships within knowledge.

Certeau opens the meanings of politics as well, by raising the question of liberty. "Politics," Certeau argues, "does not assure happiness, nor does it give meaning to things. It creates or it refuses conditions of possibility. It prohibits or it allows; it makes possible or impossible" (118). Like culture, politics are something one makes. But the space politics can open is only the beginning. The great question is, What can we do with our politics? Do politics allow for critical thought or is it the other way around? How can a political space be prepared for critical thought? If politics cannot make happiness, even as it can invoke the conditions for profound sadness, suffering, and disassociation, what other sorts of relations might be made from the now common feminist claim that the personal is the political?

Culture and politics suggest a relation between the content of teaching and the pedagogical relation. Sexuality is closer to making liberty than it is to giving meanings to things. Liberty, or the chance to make new kinds of freedom and new questions, is the basis of democratic life. Like politics and culture, sexuality either makes something possible or impossible; it is the space where one makes her or his own mark. Like culture and politics, sexuality is the imaginative site where larger social discourses attach. But culture, politics, and sexuality are also the spaces where meaning can be broken, interest can be lost, ideas can persecute, and conformity can discourage. Like culture and politics, sexuality is not something we receive from another even if others can help or impede its elaboration. Perhaps, like culture, sexuality is "an act by which each individual *marks* what others [and the self] furnish for the needs of living and thinking."

Sexuality and Knowledge

Sexuality comes before our knowledge of sexuality. Our first urges for satisfaction come before we understand how satisfaction is made. This order means that our first knowledge is precocious, curious. The experiences of the infant offers us a way to think about curiosity. In the beginning of life, the infant cannot distinguish between the urge for satisfaction and the other whose actions meet the infant's needs. It is an achievement of the human baby to begin to distinguish its body from other bodies. It is an achievement when the baby recognizes the separate existence of the other and of the self. When this occurs, knowledge, although immature in its formulation, begins to be made and used by the baby. This immature knowledge is caught in the baby's desire to be loved and the baby's growing capacity to love as she or he learns to live.

The idea that there is a developing relation between sexuality and knowledge is elaborated in Freud's *Three Essays on the Theory of Sexuality*. Freud (1905) noticed that young children had strong ideas about sexuality but these ideas were made from a strange combination of magical thinking, wishes, and attempts to make sense of the secrets of adults. Freud called children "little sex researchers," suggesting that children's theories of sexuality evolve without the permission of adults and in spite of cultural prohibitions. Of course, adults often add more magical thinking to the child's world in an attempt to keep children innocent of adult desires. The very famous childlike questions, Where did I come from?, What is the difference between boys and girls?, Can I make a baby?, or, How will my body look when I get older? all have a range of answers that partly depend upon that strange combination of what the adult can tolerate saying to the child and what the child wishes to be true. What governs these rather magical or superstitious answers the adult offers to the child is adult anxiety. They worry that too much knowledge will get children into more trouble, that somehow knowledge leads to more research. Freud suggests the desire to know is made from sexuality and that while children do experiment sexually, these experiments do not have mature meaning. Here we meet a rather curious conflict: the adult's projection of adult meaning onto the child and the child's own elusive meanings made from bodily actions.

One of the most significant speculations Freud offers is connecting sexuality to the capacity for curiosity and to having ideas. The child desires a theory of the world and this theory must be tested though questions. Sexuality inspires. Anna Freud would also make these sorts of claims whenever she spoke with teachers over the course of her long life. In her lectures to teachers and parents (1974), she emphasized the relation between sexuality and education and how education tries to forget and bury the sexual interests of children. Psychoanalysis calls this attempt to make a graveyard for instinct repression. And many in psychoanalysis claim that repression, made from the residues of anxiety, works in the service of unhappiness, loneliness, aggression, and intellectual rigidity. Repression does not solve internal conflicts, it is merely an unfinished compromise.

Miss Freud urges educators to elaborate a theory of child and adolescent development that begins in the interest of the child and the adolescent, as opposed to the interest of the institution. In later life, she would make the phrase, "in the best interest of the child" as the ethical measure of adult relations with the child. She would also suggest that adults tell children the truth about their bodies and answer children's questions in ways that neither fuel magical thinking nor shy away from their curiosity for the desire to know.

That children and adolescents have their own theories of sexuality comes as no surprise. Perhaps it seems more surprising that adults are not immune from carrying these theories into their own lives. What might seem just as strange is that education, as a social institution, is ambivalent about what role knowledge of sexuality should have in the curriculum. This ambivalence has something to do with how sexuality is defined and with the very nature of Eros as a site of ambivalence. If sexuality is defined as genital practices, then the worry becomes how and when such knowledge should be taught. But if sexuality can be thought about as the basis of curiosity, the force that allows one to make and to have ideas, and the desire to be loved and valued as one learns to love and value others, then the content of the discussion becomes very open and is crafted over the time of education. My point is that sexuality need not be viewed as a separate topic, but as the conditions for adventure in crafting ideas, in theorizing questions of love and loss of love, and in noticing the large issues that attach to our sexuality.

How does the experience of learning become pleasurable? How does one take joy in having ideas, in changing one's mind, in encountering the work of learning? What sorts of relations exists between learning to love and loving learning? We can observe the joy of very young children discovering their world, learning from mistakes, finding and using objects, telling someone what they have made or discovered. The routines of educational procedure, and how these routines can be encountered as obstacles and as an unforgiving authority, can numb and deaden this early joy. There is much to say about the relationship between rigid authority structures in education and the inhibition of making insight in learning. In my view, teachers must find a way to return to the student the conditions that allow the joy of having ideas, taking ideas apart, and then making new knowledge.

One way of thinking about this shift is to wonder if the curriculum offers students and teachers a series of conceptual positions from which students can encounter, re-find, and make knowledge. One position that might be interesting is that of the ethnographer, a position not determined by the identity of individuals, but rather by the sort of work and thinking they do. The ethnographers might explore the relations between pleasure and the making of knowledge. In this study, both knowledge and pleasure can be made complex. Part of the complexity is making the courage to study as well places where pleasure is not possible, where impediments to elaborating the self's reworking of culture make it impossible to leave one's mark, where ignorance is defended, and where refusing to make ideas vital and useful delays our capacity to make democratic experiences. The ethnographic study of knowledge and pleasure can dare to study times when there is a refusal to learn, an insistence upon ignorance, and a cruelty that inhibits the capacity to think. It can also open new questions about how people come to craft ethical relations with each other. This interest in making an affective bond in the social can also be a place where pleasure with and obligation to another come a bit closer.

Sexuality and Information

Beyond bringing into closer relations sexuality and knowledge, a certain form of knowledge is crucial. I am calling this form "information." Preventative information can be brought into relations with a series of risks in sexuality with others. By suggesting that sexuality may be a space of risks, I have in mind five risks about which students require information: the risk of venereal disease transmission, the risk of unplanned pregnancy, the risk of nonconsensual sex and sexualized violence, the risk of losing interest in living, and the risk of HIV transmission. These risks are not unrelated in our time of the global pandemic of Acquired Immune Deficiency Syndrome (AIDS). Information on the risks of sexuality is cultural and political. Culturally, one must be able to do something with information, make one's mark. Politically, information can only offer contexts for possibilities. To illustrate these dilemmas, I now turn to the questions HIV/AIDS offers to education and sketch some of the conditions new information should address.

In their introduction to *Sexuality, Politics, and AIDS in Brazil: In Another World?*, Herbert Daniel and Richard Parker note the difficult history of this virus in Brazil, describing the early experiences of the epidemic as "the night-time drama of HIV/AIDS":

> It was a night characterized above all else by the widespread prejudice and discrimination which seemed to be the only backdrop for the epidemic and its sick. It was here, within this scenery, that the degradation of those considered to be the preferential targets of the epidemic was assured—at first, particularly, behaviourally homosexual and bisexual men, and, as time passed, other similarly "marginal" groups. Quarantine. Isolation. Stigmatization. Violence. Murder. The shadows of a night at once ominous and oppressive. (1)

Richard Parker offers insight into such oppressiveness. He suggests that even before AIDS became statistically significant in Brazil, it was a topic of conversation in everyday life. Herbert Daniel's chapter makes the same point when he writes: "The first impact of AIDS in Brazil was on the public imagination" (35). But the public imagination was not made from any adequate knowledge. Rather, the public imagination was limited by popular fears, stereotypical views on who was at risk, and social class divisions. In the second decade of the epidemic, popular fears continued to inhibit any understanding of how HIV is transmitted through the exchange of bodily fluids, sexual activity, blood transfusions, and injecting drugs with shared needles. This situation became more compounded with lack of medical care and the difficulty of medical treatment opportunities. Parker's overview also suggests significant differences from North American models of HIV/AIDS education campaigns. In North America, education campaigns have been structured around the view that sexuality is an identity, while in Brazil sexual cultures are fluid and not focused on claiming an identity. Rather, the question concerns the sorts of practices that occur between people and the roles people have in these practices. Finally, because the HIV/AIDS epidemic began during the military rule and continued through various collapses of the economy, the response to developing HIV/AIDS education campaigns has occurred while Brazil transitions from an authoritarian military dictatorship to democracy and continued economic crisis.

The conditions under which the HIV/AIDS pandemic is occurring requires new responses on the part of education. Herbert Daniel makes such connections when he writes:

> A response to AIDS on behalf of *life* entails national and local programming ranging from funding to meet the material needs of a growing population, to the mobilization of social and human resources to guarantee the full exercise of people's rights as citizens. AIDS cannot be spoken of as a problem on the planet. The epidemic is a fact of the planet . . . We are living and learning with AIDS. (1993, 47)

Daniel begins with the universalizing axiom that illness must be brought into our everyday world as a question of learning to live. And he believes that this global and inclusive view is the basis for responding well to the pandemic and making the pandemic believable and relevant to every person. However, if this view is to become crucial, education will have to create new conditions for thought, new conditions for the popular imagination. This means that educators will have to consider not just the specific information that they bring to their students, but the myths students and teachers bring to the pedagogical relation. If technical information does not help everyone unlearn the myths and stigmas that can emerge from sexuality, then technical information will not be used and invested with ownership and a commitment to care for the self.

One of the lessons offered in a comparative study of HIV/AIDS campaigns is that it is not enough to dispense facts. Technical information, in and of itself, is not sufficient, nor does it even settle much.[15] Pedagogical efforts make information relevant. These creative efforts involve the capacity to craft affective communities that touch what individuals care about, that allow individuals to find something relevant in new views, and that appeal to imagination, desires, and ethical relationships. Moreover, if these campaigns are to affect youth, youth need opportunities to take leadership, speak with each other, create their own language for making their mark in the world. Curricular efforts can and should move beyond the confines of the classroom walls and into the communities and neighbourhoods of the people involved. Essentially, research-based projects and cultural activities become part of learning to live in AIDS.

The study of AIDS is a study in multiple inequalities, in multiple ethics, and in the imaginary domain.[16] The information that can address this inequality is changing. And so, in bringing pedagogical content closer to pedagogical relations, education, itself a site of popular imagination, can also help the popular imagination ready itself to view knowledge as changing, as subject to revision, and as never completed. But to do so, education will have to address its own anxieties, another symptom of the popular imagination.

Sexuality and Living Creatively

One of the most important questions each of us can ask is, What is life about? This question makes us all philosophers, people who think and dream. I want to suggest that there is a relation between how this question is engaged and what some have called "care of the self." To do so, I will use D. W. Winnicott's definition of creativity: "the doing that arises out of being . . . the ability to create the world" (1986, 39–40). This ability to create the world is the first experience of the infant. Of course the world exists without the infant's creation. But Winnicott suggests that this early experience with making meaning and using objects allows desire its closeness to creativity and, in later life, the capacity to see things freshly. Winnicott contrasts creative living with compliance to others, boredom, and withdrawal from participating in one's own life. He also suggests that not being able to see that others have their own views and creativity is a sign of responding only to the harshness of the world. "Creativity," writes Winnicott, "belongs to being alive—so that unless at rest, the person is reaching out in some way or so that if an object is in the way there can be a relationship" (41). Reaching out physically or mentally becomes meaningful only if there is a self who reaches out and paradoxically in that reach, meets others in the world. If there must be a being before a doing, the doing is also a means to invoke a being. This tension is the space of creativity.

When educators think about creativity, they may limit their imagination to artistic creativity, to innate talent, and to finely honed skills. Artistic creativity, something that is extraordinary, is different from living creatively. Living creatively should be an extraordinary experience but it does not require special talent. Living creatively requires a self who is not overwhelmed with blind compliance to outside demands. One cannot live creatively if the only relationships offered are authoritarian. The self must have opportunities to make her or his own demands to live creatively, to create something more than what she or he finds in the world. Winnicott calls this experience a philosophical dilemma, for while the world exists without us and demands many things from us, for the world to become meaningful, we must create what is already there, we must learn to make our own demands to the world. In this way, living creatively is also a condition of making democracy.

This is creative work and is part of living creatively. We only create, according to Winnicott, what we find. But to find something, we have to reach out into the world and the world must respond in good enough ways so that we can try again. What then does living creatively have to do with sexuality? The individual makes something out of urges, desires, and wishes for attachment. And, in making relations with others, in the experience of reaching out, the individual creates new meanings from the meanings that already exist, that are found. What does living creatively have to do with citizenship? Again, each generation does something more with what the previous generation has left them. The new generations somehow reinvent, and not just receive as changeless, the experiences of those who have come before. My definition of citizenship is very close to the definition of culture Certeau offers: Citizenship "consists not in receiving, but in positing the act by which each individual *marks* what others furnish for the needs of living and thinking" (68).

Sexuality, Citizenship, and the Curriculum

Many educators are well aware that if the school curriculum is to have any relevancy to students, the curriculum must somehow "speak" to an extension of student experience.[17] And yet in curious ways educators are often unprepared to respond to student views. When students begin to speak back to the curriculum, to interpret the curriculum, educators can begin to listen differently, to receive differently, what students make. For this to occur, both educators and students have to learn to see knowledge as something that is made in and altered by relationships. In this view the curriculum becomes an opportunity to explore the significance knowledge has to the lives of others and to one's own life. In conversations then, the teacher's work begins with three kinds of interpretations: The teacher interprets the curriculum and as the teacher interprets the student's interpretation, the teacher can also consider how her or his own fears and desires are shaping the response. In this unfinished and uncertain exchange of ideas, pedagogical content comes closer to the pedagogical relation. Learning is the work of making interpretations, experimenting with the potential force or power of what knowledge can do, and with *marking* knowledge with new significance.

Jonathan Silin's book has the provocative title *Sex, Death, and the Education of Children: Our Passion for Ignorance in the Age of AIDS.*[18] He argues for a curriculum that is socially relevant to children, youth, and adults. But for this social relevance to be made, educators must be willing to surpass the myth that children do not bring their own knowledge of the world to the curriculum. To surpass this myth, educators can question the distance between adults and children, specifically the distance that assumes that adults are people who already know and that children are people who do not know. To move beyond this distanced view, both students and educators can be viewed as people in the world. This requires that educators notice what students do with knowledge and how the knowledge they bring becomes transformed into new experiments. This also requires that everyone have continuous opportunities to explore different views of the world; to become ethnographers of imagination; to research how people make meanings, change their minds, use knowledge, pose problems, create new opportunities for living a life.

What would a curriculum be like if the curriculum began with the problem of living a life? One direction such a curriculum would take is a study of love and hate. These emotions are well known by everyone. They are perhaps our earliest emotions and these emotions of love and hate direct the problem of attachment, belonging, and defense against unknown and unlikable things. Love and hate inspire experiences such as jealously, betrayal, honesty, selflessness, anxiety, boundlessness, wonder, awe, defense, authority, the breakdown of meaning, and permissiveness. Most simply, love in learning is not the idealization of knowledge but the interest in exploring new ideas to see what might happen. Hate in learning emerges when one feels persecuted by the authority of knowledge. But even these simple observations are not so simple, for humans have the capacity to both love and hate and even change their feelings from hate to love and from love to hate. The curriculum should provide the occasion for students to become ethnographers of love and hate.

While the curriculum can allow opportunities to investigate the drama and passions of everyday life, to make a person interested in the work of the citizen, it can also address the histories of the nation in ways that do not repeat national traumas. Each nation wishes to be seen as glorious but history is also troubled and haunted by what is done in the name of glory, in the name of violence. Every nation offers children a legacy, but education might help this future to come to terms with the losses and disregards of nationhood. This is always a difficult question, for the ideals of a nation will change over time, and if history is encountered as a closed book, a finished record, the dramas, passions, and explorations of everyday life cannot be marked.

Throughout my discussion, I have used the term ethnographers and philosophers in a number of places. I now want to suggest some of the qualities of work ethnographers and philosophers undertake and mark. An ethnographer studies culture and the meanings and marks people make in culture. The work of the philosopher is different; philosophers grapple with the ethics of life, they are interested in the qualities of goodness and badness, of justice and of injustice. Sometimes the ethnographer enters a new culture and then her or his work is to make this strange culture familiar to those who do not live there. At other times, the ethnographer studies the culture she or he belongs in. Then the work of the ethnographer is to make what is so familiar a little strange so that one can learn something new from what is taken for granted. Philosophers are interested in the strangers of society. They may identify as strangers, taking courage in commenting upon the things forgotten, lost, or devalued. They are interested in looking again at what everyone thought was settled. Both positions encourage observation and speculation, actions that invoke curiosity.

Making knowledge both strange and familiar is the work of learning and teaching. We must do both things in order to live and to learn creatively, in order to elaborate our sexuality, in order to imagine the possibilities of citizenship. The experiences of becoming an ethnographer and a philosopher are very close to that earlier experience of little sex researchers. At first, our theories of the world are made from a strange combination of what we receive from others, what we wish to have happen, what we notice in the world. But for these theories to be helpful to how we can live, we must also decide how a theory becomes persuasive to others, worthy to ourselves, and productive in the sense that it does not stop or inhibit our curiosity or the curiosity of others. This sort of work—how ideas or objects become important—is shared by the philosopher and the ethnographer. And for the ethnographer to do this work, the ethnographer learns to slowly leave her or his own cultural preconceptions in order to find new forms of logic that are only available when preconceptions or cultural prejudices are checked. For the philosopher to do this work, the philosopher must work at living creatively.

Precocious Knowledge, Precocious Education

In discussing some of these ideas addressed throughout this chapter and in listening to the questions of teachers about how to think about the identities, wishes, troubles, and passions of their students, I am struck by something particularly common. This has to do with the worries of educators over how to approach sexuality in education and how they might listen to startling questions and statements of their students without closing down polymorphous meanings, without projecting their own worries onto the student, and without hiding behind preconceptualization and prejudice. While it is often the case that teachers wonder what to do in particular situations and thus, at first glance seem interested in creating a reply that can somehow settle what seems unsettled, the anxieties expressed may also have to do with the structural constraints of education. But if, as the analysts suggest, we learn before we understand, educators are also implicated in this psychic design. They will have to prepare themselves not so much with gathering more knowledge, but with making experiments that can tolerate the trajectories of learning, the detours made in social encounters, the misrecognitions that invoke or stall reality and pleasure testing, and the workings of anxiety in education. Perhaps most difficult, educators will have to assume the position of philosophers and ethnographers and allow the idea that knowledge can be more than certainty, authority, and stability.

When Sigmund Freud suggested the human's utter susceptibility to Eros and Thanatos; to the vicissitudes, turns, and demands of instinct, affect, and thought; and to the vulnerabilities made in recognizing another human's desires, he offered us a stunning theory of learning that exceeds the consolations of knowledge and even interpretation. The old Freudian joke, "sometimes a cigar is only a cigar," that not everything should be tied to sexuality, suggests our constitutional ambivalence that perhaps sexuality can somehow become apparent, stable, and tamed to its proper place. And if we also seem prone to another educational joke, "sometimes education is only education," we might also consider the problem of our own limits and think in more precocious ways. Then, the question is not which policy to make on which sexuality but how the strange workings of sexuality can allow for the rethinking of education.

Notes

1   This chapter is a revision of an earlier work, published in Portuguese, "Sexualidade e cidadania democratica," in *A Escola Cidada No Contexto Da Globalizaçao,* ed. Luiz Heron Da Silva (Petropolis, RJ: Editora Vozes, 1998), 154–171. Aspects of this earlier work were presented at the Fifth International Conference on Curriculum Restructuring Seminar in Puerto Alegre, Brazil in July 1998. I have left a few references to Brazil in this version because the issues raised are pertinent to questions of globalization and to a richer understanding of the ways sexuality, democracy, and citizenship might be brought closer together.

2   One of the most difficult insights psychoanalysis offers concerns how it imagines questions of boundaries, directionality, and time or the strange relations made between the inside and the outside. Freud's discussion of the term instinct in "Instincts and Their Vicissitudes" suggests this dilemma when he attempts to discuss its "pressure," "aim," "object," and "source." He speculates that instinct is a constant relation elaborated over the course of life. The instinct "impinges not from without but from within the organism, no flight can avail against it" (118).

    Oddly, the instinct requires a representative in the form of an idea. And then, the instinct becomes a problem of meaning and satisfaction. This postulate leads Freud to view the instinct "as a concept on the frontier between the mental and the somatic, as reaching the mind, as a measure of the demand made upon the mind for work in consequence of its connection to the body" (121–22). Thus even in the inside, the demand for working through the instinct requires thought and dynamic relationality.

    In his essay "Instinct in the Late Works of Freud," André Green suggests the instinct can also be considered a mode of address: "If we call this an object relation, we are emphasizing the fact that the bodily demand presupposes not only a 'something' but also a 'someone' with whom it wants to be connected. . . . The concept of instinct relates to a reality that is unknown but can be described as a wondering force that searches without knowing exactly why what it is searching for" (136). The instinct inaugurates the interminability of conflict and the work of bringing psychical and social relations into tension. The instinct is precocious, akin to the dynamics of curiosity.

3   For a discussion of the Lacanian subject-presumed-to-know and how this position is assumed and resisted by the teacher, see Shoshana Felman, *Jacques Lacan and the Adventure of Insight,* and Elizabeth Ellsworth, *Teaching Positions: Difference, Pedagogy and the Power of Address.* For a discussion of the concept of resistance in educational research, see Alice J. Pitt, "Qualifying Resistance: Some Comments on Methodological Dilemmas."

4   When asked whether homosexual teachers are a danger to children, Michel Foucault replied:

> The fact that a teacher is a homosexual can only have electrifying and intense effects on the students to the extent that the rest of the society

refuses to admit the existence of homosexuality. . . . As for the problem of
a homosexual teacher who actively tries to seduce his students, all I can say
is that in all pedagogical situations the possibility of this problem is present;
one finds instances of this kind of behaviour much more rampant among
heterosexual teachers—for no other reason than there are a lot more heterosexual teachers (1997a, 144–145).

Also see Jane Gallop, *Feminist Accused of Sexual Harassment* for discussions
of the possibilities and breakdowns of Eros between teachers and students.

5   See, for example, the work of Cindy Patton, *Inventing AIDS*, and "Safe Sex and
the Pornographic Vernacular"; and William Haver, "Queer Research: Or, how to
practise invention to the brink of intelligibility." The following assumptions structure such work: There is no relation to acquiring facts and practising safer sex;
instructional techniques are not outside of the problems they attempt to cure; and
queer orientations to research, for example, are not a cure for knowledge. We can
consider the workings of sexuality as queer research. In the words of William
Haver, "it would be more useful to ask what queer research does, to ask what
happens in queer research, than to ask what it is" (1997, 284).

6   I have found it useful to read queer theory not as a set of contents to be applied
but as offering a set of methodological rules and dynamics useful for reading,
thinking, and engaging with the psychical and social of everyday life. In Sue
Golding's (1997) anthology, authors offer eight technologies of otherness or the
everyday strategies used to craft relationality and singularity: curiosity, noise, cruelty, appetite, skin, nomadism, contamination, and dwelling.
       Some curious rules made in queer theory include: taking the side of dispar-
aged objects; making impertinent relations, attending to the conditions that allow
normalcy its hold; considering the play of ambivalence in constituting experience;
beginning in the fault lines of ideas to encounter where meaning breaks down,
defies its object, and unconsciously reverses its intentions; and supposing the
play of difference, division, and alterity in reading practices. For a longer discussion of these methods, see Britzman, *Lost Subjects, Contested Objects: Toward
a Psychoanalytic Inquiry of Learning.* For a discussion on sexuality, see Teresa
de Lauretis, "The Stubborn Drive."

7   This study is quite different from Foucault's first volume on sexuality where he is
struggling with the question of how sexuality became a site for the incitement of
discourse. In this last volume, Foucault seems most concerned with the question
of how one becomes an ethical subject through self-work, or askesis, which is a
knowledge made not just from subjection but also from the ethics of pleasure.
Foucault writes:

       The task of testing oneself, examining oneself, monitoring oneself in a
       series of clearly defined exercises, makes the question of truth—the truth
       concerning what one is, what one does, and what one is capable of doing—
       central to the formation of the ethical subject. . . . The end result of this
       elaboration is still and always defined by the rule of the individual over
       himself. But this rule broadens into an experience in which the relation to

self takes the form not only of a domination but also of an enjoyment without desire and without disturbance. (68)

8   For a discussion of possibilities of learning from homosexual sex, see Michel Foucault, "The Social Triumph of the Sexual Will."

9   Many critiques of psychoanalytic orientations to the study of individual and social life argue that psychoanalysis depends upon essentialist, binary, and biological notions of the subject. However, for an argument that suggests the flaws of such conceptualizations, and how Freud did reject nineteenth-century biological explanations so tied to racism and discourses of degeneracy, see Charles Shepherdson, "Human Diversity and the Sexual Relation," Adam Phillips' discussion of sexes in *Terrors and Experts*, and Sander Gilman, *Freud, Race, and Gender*.

10 Cornell offers a theory of equal protection under the law that can sustain the value of freedom. She argues that for equality to become a possibility for people, three conditions must be met: "1) bodily integrity, 2) access to symbolic forms sufficient to achieve linguistic skills permitting the differentiation of oneself from others, and 3) the protection of the imaginary domain itself" (4).

11 For a discussion of schooling and libidinality, see for example Melanie Klein, "The Role of School in the Libidinal Development of the Child" and my discussion of the history of psychoanalytic critiques of education in *Lost Subjects, Contested Objects*.

12 Research on the historicity of sexuality has been central to discussions in queer theory. A brief sampling includes Michel Foucault, *The History of Sexuality: An Introduction, Volume 1*, Jeffrey Weeks, *Against Nature*, Eve Sedgwick, *Epistemology of the Closet* and William Haver, "Queer Research," to name just a few central studies.

13 The idea that modern sexuality has become an object of knowledge is found in the writings of Michel Foucault and others who worked with this idea. Foucault is interested in when sexuality became viewed as a problem and the various discourses mobilized to elaborate the problem, modes of research, and modes of cure. By "object of knowledge" Foucault was interested in the history of knowledge in terms of its application in contexts of schools, the medical and scientific establishment, the human sciences such as anthropology and sociology, and government procedures. See Michel Foucault, *The History of Sexuality: An Introduction, Volume 1*, and Richard G. Parker, *Bodies, Pleasures, and Passions: Sexual Culture in Contemporary Brazil*. For a discussion of how discourses of sexuality work in schools, see Debbie Epstein and Richard Johnson, *Schooling Sexualities*.

14 The play of knowledge as the grounds of both illusion and disillusion, of both joy and frustration, is borrowed from the work of Donald Winnicott (1986) and his sense of the work of the "good-enough" mother. In Winnicott's view the mother must attempt contradictory actions upon the infant. The mother must sustain the illusion that the infant's needs will be met. And the mother must try to help the infant tolerate frustration in times when needs cannot be met. We can bring this

insight into pedagogical relationships, where the teacher must help the student believe in the illusion that knowledge can serve as a force for stabilizing identity and one's place and perceptions in the world and help the student tolerate times when meaning and knowledge lose their purpose, cannot match the object, or become dissolved in new imperatives.

15   Early research in North America on pedagogical campaigns to prevent HIV transmission has shown that knowledge of the facts of transmission does not easily translate into safer sex practices. Much of the research was influenced by the work of Cindy Patton and her book *Inventing AIDS*. There, Patton suggests that accepting new knowledge is also a question of belief and of making new knowledge relevant to one's present life. In the case of adolescents, many adolescents believe that AIDS happens to other people. Thus the insistence by Herbert Daniel that we are all living and learning in AIDS is one that may help make information on the transmission of HIV relevant.

16   This orientation to the study of HIV/AIDS organizes the polyphonic narrative devices of Patti Lather and Chris Smithies' *Troubling Angels: Women Living with HIV/AIDS*. Also see my discussion of AIDS education, "On Some Psychical Consequences of AIDS Education."

17   These points are well developed in Debbie Epstein and Richard Johnson's study, *Schooling Sexualities*.

18   Silin's book was the first North American study that addressed questions of AIDS education for young children. He offered both a theory of knowledge and a theory of learning that moved beyond the developmental stage theory discourse so common in early childhood education in North American contexts. The book is also a very personal statement in that Silin uses his own stories to illustrate the importance of connecting the teacher's personal history to larger historical questions.

Works Cited

Bernfeld, Sigfried. 1973. *Sisyphus: Or the limits of education.* Translated by Frederic Lilge. Berkeley: University of California Press.

Britzman, Deborah. 1998. "On some psychical consequences of AIDS education." In *Queer Theory and Education,* edited by William Pinar. New York: Lawrence Erlbaum.

———— 1998. *Lost subjects, contested objects: Toward a psychoanalytic inquiry of learning.* Albany: State University of New York Press.

de Certeau, Michel. 1997. *Culture in the plural,* edited by Luce Giard. Translated by Tom Conley. Minneapolis: University of Minnesota Press.

Cornell, Drucilla. 1995. *The imaginary domain: Abortion, pornography and sexual harassment.* New York: Routledge.

Daniel, Herbert. 1993. "The bankruptcy of the models: Myths and realities of AIDS in Brazil." In *Sexuality, politics, and AIDS in Brazil: In another world?,* edited by Herbert Daniel and Richard Parker. London: Falmer Press.

Daniel, Herbert and Richard Parker, eds. 1993. *Sexuality, politics, and AIDS in Brazil: In another world?* London: Falmer Press.

Ellsworth, Elizabeth. 1997. *Teaching positions: Difference, pedagogy and the power of address.* New York: Teachers College Press.

Epstein, Debbie and Richard Johnson. 1998. *Schooling sexualities.* Buckingham, UK: Open University Press.

Felman, Shoshana. 1987. *Jacques Lacan and the adventure of insight.* Cambridge: Harvard University Press.

Foucault, Michel. 1997a. "Sexual choice, sexual act." In *Michel Foucault: Ethics, subjectivity and truth,* Vol. I of *The essential works of Foucault 1954–1984,* edited by Paul Rabinow. New York: New York University Press.

————— 1997b. "The social triumph of the sexual will." In *Michel Foucault: Ethics, subjectivity and truth,* Vol. I of *The essential works of Foucault 1954–1984,* edited by Paul Rabinow. New York: New York University Press.

————— [1978] 1990. *The history of sexuality: An introduction. Volume 1.* Translated by Robert Hurley. New York: Vintage Books.

————— 1988. *The history of sexuality: The care of the self. Volume 3.* Translated by Robert Hurley. New York: Vintage Books.

Freud, Anna. 1974. "Four lectures on psychoanalysis for teachers and parents." In *The writings of Anna Freud. Vol. 1, 1922–1935.* New York: International Universities Press.

Freud, Sigmund. 1905. *Three essays on the theory of sexuality.* Vol. 7 of *The standard edition of the complete psychological works of Sigmund Freud.* Edited and translated by James Strachey. London: Hogarth Press and Institute for Psychoanalysis.

————— 1915. "Instincts and their vicissitudes." In vol. 14 of *The standard edition of the complete psychological works of Sigmund Freud.* Edited and translated by James Strachey. London: Hogarth Press and Institute for Psychoanalysis.

Gallop, Jane. 1997. *Feminist accused of sexual harassment.* Durham: Duke University Press.

Gilman, Sander. 1993. *Freud, race, and gender.* Princeton: Princeton University Press.

Golding, Sue, ed. 1997. *The eight technologies of otherness.* New York: Routledge.

Green, André. 1991. "Instinct in the late work of Freud." In *On Freud's "Analysis terminable and interminable,"* edited by Joseph Sandler. New Haven: Yale University Press.

Haver, William. 1997. "Queer research: Or, how to practise invention to the brink of intelligibility." In *The eight technologies of otherness,* edited by Sue Golding. New York: Routledge.

Klein, Melanie. [1923] 1994. "The role of school in the libidinal development of the child." In *Love, guilt, and reparation and other works, 1921–1945.* London: Virago Press.

Lather, Patti and Chris Smithies. 1997. *Troubling angels: Women living with HIV/AIDS.* Boulder, Colorado: Westview Press.

de Lauretis, Teresa. 1998. "The stubborn drive." *Critical Inquiry* 24, no. 4: 851–877.

Parker, Richard G. 1991. *Bodies, pleasures, and passions: Sexual culture in contemporary Brazil.* Boston: Beacon Press.

————— 1993. "AIDS in Brazil." In *Sexuality, politics, and AIDS in Brazil: In another world?*, edited by Herbert Daniel and Richard Parker. London: Falmer Press.

Patton, Cindy. 1990. *Inventing AIDS.* New York: Routledge.

————— 1990. "Safe sex and the pornographic vernacular" in *How do I look?: Queer film and video*, edited by Bad Object-Choices. Seattle: Bay Press.

Phillips, Adam. 1996. *Terrors and experts.* Cambridge: Harvard University Press.

Picard, André. 1998. "Rates of infection climbing for women," *Toronto Globe and Mail*, 30 June, A5.

Pitt, Alice J. "Qualifying resistance: Some comments on methodological dilemmas." *International Journal of Qualitative Studies in Education*, in press.

Sedgwick, Eve. 1990. *Epistemology of the closet.* Berkeley: University of California Press.

Shepherdson, Charles. 1998. "Human diversity and the sexual relation." In *The Psychoanalysis of race*, edited by Christopher Lane. New York: Columbia University Press.

Silin, Jonathan. 1995. *Sex, death, and the education of children: Our passion for ignorance in the age of AIDS.* New York: Teachers College Press.

Weeks, Jeffrey. 1991. *Against nature.* London: Rivers Oram Press.

Winnicott, Donald W. 1986. "Living creatively." In *Home is where we start from: Essays by a psychoanalyst.* New York: W. W. Norton.

Chapter 4

Identity Politics, Institutional Response, and Cultural Negotiation: Meanings of a Gay and Lesbian Office on Campus

Susan Talburt

> If coming out says, "We're queer, we're here, get used to it," new-right identity appropriates this to say, "We knew it," and to society, "We told you so." What operates as a performative act of identity assertion for "queers" is read by the new right as *descriptive*, as not performative at all.
>
> —Cindy Patton, 1993, 145–46

> I think that most of those responses [the creation of a gay and lesbian support office] are sort of token responses and not really substantive responses. I think this university in general is very good at constructing messages that are, for lack of a better term, sort of politically correct without really getting at the roots of most of the problems. . . . But the university is smart enough as an institution, and the leadership is smart enough to know that in the world of academia, it's very important to make those symbolic gestures. In terms of the national reputation of the school, in terms of being able to recruit faculty, staff, and students, and all those kinds of things. You know, it means that they're not completely clueless, it means that the school subscribes to basic sort of liberal values. Again, in comparison to the backlash at a lot of universities and colleges, that's certainly a positive.
>
> —A Liberal U faculty member

The advent of campus activism in the form of identity politics throughout the 1970s and 1980s encouraged the institutionalization of such interdisciplinary courses and programs as Women's and African American Studies, hiring and admissions practices that included "minorities," and the creation of centers and campus programming related to "diversity." In the context of post–Civil Rights and post–Stonewall social movements, the

recognition of gay men and lesbians at universities has also increased, a
trend many scholars attribute to gay and lesbian visibility on campuses
(see, for example, D'Augelli 1991; D'Emilio 1992; Rhoads 1994; Tierney
1993a). The constitution of student organizations, support and counseling services, and the emergence of gay and lesbian studies have been the
prevalent forms of social and academic change on campus. As gays and
lesbians have gained a sort of semi-codified minority status at many universities in the 1990s, a concomitant rise has occurred in conservative
student organizing and in legal battles against official recognition and
support (see, for example, Mangan 1995), a trend that suggests a need
for inquiry into the possibilities and limitations of practices of gay and
lesbian identity politics on campus. What constitutes being *recognized* as
a visible group? What are the meanings of the services and programs
created for a visible group within the structures of liberal democratic educational institutions?

In this chapter, I examine the highly contentious opening of a gay/
lesbian/bisexual support office at Liberal U, a public research university.[1]
Underlying my inquiry into the creation of the office is a concern with
what it means for gays and lesbians to become the most recent "diversity"
in an epoch in which there is growing backlash against "special-interest"
groups and in which institutional policy and practices construct group
identities as having fixed meanings that pose specific problems to be
accommodated and managed. However, a tension runs throughout my
discussion: Although there are always dangers of reification and exclusion
involved in claiming a group identity, the efficacy of gay/lesbian identity
politics on campus may derive from its consonance with university structures that are based on serving specific constituencies.[2] In addition, although the social and institutional recognition of gays and lesbians under
the aegis of "diversity" may discipline identities and limit the transformative potential of group organizing, the constitution of gay and lesbian
groups may also create new forms of socializing and organizing that challenge the boundaries of institutional acknowledgment. To determine both
what is made possible and what is limited by the use of group identity
takes up challenges posed by writers such as Steven Seidman (1993),
who argues that poststructural critiques of identity politics "fail to theo-
retically engage the practices of individuals organized around affirmative
gay and lesbian identities" and ignore the ways that identities "are enabling or productive of social collectivities, moral bonds, and political
agency" (134). How, without categorically dismissing identity politics, can
the use of group identity be understood as creating new spaces for inter-

vention? Following Cindy Patton (1993), where can the movement between describing (or reinscribing) an identity and performing new sets of
relations be located? And, despite their limitations, what do the symbolic,
accommodating gestures of universities enable?

To situate my analysis of the limitations and openings involved in gay
and lesbian visibility and recognition in concrete practices, I discuss social
and institutional contexts within and beyond Liberal U and relate practices of diversity and gay and lesbian identity politics to tenets of liberal
education. I begin by depicting the relations of the state, the town of
Oasis, and Liberal U as they inform understandings of policy, practice,
and social life at the university. As my discussion of the university pro-
ceeds, it is crucial to understand that what it sets forth in policy and what
I present as prevailing social and academic discourses are hardly uniform
but are interpreted and enacted differently in different locations. Nonetheless, these institutional contexts play a part in defining the interventions
available to gay, lesbian, and anti-homophobia activists as they seek to
create new forms of exchange.

Let me note at the outset that although I at times appear critical of
these activists and of the gay and lesbian office they fought for, I mean
neither to condescend to those who use possibilities at hand to create
tangible forms of change nor to ignore the needs of young people who
may benefit from the services the office provides. Rather, I wish to point
to the ways in which institutionalized gay and lesbian identity politics can
result in psychologizing gay men and lesbians at the expense of considering the social and institutional production of identities. At the same time,
I wish to suggest that a focus on concrete social and institutional changes
made possible by the deployment of identity forecloses theorists' attention to the spaces created by alliances and forms of activism that are not
predicated on group identity models (see, for example, Martin and Mohanty
1986; and Sandoval 1991).

Locating the Liberal U Campus

As we strive to create a new idea of the public university, the circles in which we
move expand in size and complexity. But always at the center of these many
circles, firmly rooted in honorable traditions and civilizing activities, remains the
campus. —from the Liberal U Strategic Plan

Liberal U is a well-known public research university with a population of
nearly 40,000 students. It is situated in a politically and socially conservative, racially homogeneous Midwestern state.[3] While the state government

and overall state voting patterns are predominantly Republican, the town of Oasis, in which Liberal has a prominent place, has a strong pattern of Democratic voting. Despite a pronounced lack of interaction among racial and ethnic groups, people at the university and in town almost invariably described Oasis as a protective sphere distinguished from its surroundings by its history of social compassion and activism. In fact, several years ago the predominantly Democratic city council passed a human rights ordinance that includes sexual orientation. As a faculty member who does anti-homophobic work in town explained, "Oasis is a caring place, a sort of a liberal island in a fairly conservative environment." Others, however, have questioned the positive dimensions of this refuge. A young lesbian student, for example, mapped the town and the university ideologically and geographically, speaking of those beyond her sphere in totalizing terms:

> I can't emphasize this enough, that Oasis is an island. I've been told by people not to drive alone out in the country because this is KKK territory. It's an island, if you cross a certain line. People can feel really "out" here in Oasis, but it's not real, it's just an artificial set-up, situation. There's nothing inherently gay-lesbian friendly in Oasis, the gay-lesbian population in Oasis can feel out because of the university. I don't know what the community would be like without the university. . . . When you get into the townies section, outside the university section, it turns into standard conservative redneck . . . right-wing conservative, low middle-class, low-class people who've been brought up in racist, homophobic, anti-Semitic homes, and that clashes incredibly with the university.

Sociopolitically Liberal U is curiously positioned in relation to its surroundings. While Oasis is markedly different from the state, Liberal U is also distinct from Oasis. Furthermore, university policy constructs the institution as distinct from its surroundings: It offers access to excellence, "honorable traditions," and "civilizing activities" to those outside its circle. In the logic of twentieth-century liberalism in education, self-definition through opposition with what is outside creates a situation in which the university represents, serves, and educates the very people, its constituencies, against whom it is defined—a paradox that creates a number of tensions as the university seeks to justify and enact its mission as a public institution.

One tension created by the disjunctures that exist among the state, town, and university lies in the fact that the state places legislative and budgetary constraints on the university; thus, Liberal U must define its mission with an eye to the support of legislators, the needs of constituencies, and the public's responses to its purposes and methods (see Piven

1983). In fact, the administration has been succumbing to what Joan Scott (1995) describes as the "rhetoric of crisis in higher education," allowing public dissatisfaction with higher education to dictate much of its policy talk. Although the state legislature has granted funding increases to the university throughout the 1990s, they have been more modest than the university has requested. In this context, the administration seeks public credibility by defining the university's purposes in terms of individual and economic development (see Apple 1995) and has appropriated the language and practices of business and industry in projecting an image defined by accountability, efficiency, and productivity: input, output, access, and excellence form the basis of the university's public justification of self.[4]

The "managerial culture" (Bergquist 1992) of Liberal U, combined with its internally contradictory identity, plays a role in structuring diversity in policy and practice. In this context, I find helpful David Trend's (1995) remark that administrative documents "never assert a virtual authority. Their meanings are constructed in communicative exchange, so they are always open to subversion or revision" (103–4). This communicative exchange, in which policies and their enactment are not given products but are both processes, offers an understanding of how diversity and academic and social life are officially defined and subsequently redefined in practice—and what interventions those definitions allow. I employ this analysis to understand how institutional access and efficiency intersect with discourses of gay and lesbian identity to define some of the uses and effects of gay and lesbian identity politics at Liberal U.

Social and Academic Diversity in Policy and Practice

The president of Liberal U has explained that because Liberal U constitutes "a microcosm of the values and ideals of the state and the nation, [it is] uniquely situated to influence the development of our students by exposing them to a truly diverse educational experience." As Liberal U institutes social and academic programs meant to enrich community members' perspectives, however, it is caught in a peculiar situation. Although it is *accountable* to "the values and ideals of the state and nation," it is not a microcosm, embodiment, or reflection of those ideals. Furthermore, in an epoch of antifeminism and affirmative action backlash, diversity is hardly a universally held value. Rather, the current trend in cultural politics constructs a focus on difference as dangerous to national unity (Giroux 1994; West 1993). There is thus a tension between academic excellence and social access in the university's support for diversity that surfaces in official statements: "There is much to be done, much that requires creative balancing. The campus must ensure, for example, that it attracts the best students in the state and nation and also supports and aggressively seeks out disadvantaged students" (Strategic Plan). The balancing the institution performs between equitable access and excellence directly affects the locations and means by which differences gain recognition.

Liberal U's mission is predicated on what Torres (1995–96) has described as a "liberal view [that] suggests that the state is the collective creation of its members, providing a set of common social goods" (275). As it aligns itself with democratic progress, the university must provide those social goods to all students. The strategic plan's description of educating students, "not solely to certify them for professional employment, but to leave them with a sense of ethical and social vision, a love of learning, and a complex, nimble intellect," reflects three principal functions of liberal education: "cognitive and moral socialization, skills training, and certification" (277), or what could more crudely be described as providing academic, social, and economic goods to constituents. Across these three categories, diversity is ambivalently constructed and relegated to the domain of the social, removed from economic structures and definitions of academic knowledge and purposes. For example, to achieve the balance between quality and democracy in its academic mission, the university has organized knowledge by subject areas "which, though constantly changing, are delineated by custom, necessity, and tradition." This "foundation of undergraduate education" is then supplemented by "programs that focus on the cultures of ethnic and racial minorities and other groups that have experienced disadvantage and discrimination" in a center-periphery model of defining knowledge of worth.[5] Reinforcing the social definition of "diversity," a statement that "discrimination on the basis of race, gender, age, sexual orientation, nationality or any other such arbitrary criteria will not be tolerated on the Liberal U campus" is placed in the Strategic Plan's section on social development. According to a logic that relegates work against "discrimination" to social relations and disavows needs for transformations of academic and economic structures, the emphasis in policy is based on "the belief that opportunities to interact with others from diverse backgrounds can result in increased understanding and appreciation of differences, immeasurably enriching the perspective of all members of the academic community." Discrimination becomes a social problem and diversity (or diverse perspectives) a social asset. Neither, however, bears on academic knowledge; in fact, diverse perspectives conflict with the university's academic ideal that "a scholar recognizes a primary responsibility to seek and state the truth without bias."

The tension between excellence and access in Liberal U's policy statements surfaces in frequently articulated student discourses. Students who speak against diversification (read: race) argue that promoting diversity involves lowering standards of excellence, is divisive insofar as it calls attention to differences that are irrelevant in a meritocratic system, and discriminates against those who excel, offering them no "special services." Talk of diversity, then, constructs equality as the opposite of difference, mistakenly confusing sameness and equality and ignoring the fact that "the political notion of equality thus includes, indeed depends on, an acknowledgment of the existence of difference" (Scott 1988, 44). Thus, although perspectives are said to be sought after, the differences assumed to generate these perspectives hinder both excellence and equality understood as sameness.

In the context of increasing institutional recognition of difference, Chandra Mohanty (1994) has argued, "The central issue, then, is not one of merely *acknowledging* difference; rather, the more difficult question concerns the kind of difference that is acknowledged and engaged" (146). *How* those differences are attended to is significant, as well as for what reasons and in what contexts. Both in policy and lived experience, the "diverse communities" constituted at Liberal U function as distinct enclaves with clearly delineated borders that define the affiliations and activities of individuals. In campus discourses, gay and lesbian persons are represented as white, women as white and heterosexual, and "raced" persons as African American and heterosexual. Thus, each singular category is understood to be continuous with a set of experiences that flow from intact identities, which in turn form the basis of needs and responses from the institution, which manages them through support or representation in a system Michael Warner (1995) calls corporate multiculturalism, "a pluralist affirmation of cultures, where cultures are conceived on a racial or ethnic model . . . in which irreconcilable demands are dealt with by giving every constituency its own course or, if necessary, program" (289–290). By such logic, African American students and faculty members are sought after by the administration, which employs rhetorics of perspective enrichment and democratic access. At the same time, they pose a potential danger to meritocracy, standards of excellence, and the unbiased pursuit of knowledge. Women faculty members are needed for equitable representation, but they pose threats to academic knowledge if they bring a feminist perspective. Because gays and lesbians are not a group codified in many spheres, their recruitment, retention, and the valuing of their perspectives are non-issues. Instead, the results of gaining a semi-codified group status have been heightened talk of equitable educational opportunities and of the problems stemming from their identities, including psychology, disease, and immorality.

In order to grant various social and ethnic groups access and bring multiple perspectives to campus life, Liberal U has committed significant resources—specifically, several decentralized offices—to the recruitment and retention of students. As an institution funded and regulated by society and its constituencies, however, Liberal U operates within the dictates of a liberal politics that conceives of individuals abstractly (Jaggar 1983) and of public institutions as neutral in sociopolitical relations (Torres 1995–96). Because policy focuses on numerical representation and diversity as social interaction, university programs inadequately address material and structural oppressions that block easy incorporation of "diversity."[6] Instead, the underlying ethos is one of accommodation in response to external social change. Meg, a graduate student activist and member of the Lesbian Avengers, asserted in a conversation about the administration and various diversity initiatives:

> I don't know how much the university can do because it's so much the norm. I mean, university administrations are middle America, they have to be, they're public institutions. If Liberal U has instituted a diversity program, that means it has become part of American consciousness, that means it's like *Newsweek* culture. I can't imagine asking the Liberal U administration to do things that *Newsweek* wouldn't do. Or that *Time* wouldn't do. What else can you say? It is the system, it loves the system, it will be the system, and it won't be radical, that's it by definition, which doesn't mean there aren't things that can't be done that will make life more livable for people.

Although diversity initiatives and programs are largely reactive—that is, instituted in response to social demands—their increasing presence at Liberal U suggests that what "the system" will do is open to pressure and change. Officially, diversity is a managed and measured numbers game of representation, in which efficient performance is won through programs to recruit and retain faculty and students. Meanwhile, unofficially, groups may use the resources provided by such programs for purposes not officially codified. In this way, although representational politics has limitations, it constitutes a process of ongoing negotiation and change.

Into a liberal system of diversity predicated on accountability, representation, and access, enters a newly vocal group to be served. The constituency logic of the university allows talk of serving its needs; yet, the problems it seems to bring to the campus are articulated through the prism of diversity discourses, which structure the immediate limits of institutional response and social change. These problems, naturalized as stemming from gay and lesbian "identities," pose further threats to unity, excellence, and equality.

Centering Gay and Lesbians

This is a WASP university, and they don't talk about these things. Meanwhile everybody knows that there are lesbians, and a lot of them. I mean this is not a small category.   —A Liberal U faculty member

It's a campus that talks about these things.   —Another faculty member

Until the formation of an activist group several years ago, gay and lesbian organizing at Liberal U had previously been, if not submerged, then somewhat behind the scenes. While some undergraduate and graduate students have "come out" on campus, few gay and lesbian faculty are open about their sexuality. Despite some incidents of harassment among students, faculty members and students consistently explained that homophobia was less "overt" than subtle. One faculty member explained, "With faculty, it's still the same don't talk about it and it's okay kind of stuff. But I don't think anybody's actively harassing. I don't think it fits their image of being liberal. We're open-minded individuals here." According to many students and staff members, the ethos that prevails is one of "don't ask, don't tell," in which structures of willful ignorance relegate sexuality to private domains. Despite an environment of disacknowledgment, pockets of activism have contributed to such changes as the inclusion of sexual orientation in the university's non-discrimination clause several years ago. Actually, sexual orientation was added gradually, first in student handbooks, then in faculty handbooks, and finally in hiring and other policy statements. Domestic partnership benefits, however, have yet to gain acceptance. Although the faculty council passed domestic partnership benefits, the board of trustees tabled the proposal, citing economic viability and problematic "proof" of partnership, thus officially constructing same-sex relationships as both exceptions to the rule (special privileges) and as unverifiable.

Despite social and institutional pressures to suppress homosexuality, cultural change and local activism have forced Liberal U into becoming "a campus that talks about these things," which surface with increasing frequency in official and unofficial conversations. In particular, the polemics around the opening of the support office for gay and lesbian students and its galvanization of a number of groups and individuals resulted in discussions of homosexuality predominating in the student and local newspapers for several months. The talk and activities surrounding its inception dramatize the intersections of gay and lesbian identity politics, campus diversity discourses, and liberal democratic educational policy and practice. In addition, the propaganda created by the multiple sides claiming stakes in the debate and the events that occurred reveal the operations of what Eve Kosofsky Sedgwick (1990) has identified as minoritarian and majoritarian discourses around (homo)sexuality. As she describes these contradictory yet simultaneously circulating sets of beliefs, the minoritarian view holds "that there is a distinct population of persons who 'really are' gay" and that homosexuality is "an issue of active importance primarily for a small, distinct, relatively fixed homosexual minority." The universalizing, or majoritarian, view maintains "that sexual desire is an unpredictably powerful solvent of stable identities" and thus homosexuality is "an issue of continuing, determinative importance in the lives of people across the spectrum of sexualities" (1, 85). These incoherent stances intersect with rhetorics of identity politics, minority rights, and diversity to produce multiple effects. I begin with a chronicle of the events leading to the Liberal U controversy.

The Liberal U Controversy: Chronology and Analysis

After staff in several offices documented numerous incidents of gay and lesbian harassment in the late 1980s, Liberal U formed a task force that eventually recommended an office for educational and support services. The proposal was approved in the spring of 1994. After the administration announced that the office would be allocated $50,000 a year, letters from the local constituency and from within the university reached the administration protesting the use of university (public) money to support the office. In newspaper interviews, administrators described the letters as arguing that the office was intended for a special-interest group, and would be a social club ("recruitment center") that promoted a "homosexual lifestyle."

Basing its rhetorical stance on equity issues of creating a safe learning environment for all students through support and education, the administration pointed to increased reports of gay and lesbian harassment on the campus to defend the office. Thus, the polemic of the office began around three discursive strands: (1) a liberal rights discourse suggesting that an identifiable minority population is failing to receive educational equity; (2) an unwitting invocation of majoritarian discourse that recognizes the instability of categories of sexuality and implicitly denaturalizes heterosexuality through the fear that homosexuality can be promoted; and (3) a minoritarian discourse of gays and lesbians in need of special institutional support and protection and a general public in need of education about a discrete population.

When the following academic year began, a state representative entered the fray, combining morality, money, and willful ignorance in an argument that the university was promoting an immoral lifestyle by publicly recognizing homosexuality. The legislator threatened to hold the university's budget hostage in the next legislative session if the office were funded. For several months, student and local papers printed articles, editorials, and letters to the editor, as protests on both sides began and further events unfolded. Gay and lesbian student groups formed a coalition, mounted protests, undertook letter-writing campaigns, and participated in meetings with the legislator and administration. Concurrently, but with more than the usual fanfare, the newly traditional gay and lesbian fall events at the university took place: a kiss-in (complete with two front-page newspaper photos) and a rally for National Coming Out Day. To counter these events, a group held a "Straight Pride Week," during which its members staged a hug-in, wore T-shirts that said "Damn Straight," and held a "debate" over the advisability of the gay and lesbian office. Finally, the university announced that the office would be funded by an anonymous donor, thus leaving intact the goal of having the office while escaping legislative budgetary threats.

The ability of a single legislator, although external to Liberal U (from a different district, in fact), to represent the university's constituencies and to shape the administration's actions and policies offers an example of the constraints on Liberal U's ability to respond to social changes. The responses of students to his actions also constitute a part of the process of change, in this case a proliferation of campus talk and mobilization. However, although gay and lesbian groups continued to protest the delegitimation implicit in the change in funding, with the office's existence assured, interest waned and protests slowed.

The stances and tactics marshaled in favor of the office reveal the discourses that circulated throughout the events. The arguments posed by gay and lesbian persons, their supporters, and the administration combine three elements:[7] First, identity politics was invoked to argue that gay men and lesbians are a pre-constituted minority group that pays taxes, is discriminated against, and merits its own office. In the logic of rights, this discourse included the argument that the administration had a responsibility to represent the needs of gay and lesbian students. In addition, liberalism was invoked to defend the separation of "private" judgments of groups and individuals from the domain of public affairs (Phelan 1989). *"You are not regarding a population that should be your constituency." "As a public university, we both lead and respond to concerns expressed throughout the state. Sometimes our multiple constituencies come into conflict." "Liberal U is a secular institution. The goal of the university is not to make moral judgments, but to educate."*

Second, the pathology model of gay and lesbian needs attributable to harassment was expanded as a justificatory rationale, displacing the political implications of the creation of the office. In this defensive posture, support and counseling neutralized politics. *"Our energies should be focused on providing services to the gay and lesbian community. In the last four years, the incidence of harassment against gays, lesbians, and bisexuals more than doubled." "The intent is to provide a safe learning environment and not to advocate a lifestyle or political agenda." "The office is not a political statement, but a support service to a population of students in need." "It's important for people to know this isn't going to be a hotbed of political activity."*

Third, identity politics, educational equity, and pathology combined to form an argument for the symbolic importance of institutional legitimation of the gay and lesbian population by funding the office. Thus, gay and lesbian identity politics became intertwined with the rhetoric of the purposes of education and the role of the university in allowing equal access to learning, educating the general public, and validating a population. *"The first problem is that education can only take place in an environment in which everyone has free access to educational resources." "The university's unwillingness to publicly fund the center sets up an official closet and suggests gays and lesbians are not of equal value." "Our university appears on the brink of denying identity to a large number of students based on their sexuality." "The university should provide support to the sexual minority community and increase awareness within the general population."*

Fourth, academia, a sphere separate from the "real" world, was simultaneously figured as responsible for leading and responding to social change. *"Tolerance and diversity are 'in' and the university will ap-*

pear to be a backwater if it does not acknowledge gay men and lesbians by funding the office." "It is unethical . . . for a university to extend the closet mentality of the general world to the campus."

Stances against the center operated within a similar discursive field with four identifiable sectors. First, minoritarian arguments stated that public funds should be spent on services that benefit all students rather than a small minority. In other words, (homo)sexuality is not the concern of all students. Paradoxically, majoritarian discourse, in the form of fear of promotion and recruitment of the majority, intersected with this outrage at the legitimation of the minority. *"Tax money should not pay for the agendas of special interest groups." "Many of the majority feel alienated and ask themselves why there are no 'special' funds designated for them." "I believe it's going to be used as a tool to say, 'the state university promotes us, so that gives us an excuse to promote our lifestyle.'" "It's still promoting a certain lifestyle above all others." "It gives credence to an immoral lifestyle and may sway people on the fence about which way to go." "Why should the majority be forced to pay for an office they will never step foot in?"*

Second, public acknowledgment and display of difference were said to increase hostility and homophobic acts and limit possibilities of equality (sameness) and acceptance of gays and lesbians by the mainstream. *"If they're trying to get all this equality, why make such a big deal?" "They aren't going to be accepted if they insist on being different." "It's strange they're showing their emotions to prove something [at the kiss-in]." "The office will just further exclude homosexuals from the mainstream campus." "When people are going to do things that aren't mainstream American, they're going to be discriminated against more." "I don't have any problem with them personally, but the way they are going about it is disruptive to the campus. They should just talk to each other about it."*

Third, ethnic models of identity politics were challenged in arguments that (dangerous) gay men and lesbians are not a legitimate or authentic minority because they choose homosexuality and also choose whether to reveal or conceal it. *"Gays and lesbians can avoid discrimination if they want to, not like racial minorities." "They elect to make it public or private." "True minorities are different than special interest groups because they look different." "It is only a matter of time before the bathrooms of [ ] Hall will be used nonstop for activities that defy the original purposes of bathrooms." "There are health hazards associated with the gay lifestyle."*

Fourth, diversity was said to take priority over academics in arguments that the university was bowing to political correctness pressures, creating an academic culture of oppressed groups whose ideas matter without regard to their content. *"Support? What ever happened to emotional self-sufficiency?" "It's just part of an effort to bring liberal ideas to the Liberal U campus." "Once again Liberal U has sold its soul to diversity. Once again it has designated a disproportionate amount of student funds to promote the different lifestyle of a small student group. Once again, the university has attempted to assuage tensions by promoting the very differences that created them." "The office shows just how far the administration has been distracted from the true mission of the university: the education of great ideas. [They are] letting standards decline from the exposure of students to great ideas to the ideas of the latest group to achieve 'victim' or 'oppressed' status." "I don't need to be educated. I know what homosexuality is, that there are many homosexuals, and that it's wrong to hate someone because he or she is gay. That's all I need to know."*

Many of the arguments for and against the office revolved around issues of minority status: defining, recognizing, and legitimating a minority, and invoking or arguing against that group's rights. Although constituting themselves as an aggrieved group seeking equitable educational access is consonant with the constituency logic of Liberal U and ultimately won students the office, it has done little to shift discourses of sexuality at Liberal U and may very well reinscribe them. Tenuous minority status, "special interest" hostilities, and the binary opposition of equality/difference remain unchallenged. On the other hand, one effect of the discourses has been to chip away at institutionalized ignorance. As Michael Warner (1995) has observed, "Because being queer necessarily involves and is defined by a drama of acknowledgment, a theater of knowledge and publicization, the institutions that transmit and certify knowledge take on special importance" (285). At Liberal U, the gay and lesbian presence has been certified on the institutional stage; gay and lesbian identity has received quasi-legitimation in the institutional public sphere with the specially earmarked private money. But precisely what is acknowledged, where it is acknowledged, is an identity *from* which differences are presumed to emanate. In other words, identity is thought to precede difference rather than the other way around. Acknowledgment of gay men and lesbians at Liberal U is less acknowledgment of the construction of queerness per se or of the effects of institutionalized heterosexism and homophobia than it is an acknowledgment of individualized homosexual problems emanating from a pre-existing identity. Furthermore, the negative differences thought to follow from this pre-existing identity are reinscribed in the existence of the office, which accommodates through counseling the special problems of this newly acknowledged group. Difference as produced in relations of power is displaced by a liberal humanist conception of difference as a superficial social problem (Seidman 1993; Tierney 1993b). The role of dichotomies of public-private and knowledge-ignorance in structuring sexual difference are confronted, yet shift only slightly, in the form of discussions of equity, personal support, and general education.

The values embraced in supporting and sustaining the office reveal its distance from activism and academic affairs and its focus on individuals. In fact, the recently hired director of the office emphasized the importance of social support:

> Actually, as I think about the interview process, I think the best question that was asked was . . . "This job basically takes someone who has some counseling skills and who's an educator, and is," I don't believe they used the word activist, "advocate," they said, "and each of the three candidates seems to have a specialty in each of those areas, which do you think is the most important, and why?" And I think my response is perhaps what, well, among the things that got me the job. I just said, "You need someone with some counseling background, who can build some bridges here, who understands that education is a lot about hearing the questions that are being asked and understanding the questions behind what's being asked, and also knowing that even activists need some support. But I think you need someone to build some bridges here. I network well, you need someone to build community here," so I think that suggests something of the direction they wanted to go in.

Consonant with the diversity logic of Liberal U, the function of the office has become "a space to hang out," a place to get personal support in coming out, and a source for information and referrals. In a newspaper interview, the director emphasized, "We are not an office for activists. We are really an office for students who are struggling in a *personal* way with issues, students doing research, and students who need information or referral. It is not as glamorous as organizing kiss-ins." Whether his disavowals of activism were intended to justify the office's continued funding or earnest descriptions of his intentions is difficult to evaluate, though my conversation with him suggested the latter.

After the office had existed for nearly a year, a number of faculty, staff, and students described it positively, saying that it was "a form of recognition that gay and lesbian students are important" and that the office confers credibility on gay men and lesbians, signifying "institutional commitment," as one staff member stressed, through "an office, a space, a sign." As a lesbian undergraduate explained, "It's a real source of pride. It legitimizes it for a lot of people. We're accepted by the university, and that's true for straight people and people coming out." A faculty member found value in the office "for the quieter students who are trying to figure things out, what's right and what's wrong, university values." Thus, although the explicit function of the office, in keeping with the functions of other diversity offices at Liberal U, is less to promote institutional change than to support individuals, some members of the university understand it as representing and promising institutional transformation.

Not all, however, agree that the office's importance lies in recognition and support. Meg, who organized protests in favor of the center, spoke of the importance of uncovering the workings of institutionalized homophobia:

> I'm not invested in the final product. I was invested in the struggle and making a lot of noise about the wheeling and dealing that was happening in terms of the ways that state governments and big business are involved in university affairs and the very pernicious kinds of—it's disturbing to me the discrepancy between what people think is going on and what's really going on, as was the case here. . . . And the kinds of interests that determine university policies in a number of ways, this was just a particularly ugly incarnation of it.

She based her concerns on the failure of campus activists to take into account the external pressures on the administration. A faculty member expressed a second set of concerns about subjecting gay and lesbian students to psychologizing:

> I have mixed feelings about it. I mean, I'm glad if there's a student organization, I think that that's important. When I hear that they've got peer counseling over there and they're trying to get a library of coming out novels and stuff like that, I start to worry a little bit that they're adopting the medical model and understanding the job of the institution as nurturing somebody through a deep and dark and painful psychological experience. And I don't think that that's what the university's job is in relation to this cohort of students. And I think it's dangerous in the long run to pathologize gay and lesbian students. I think what they should be doing instead, and what I'm in favor of, is culture-building, the office sponsoring events that allow students to network, that allow students to explore questions of sexuality and cultural difference in a variety of ways, you know, reading groups, drag shows, dances, bringing in gay and lesbian performers to campus, or speakers, or things that would be defined as more cultural. I think that that's another way of dealing actually with the difficulty of coming out. It's a way of providing forums and community for people in order for them to work through that. . . . You know,

the cultural and intellectual thing, that's not like the medical model that says you need to be counseled because we don't want you to kill yourself sort of thing.

One year after the events around the opening of the office, gay and lesbian political activism was less prevalent on the campus than it had been during the previous fall. However, the messages I received from the office's e-mail distribution list indicate that the existence of the office was making possible new forms of community-building both at Liberal U and in Oasis. Notices ranged from announcements of movie series, speakers, dances, and picnics, to the announcement of a new course in gay and lesbian studies, to meetings of new groups at a local coffeehouse, to requests for roommates, and to announcements of local, state, and national political news, rallies, and conferences. In addition, several students spoke to me of groups they had formed or were planning to form that would meet in the office's space. These groups went beyond support and coming out issues to consider the political implications of queer sexualities, to advocate for gay and lesbian studies courses in the curriculum, and to consider the intersections of race and sexuality. Thus it appears that individuals and groups may be appropriating the office as a resource for social, academic, cultural, and political networking beyond its stated purposes. In other words, while it continues to have an official focus on individual counseling and community education, the office may be encouraging new coalitions, in the forms of culture-building and activism, that move beyond the institutionally sanctioned social domain to include academic and political domains.

Cultural Negotiation

Gay men and lesbians at Liberal U have gained institutional recognition in a system of diversity where the identities and perspectives thought to accompany them are acknowledged at the social level, but not as they relate to knowledge production or political structures. In discussions of accountability and access, practices and policies of diversity specify and distinguish groups, creating rhetorics that reify differences as positive (enhancing perspectives) or negative (threatening meritocracy and standards of excellence) in relation to campus norms. Even as identities are conceived as vehicles of institutional legitimation—for example, in light of federal hiring mandates, disciplinary demands for scholarship, and exigencies of accreditation—these identities become construed as discrete problems to be dealt with through centers and programs. Within these

institutional diversity discourses, the constitution of a visible gay and lesbian group makes institutional policies for equitable educational access
imperative. By the logic of identity politics, an institutional shift has occurred at Liberal U. For example, in his ethnographic study of gay males
at one campus, Robert Rhoads (1994) suggested that students "forged a
group identity that has enabled them to enter their agenda into the political terrain of the University" (23). Although Rhoads cautions against the
essentialism of identity politics, he attributes changes in university policy
to the students' intertwined uses of politics, visibility, and education in
the context of a positive queer identity, one akin to the positive gay identity Seidman (1993) argues poststructuralism does not engage. However,
while the changes at Liberal U resemble those Rhoads identifies, and
were made possible by identity politics, those changes are limited in a
system that circumscribes forms and locations of recognition and that is
predicated on granting (and taking away) services and rights to narrowly
defined groups.

It may be more helpful to consider the recognition and resources won
through group identity as just one aspect of ongoing negotiation that may
in the long term bring change whose aim, as Seidman (1993) has said of
postmodern politics, "is less 'the end of domination' or 'human liberation' than the creation of social spaces that encourage the proliferation of
pleasures, desires, voices, interests, modes of individuation and democratization" (106). The events at Liberal U suggest that although services
won through the constitution of visible and vocal groups do not significantly shift social discourses, they do represent a means by which individuals and groups can begin to enact new practices. Codification in social or academic spheres can correspond to forms of containment—or a
Foucauldian disciplining—and is not an end in itself. Policies and offices,
however significant, should be understood less as final products of change
and more as vehicles for ongoing change within liberalism. To understand processes of change, one might ask, How are policies and the
programs they allow subject, in practice, to reinterpretation and ongoing
negotiation? And, even as the tactics of identity politics employed in the
struggle for the office closed down certain discourses, what other openings did they make possible?

Understanding policy and the garnering of services as one aspect of
processes of cultural negotiation is, in this case, to shift attention to the
students' appropriations of institutional resources for purposes beyond
the official, such as creating formal and informal social, political, and
academic networks. In his theory of practice, de Certeau (1984) has out-

lined his understanding of the ways systems may be appropriated by those who use them: "The order of things is precisely what 'popular' tactics turn to their own ends, without any illusion that it will change any time soon. . . . Into the institution to be served are thus insinuated styles of social exchange, technical invention, and moral resistance" (26). In just this way, gay and lesbian groups may be understood as putting to their own uses practices of identity politics to make spaces within the institution for new forms of exchange and possibilities for resistance. The conditions for recognition have been made possible by the ongoing work of identity-based social movements. While that recognition is limited, it has the effect of creating new conditions that may or may not call for the deployment of identity to rescript recognitions and to insinuate new styles of exchange into the institutional space. Attention to the planned and unplanned interventions that institutional policy and official response allow may yield significant insight into social and academic change, its limitations and possibilities, and the ongoing articulations of policy and practice. Rather than positing institutional stasis or transformation, social theory might attend more closely to the relations of institutional practices to identity-based movements, as those practices both sustain and make identity necessary and as new practices, not always predicated on identity but enabled by the new spaces identity creates, are enacted.

Notes

1   All names are pseudonyms. The data and analysis presented here comprise a
    portion of an ethnographic study focused on the academic practices of lesbian
    faculty at Liberal U (Talburt, 2000). The fieldwork discussed includes analyses of
    the university's mission statement and strategic plan, campus and local newspa-
    pers, statements produced by a number of diversity offices, and some twenty
    interviews with faculty and staff members and students across campus. My narra-
    tive pertaining specifically to the opening of the gay and lesbian support office is
    based on extensive newspaper coverage of events, internal and external docu-
    ments, and interviews with a number of participants and observers.

2   For critiques of the liberatory nature of identity politics and discussions of the
    disjunctures between poststructural analyses and identity politics, see Alcoff (1988),
    Butler (1990), Fuss (1989), Phelan (1989), and the essays in Warner (1993).

3   White people constitute nearly 90 percent of the state's population, African
    Americans (grouped primarily in two urban centers) under 8 percent, and generi-
    cally grouped "Hispanics" under 2 percent.

4   Symptomatic of the vilification of the public sector and the glorification of the
    private sector that currently prevail in public discourse (Apple 1995), the inter-
    twining of public and private languages to establish accountability reinscribes an
    "us" (the university) that must respond to a "them" (the public) that "we" claim to
    represent and by which "we" are ostensibly constituted, thus highlighting the
    problem of the university's representing that from which it is distinguished. See
    Nelson and Bérubé (1995) for a discussion of the ways partisan attacks that decry
    "politicized" university curricula and admissions procedures have combined with
    nonpartisan critiques that proclaim the failure of universities to educate and cre-
    dential, creating public uneasiness with higher education and "a climate in which
    universities are vulnerable and in which public resistance to [funding] cuts is al-
    most non-existent" (7).

5   Liberal U offers a major in African American Studies and a *non-degree* program
    in women's studies. It offers no programs in gay and lesbian or sexuality studies.

6   In a system constructed largely in terms of input and output, the addition of
    offices and programs may actually distract attention from the quality and effects
    of institutional structures. As an example, an administrator explained in a news
    interview, "For Liberal U to be among the top universities in the world it must
    continue to attract the best and brightest African American students and faculty."
    Toward this end, the administration has recently enhanced the Black Cultural
    Center, a space that includes a library, tutoring center, and other resources. A
    dean explained that it is a place for "African American students to feel at home,"
    and gives them "an extra hand in coping with a white campus." Although the
    center offers students a resource that they may appropriate for their own uses, it

does not signify institutional commitment to structural change, as suggested by the dean's assumption that the campus will continue to be white, a place for black students to "cope with." As the director of a multicultural office explained, "I think they [the administration] look for groups like this to sort of take the heat off them sometimes. If we have a [multicultural office], then we must be doing okay with issues of diversity. But institutionally, I think the institution welcomed the office. Now they don't always pay a great deal of attention to us and they don't give us adequate funding to do what we need to do, but it looks good."

7   The italicized statements constitute part of the flow of words and rhetoric around the creation of the office. Sources include newspaper articles, editorials and letters, brochures, documents, and leaflets. Speakers include the legislator, administrators, students, faculty, staff, alumni of Liberal U, and citizens of Oasis.

Works Cited

Alcoff, Linda. 1988. Cultural feminism versus post-structuralism: The identity crisis in feminist theory. *Signs: Journal of Women in Culture and Society* 13, no. 3: 405–436.

Apple, Michael. 1995. Cultural capital and official knowledge. In *Higher education under fire: Politics, economics, and the crisis of the humanities*, edited by Michael Bérubé and Cary Nelson. New York: Routledge.

Bergquist, William H. 1992. *The four cultures of the academy: Insights and strategies for improving leadership in collegiate organizations*. San Francisco: Jossey-Bass.

Butler, Judith. 1990. *Gender trouble: Feminism and the subversion of identity*. New York: Routledge.

de Certeau, Michel. 1984. *The practice of everyday life*. Translated by Steven F. Rendall. Berkeley: University of California Press.

D'Augelli, Anthony R. 1991. Lesbians and gay men on campus: Visibility, empowerment, and educational leadership. *Peabody Journal of Education* 66, no. 3: 121–141.

D'Emilio, John. 1992. *Making trouble: Essays on gay history, politics, and the university*. New York: Routledge.

Fuss, Diana. 1989. *Essentially speaking: Feminism, nature, and difference*. New York: Routledge.

Giroux, Henry A. 1994. Living dangerously: Identity politics and the new cultural racism. In *Between borders: Pedagogy and the politics of cultural studies*, edited by Henry A. Giroux and Peter McLaren. New York: Routledge.

Jaggar, Alison M. 1983. *Feminist politics and human nature*. Totowa, N.J.: Rowman and Allanheld.

Mangan, Katherine S. 1995. Conservative students challenge support for campus gay organizations. *The Chronicle of Higher Education*, January 27, A38.

Martin, Biddy and Chandra Talpade Mohanty. 1986. Feminist politics: What's home got to do with it? In *Feminist studies: Critical studies*, edited by Teresa de Lauretis. Bloomington: Indiana University Press.

Mohanty, Chandra Talpade. 1994. On race and voice: Challenges for liberal education in the 1990s. In *Between borders: Pedagogy and the politics of cultural studies*, edited by Henry A. Giroux and Peter McLaren. New York: Routledge.

Nelson, Cary and Michael Bérubé. 1995. Introduction: A report from the front. In *Higher education under fire: Politics, economics, and the crisis of the humanities*, edited by Michael Bérubé and Cary Nelson. New York: Routledge.

Patton, Cindy. 1993. Tremble, hetero swine! In *Fear of a queer planet: Queer politics and social theory*, edited by Michael Warner. Minneapolis: University of Minnesota Press.

Phelan, Shane. 1989. *Identity politics: Lesbian feminism and the limits of community*. Philadelphia: Temple University Press.

Piven, Frances Fox. 1983. Academic freedom and political dissent. In *Regulating the intellectuals: Perspectives on academic freedom in the 1980s*, edited by Craig Kaplan and Ellen Schrecker. New York: Praeger.

Rhoads, Robert A. 1994. *Coming out in college: The struggle for a queer identity*. Westport, Conn: Bergin & Garvey.

Sandoval, Chela. 1991. U.S. third world feminism: The theory and method of oppositional consciousness in the postmodern world. *Genders* 10: 1–24.

Scott, Joan W. 1988. Deconstructing equality-versus-difference: Or, the uses of poststructuralist theory for feminism. *Feminist Studies* 14, no. 1: 33–50.

——— 1995. The rhetoric of crisis in higher education. In *Higher education under fire: Politics, economics, and the crisis of the humanities*, edited by Michael Bérubé and Cary Nelson. New York: Routledge.

Sedgwick, Eve Kosofsky. 1990. *Epistemology of the closet*. Berkeley: University of California Press.

Seidman, Steven. 1993. Identity politics in a "postmodern" gay culture: Some historical and conceptual notes. In *Fear of a queer planet: Queer politics and social theory*, edited by Michael Warner. Minneapolis: University of Minnesota Press.

Talburt, Susan. 2000. *Subject to identity: Knowledge, sexuality, and academic practices in higher education*. Albany: SUNY Press.

Tierney, William G. 1993a. Academic freedom and the parameters of knowledge. *Harvard Educational Review* 63, no. 2: 143–160.

———— 1993b. *Building communities of difference: Higher education in the twenty-first century*. Westport, Conn.: Bergin & Garvey.

Torres, Carlos Alberto. 1995–96. State and education revisited: Why educational researchers should think politically about education. *Review of Research in Education* 21: 255–331.

Trend, David. 1995. *The crisis of meaning in culture and education*. Minneapolis: University of Minnesota Press.

Warner, Michael. 1995. No special rights. In *Higher education under fire: Politics, economics, and the crisis of the humanities*, edited by Michael Bérubé and Cary Nelson. New York: Routledge.

Warner, Michael, ed. 1993. *Fear of a queer planet: Queer politics and social theory*. Minneapolis: University of Minnesota Press.

West, Cornel. 1993. The new cultural politics of difference. In *Race, identity, and representation in education*, edited by Cameron McCarthy and Warren Crichlow. New York: Routledge.

Chapter 5

Paranoid Politics, Extremism, and the Religious Right: A Case of Mistaken Identity?

V. Darleen Opfer

In June 1998, the city council of Orlando, Florida, approved the flying of rainbow flags from city light posts. The flags were paid for by a private group and were flown to show support for Walt Disney World's "Gay Days." Gay Days is a weekend event at Walt Disney World that attracts thousands of gay men and women. The weekend itself has attracted negative comment in the past, but the flying of the flags in support of the Gay Days weekend created an entirely new conflict. On the June 8, 1998 broadcast of the *700 Club*, Pat Robertson, a leading spokesperson for the religious right, stated:

> We'd better respond according to what the Bible says. The Apostle Paul made it abundantly clear in the Book of Romans that the acceptance of homosexuality is the last step in the decline of Gentile civilization.
>
> So if the United States wants to embrace "degrading passions"—according to the Bible, something that the Bible says is an abomination against God—we're not in any way, shape, or form hating anybody. This is not a message of hate; this is a message of redemption. But if a condition like this will bring about the destruction of your nation, if it'll bring about terrorist bombs, if it'll bring earthquakes, tornadoes and possibly a meteor, it isn't necessarily something we ought to open our arms to. And I would warn Orlando that you're right in the way of some serious hurricanes and I don't think I'd be waving those flags in God's face if I were you. (Transcript of broadcast, June 8, 1998)

Within two weeks of this statement, devastating fires engulfed a large portion of central and north Florida. Pat Robertson explained the presence of these fires on the June 24, 1998 broadcast of the *700 Club*:

> This is a terrible tragedy in Florida. And you know, as I've been reading and
> praying, we had quite a flap the other day when we were talking about that gay
> pride day in Orlando and everybody laughed, but nevertheless, here's what I saw
> in the Bible. There are two things that I think are every significant. And what
> happens to these fires in Florida could be a prelude to some things that are going
> on all around the world. It just has to do with terrible drought, but it also is caused
> by lightning. Lightning keeps striking.
>   And this is in the Book of Revelation; you'll find it interesting. [Quoting Rev-
> elation 8:7] "There was an angel who sounded," it said, "his trumpet and there
> came hail and fire"—and, of course, fire is lightning—"and it was hurled down
> upon the earth. A third of the earth was burned up, a third of the trees were
> burned up, and all the green grass was burned up." And that's exactly what is
> happening. It was lightning strikes. And I saw on CBS last night the reporter said
> these fires cannot be stopped by man and says nature is not cooperating. (Tran-
> script of broadcast, June 24, 1998)

Scholarly literature has consistently characterized the discourse of the
religious right as "extremism" and "paranoid politics."[1] Is Pat Robertson
being "paranoid" when he states that the Florida fires are the result of
Orlando's support of Gay Days? Or is his call for fellow fundamentalists
to stop the spread of homosexuality a manifestation of "extremism"? The
terms extremism and paranoia, which have been used to characterize the
religious right, come from a larger body of socio-political theory that builds
on the work of Smelser (1963) and Parsons (1954). Scholars who write
about the religious right cite Lipset and Raab's (1970) conception of extremism and Hofstadter's (1965) understanding of paranoid politics when
trying to explain or characterize actions taken by the religious right. Are
those labels accurate? Are the actions of the religious right paranoid and
extreme?

For Lipset and Raab (1970) and Hofstadter (1965), "extremism" and
"paranoid politics" result when corporate status displacement becomes
anomic status displacement. Individuals have real social displacement, of
an economic nature, that they then attribute to a target population. The
target population is blamed for the change in social status, and is further
seen as engaging in a conspiracy to deliberately take over the status of the
affected group. Individuals make this inferential leap, from personal economic dispossession to a generalized social conspiracy, because of their
low educational backgrounds and susceptibility to monistic political appeal.

It is my intent in this chapter to show that characterizing the Christian
right as engaging in "paranoid politics" and "extremism" is a misapplication of the socio-political terms. The religious right has experienced neither economic instability as a result of a rise in the gay and lesbian
population's status, known as "the quondam complex," nor have they
attributed a status strain to gays because of a susceptibility to monistic

political appeal, referred to as "low democratic restraint." Posing an alternative conception of the religious right's actions is beyond the scope of this paper.[2] However, it is important to illustrate that the terms with which we have been labeling the religious right have a very narrow application. And while the terms may reflect how we feel about the actions of the religious right, such characterizations limit our available responses.

In order to demonstrate that the religious right is neither paranoid nor extreme, I will explain: (1) how a quondam complex occurs and its necessity for paranoid politics; (2) how the necessity of the quondam complex for paranoid politics and extremism rules out the application of the terms to the religious right; (3) how low democratic restraint occurs; (4) how the religious right's actions fail to qualify as low democratic restraint; and finally, (5) the implications of misapplying the terms paranoid politics and extremism to the actions of the religious right.

Throughout the paper, I will use the terms extremism and paranoid politics interchangeably. While they may be defined differently in other contexts, in Hoftsadter's and Lipset and Raab's work they result from the same economic and social context. The social conditions that lead to paranoid politics (as defined by Hofstadter) also lead to extremism (as defined by Lipset and Raab). Since I am interested in determining whether the social conditions that lead to either of these terms have been present during the religious right's actions against homosexuality the terms can be used interchangeably.

Quondam Complex

The term quondam complex comes from Lipset and Raab's *The Politics of Unreason* (1970), but the concept is similar in Hofstadter's (1965) and Smelser's (1963) work. The quondam complex results from economic and political dispossession. That is, the people within the paranoid movement feel that the targeted group has usurped their economic status and that they have no political channels open to them in which to make their grievances known.

Hofstadter describes the anti-Catholic sentiment of the nineteenth century to illustrate how paranoid politics results from status strain. During the nineteenth century, immigrants, many of whom were Catholic, were displacing skilled Americans from jobs. Americans, particularly rural Protestants, felt their economic status threatened by these immigrants. Rather than attribute their displacement to particular individuals, Protestant Americans generalized their anger toward the Catholics as a group. Protestant Americans began to see Catholics as libertine, "the confessional as an opportunity for seduction, licentious convents and monasteries, and the like" (Hofstadter 1965, 21–22). Additionally, the depression of 1893 was alleged to be an intentional creation of Catholics, who caused it by starting a run on the banks.

Lipset and Raab (1970), in describing social strain, reference the anti-Catholic movement and the rise of the Ku Klux Klan (KKK). In attributing the KKK movement of the nineteenth century to social strain, the authors indicate that "the disaffection of members of the white lower middle-class [sic] and working class is inevitably set against what they feel is not just the rise of the Negro population but a rise which is taking place at their inordinate expense" (510). Thus, the increase in economic mobility of black Americans, coupled with an increase in tax-supported programs for black Americans, led some white Americans to feel economically dispossessed. This dispossession was generalized to the entire black population, resulting in the KKK movement.

In these illustrations the structural strain necessary for extremism or paranoid politics develops first as personal displacement from some social and economic status and then becomes generalized or nativist bigotry. Four conditions appear to be necessary for extremism or paranoid politics to result from social strain. First, people are attracted to a movement because they have personally felt the strain. Second, this strain relates to a livelihood or status defined by income. Third, the targeted population has benefited from the social strain, but not to the extent that the movement comes to believe. Fourth, a leader or "paranoid spokesman," who has also been negatively impacted by the social strain, emerges to unify those who have been affected.

Economic Status Loss and the Religious Right

If this type of economic and social status loss is necessary for extremist movements to result, then the religious right's campaign against homosexuality does not qualify as paranoid. Neither the current economic situation in the United States nor the religious right's discourse about homosexuality indicates that gays and lesbians are displacing religious fundamentalists in any economic sense. To begin with, religious fundamentalists do not all share the same economic status. Those professing fundamentalist beliefs come from all economic strata: low, middle, and high. Thus, they do not have a shared social status that can be taken away. A paranoid movement, however, begins as a perceived economic displacement.

Further, the paranoid spokesmen, necessary to unify the movement, clearly have high status and have not experienced a recent economic status loss. Pat Robertson, for example, heads an organization with 1.8 million members and an annual budget of $27 million (Salter 1998). He also recently sold his Family Entertainment Network to Rupert Murdoch's News Corporation for a reported $1.7 billion. The most outspoken members of the religious right's movement are the least susceptible to the type of status loss necessary for paranoid politics or extremism.

The social status of religious fundamentalists, as well as that of the majority of Americans, has been on the rise for some time. Unemployment is low, mortgage rates are at a thirty-year low, and our national deficit is on the decline (NBC News, September 21, 1998). If Hofstadter's theory of paranoid politics and Lipset and Raab's theory of extremism were to hold true for the religious right, the amount of anti-homosexual action should be declining. This is not the case. People for the American Way (PFAW 1997), which tracks anti-homosexual initiatives state by state, indicates that in 1996 there were more incidents of anti-homosexual activity by religious right groups than in the four previous years.

The public discourse of the religious right relating to homosexuality does not evidence social or economic dispossession by gay men and lesbians. In fact, religious right spokesmen argue just the opposite; that is, that the numbers of homosexuals in the population are exaggerated. Lou Sheldon, leader of the fundamentalist group Traditional Values Coalition, has stated that the homosexual population "is less than 1.5%" and that "studies have proven that nearly 85% of those who ever practice homosexuality for a season either return to heterosexuality or celibacy as a lifestyle" (Letter to members, October 10, 1995). The religious right does not feel dispossessed as defined by Hofstadter and the others. They do not feel that "America has been largely taken away from them and their kind" (23) by homosexuals.

It could be argued that while the religious right has not experienced a change in social status that has economic origins, they are experiencing a change in social status that has cultural or value origins. I would agree with those who would make this argument. America is undergoing changes that are inconsistent with the culture and values of fundamentalism. For example, the decline in the nuclear family and the subsequent rise in alternative family structures undermine fundamentalist family values.

However, cultural or value status changes do not result in a quondam complex. To be labeled paranoid or extreme there has to be: (1) a change in status that has economic origins; (2) a real, individualized change in status; and (3) a change in status that is the result of an increase of status of the targeted group. To experience the quondam complex fundamentalists must perceive the breakdown of their own families. They must also attribute this breakdown to homosexuals. Thus, while it could be argued that fundamentalists have perceived a threat to their cultural status, it cannot be said that the threat has economic origins, that fundamentalists have been personally impacted, or that they have attributed the threat to homosexuals. Extremism and paranoid politics are not labels that can be used to describe action resulting from cultural or value changes.

Political Impotency and the Religious Right

If the quondam complex, and thus extremism or paranoid politics, is to apply to the religious right, there must also be an indication that they feel politically impotent. Lipset and Raab write, "In addition to identifiable group displacement, there was something more precise taking place in each of these periods [of extremism]: formal political alignments were shifting, and the conservative political party was usually in trouble" (485). Hofstadter claims that, "the paranoid style runs dangerously near to hopeless pessimism" (30) and that, "since [the movement's political] goals are not even remotely attainable, failure constantly heightens the paranoid's frustration" (31). Therefore, if we are to apply the quondam complex to the religious right we must first address whether the religious right felt that they could not address their concerns through traditional political means. Second, because extremist movements typically align themselves with the conservative party, we would have to determine that the conservative party has been in trouble and losing strength.

In regard to the first test of political impotency (that is, pessimism about political action and unattainable goals) the religious conservatives would concede very little political failure of late. Religious conservatives claim credit for the Republican Party's overwhelming victory in 1994. Brian Lopina, lobbyist for the Christian Coalition, claims that "the Christian Coalition is responsible for the election results, our grassroots got the Republicans elected. So we made them more influential" (Personal communication, October 14, 1996).

The results of an exit poll conducted by Mitofsky International indicate that the religious right deserves this credit. That poll found that 20 percent of voters in the 1994 Congressional election considered themselves evangelicals or born-again Christians. Additionally, three out of four of those Christians voted Republican. This represented "the largest single voting bloc among Republican voters. It represents just about a third of the Republican vote" (Green in Niebuhr 1995, B1).

In addition to their ability to mobilize on behalf of the Republican Party, the religious right is now afforded unprecedented access to the legislative process. Robert Raben, counsel to Rep. Barney Frank (D.-Mass.), told Gregg Zorova of the *Los Angeles Times* (1995) that Andrea Sheldon, lobbyist for Traditional Values Coalition, "is a diligent and pervasive presence at some of the most high-profile hearings. . . . She is omnipresent" (E1). Beverly LaHaye of Concerned Women for America sent a letter to her members stating:

CWA has been called upon by U.S. Senators and Representatives

- To testify before Congressional committees more times in the first five months of this year than in all of last year.
- To attend and provide pro-family input at "mark-up" meetings where vital pieces of legislation are drafted.
- To furnish senators and congressmen with research on a wide range of issues. (May, 1995)

And Dr. Robert Simmonds of Citizens for Excellence in Education, stated in an interview with the author:

Since the change in congressional majority, influencing legislation has been easier for us. Members of committees routinely call us now for information about pending policy and to get our viewpoint on issues. Republican members are receptive to our issues and make use of the research we undertake. (Personal communication, March 27, 1996)

If anything, the access to lawmakers has made the religious right feel more optimistic about their political chances today than they ever have in the past. Lou Sheldon has stated, "Give us a few more years under the belt and we will learn how the system works, we'll work the system even better than one could ever imagine" (CNN News, September 2, 1990).

To address the second task, that of showing that the conservative party has lost strength, scholars of political parties determine strength by examining two functions: the party-in-the-electorate function and the party-in-the-government function. The party-in-the-electorate function refers to a party's ability to organize its electoral capacity—to mobilize voters, to provide resources to candidates, and to get their candidates elected. The party-in-the-government function refers to a party's ability to design and implement a unified policy agenda (Herrnson 1994).[3]

The Republican Party's majority rule of Congress in 1994 is a clear indication of party strength. The Republican victory indicated exceptional electoral organization that was also accompanied by unification behind a clear policy direction—the "Contract with America." The Republican Party meets both tests of party strength. As such, it can not be claimed that the conservative party has suffered recent trouble significant enough to block conservative involvement in traditional political outlets.

Given the optimism about their political fortunes, the ability of the religious right to mobilize politically, the lack of a shared social status, and the good economic condition of the country, it seems implausible that the religious right's actions against homosexuality are due to a quondam complex. What remains to be seen is whether the anti-homosexual activity of the religious right emanates from "low democratic restraint."

Low Democratic Restraint

Low democratic restraint is caused by "conspicuous distortions of the patterns of value, and of the normal beliefs about the situation" (Parsons 1954, 169). The people suffering from the distortion of "normal beliefs" direct aggression toward the perceived source of social strain, in what Smelser characterizes as an unreasonable response to the situation. In the extremist or paranoid theories of social movements, members have low levels of education. These individuals have a general susceptibility to an uncomplicated narrative about the causes of problems and their possible solutions. Lipset and Raab indicate that the member of conservative social movements tends to "favour a simplified view of politics, to fail to understand the rationale underlying tolerance of those with whom he disagrees, and to find difficulty in grasping or tolerating a gradualist image of political change" (108). Thus, members of social movements who have low democratic restraint, characterized as paranoid, are uneducated, have distorted value or belief systems, and react unreasonably to social strain.

For the purposes of this chapter, I will not try to address whether religious conservatives can be considered, on the whole, uneducated. I will, however, discuss whether they exhibit the kind of belief system that characterizes paranoid or extremist groups and whether the organization's actions can be considered unreasonable given its members' belief system. Lipset and Raab describe the distorted belief system as one in which belief follows action. Specifically, the authors argue, "reservoirs [of belief] have typically been revitalized by and used by political developments, rather than being the genesis of them. . . . Right-wing extremist movements have not sprung up out of nativist bigotry; they have sprung up out of backlash against change which invented or reinvented nativist bigotry" (491).

To illustrate how a distorted belief system is formed, Lipset and Raab provide a small case study of extremism. The authors tell of a Jewish couple who were terrorized for over a year by a gang of boys in the early 1960s. When the boys were caught and their families questioned, there was no evidence of anti-Semitic belief. The families did not engage in anti-Semitic discourse, they did not belong to anti-Semitic organizations, and no anti-Semitic literature was found in any of the homes. Additionally, none of the activities of the teenagers outside their homes, other than the instances with the Jewish couple, had anti-Semitic proclivities.

In analyzing the year-long activity, Lipset and Raab found that it was only toward the end that the boys began making anti-Semitic references. In the beginning they were making anonymous calls randomly. The boys narrowed in on the Jewish couple because they responded especially fearfully. Even after honing in on the couple, the boys did not use anti-Semitic tactics. Well into the year, the boys discovered that anti-Jewish comments added new life to the terrorization. It was only then that their remarks became singularly anti-Semitic.

What makes the belief system distorted, then, is that the paranoid person is predisposed to certain activity and the belief system is strictly an instrument used in this activity. In discussing belief as an instrument, Lipset and Raab state:

> The juvenile gang in San Francisco had no difficulty plucking it [anti-Semitic belief] out when they had use for it, although their previous acquaintanceship with it had been no greater than that of other Americans. The level of their folk anti-Semitism was not the key to their anti-Semitic activity; the key was their inclination toward cruelty and their willingness to use anti-Semitism to further that cruelty. (495)

Low Democratic Restraint, Belief, and the Religious Right

For the religious right to be considered paranoid or extremist, they first would have to be willing to act against homosexuality, and then use a belief system to justify or further that action. The religious right however, is defined as a group by a unified, pre-existing belief system. Strict fundamentalists, open fundamentalists, and establishment evangelicals, who are generally lumped together under the label of the "religious right," believe first and foremost in the inerrancy of the Bible. For them, the "Bible is the inerrant Word of God and should be interpreted literally as such" (Hunter 1991, 68). The text of the Bible is the source of all religious and moral authority. The Bible outlines clear boundaries between right and wrong that result in absolute standards of life and thought.

This literal interpretation of the Bible leaves little room for doubt about the sinfulness of homosexuality. In Leviticus 20:9 of the New English Bible (NEB) it states, "If a man has intercourse with a man as with a woman, they both commit an abomination. They shall be put to death; their blood shall be on their own heads." In his landmark book *Homosexuality and the Western Christian Tradition*, which is considered generally sympathetic to gay and lesbian interests, D. S. Bailey (1955) finds this passage an unambiguous condemnation of all homosexual acts. This unambiguous condemnation, when combined with other Biblical passages, permits the religious right to engage in anti-homosexual politics. For example, "You shall reprove your fellow-countryman frankly and so you will have no share in his guilt" (Leviticus 19:9, New English Bible) informs the religious right's belief in the sin of homosexuality, but also allows its members to believe that those who do not speak out against homosexuality are as guilty of homosexuality as those who engage in homosexual conduct.

The story of the city of Sodom, told in the book of Genesis, further illustrates to the religious right the danger of homosexuality. In this story, God destroyed the city of Sodom with fire and brimstone. Abraham tries to intercede on behalf of those who did not engage in the "egregious" acts by asking in Genesis 18:22, "Wilt thou really sweep away the good and bad together?" He pleads with God to spare the city even if only ten good men can be found. God saves only Lot and his family, who are recent citizens of Sodom. God destroys everyone else. This story allows the reader to assume that God considers all citizens, even young children, guilty or guilty by association.

If we consider a passage by the Apostle Paul in his first letter to the Corinthians, the danger of homosexuality for the Christian fundamentalist is even greater than death. Paul writes, "Make no mistake: no fornicator or idolater, none who are guilty either of adultery or of homosexual perversion, no thieves or grabbers or drunkards or slanderers or swindlers, will possess the kingdom of God." If fundamentalists believe in the inerrancy of the Bible, if the Bible states that homosexuality is punishable by death, if it also states that they will share in their neighbor's guilt if they do not reprove his behavior, and if it concludes that the kingdom of God is denied to the guilty, then the Christian fundamentalist who does not actively speak out against homosexuality risks not only death, but the loss of salvation. Silence about homosexual issues is equated to death and then damnation.

Given this belief system, are the anti-homosexual actions of the religious right irrational? That is, can we say that their actions do not logically follow from their beliefs? Examining both national and local occurrences indicates that the anti-homosexual actions of the religious right are rational. Nationally, homosexuality has been slowly gaining acceptance among the U.S. population since the late 1960s. In a Gallup poll conducted in July 1998, 31 percent of Americans polled believe people are born homosexual, up from 19 percent in 1989 and 13 percent in 1977 (Gallup in Schneider 1998, 1838). During the same period in which homosexuality gained acceptance, the fundamentalist population declined. Smith (1992), of the National Opinion Research Center, found that the percentage of Americans who believe in the inerrancy of the Bible has actually decreased from 65 percent in 1963 to 31 percent in 1989. The trend is actually running counter to the beliefs of the religious right. Because of this trend, and during this same time period, we have seen an increase in religious right anti-gay activity.

To illustrate how these trends have led to religious right anti-gay activism, consider their most recent advertising campaign. A coalition of fifteen religious right groups launched a series of advertisements beginning on July 13, 1998, in the *Washington Post*, the *New York Times*, and *USA Today* claiming that homosexuals can be converted to heterosexuality through faith. The "Toward Hope and Healing for Homosexuals" advertisements are a direct result of a meeting of conservative group leaders in late June 1998. These leaders had specifically met to discuss the "anti-Christian" reaction to the remarks of Senate Majority Leader Trent Lott that called homosexuality sinful and the growing trend toward an essentialist view of homosexuality (Gersen 1998). The advertisements with the message that homosexuals can change were aimed at heterosexuals who believe that one is born homosexual.

Locally, these national trends get played out even more explicitly. For example, in a Brookfield, Connecticut, high school, pink triangles were placed outside seven classrooms designated as "safe zones" for gay, lesbian, and bisexual students. The parents of one student complained to the school board in a letter stating, "This is a homosexual agenda. This is homosexual recruiting. This is disgusting. This is illegal." As a result of this letter, a group of area residents called Committee for the Defense of

Classroom Tolerance and a teacher filed a libel lawsuit against the parents. The school board also voted 5–2 that the "safe zones" should remain.

The American Center for Law and Justice (ACLJ), founded by Pat Robertson, became involved to provide legal and financial support to the parents. The ACLJ also dedicated a seven-page national newsletter to the case in which Jay Sekulow, chief counsel for ACLJ, wrote, "Can you imagine, that in public schools of America today, students are being taught that homosexual conduct, which in many states is still deemed illegal, is not only a viable alternative lifestyle, but is actually equal to heterosexual relationships?" (PFAW 1997). Thus, not only did fundamentalists experience a rise in pro-gay sentiment within their community, they also felt the weight of state-sanctioned institutions, the schools, and the courts against them.

As Bruce (1984) in *Firm in the Faith* points out, "the liberals' view that conservatives are narrow-minded and bigoted misses the point that such characteristics are not characteristics of the individuals who *become* conservative evangelicals; they are logical and socio-psychological consequences of the belief system" (89; emphasis in original). The rise in anti-gay activity by the religious right can be directly attributed to a greater acceptance of homosexuality by Americans. Additionally, specific actions by religious right organizations are often taken to defend against actions by other community members, the schools, the courts, or state and national legislatures. Thus, the religious right is informed by a logically ordered belief system that justifies their actions. Paranoid groups, on the other hand, are not.

I am not contending that spokesmen such as Pat Robertson do not use the fundamentalist belief system to further their political agendas. What I argue is that the typical fundamentalist American, who does not seek personal political gain, engages in anti-gay activity because of specific and clear religious beliefs. And, because he or she is reacting to a threat that they believe leads to their damnation, neither their beliefs nor their actions can be considered of "low democratic restraint."

Discussion

Since, as I have shown, the religious right has neither a quondam complex nor low democratic restraint, they can not be considered paranoid or extremist. However, in addition to being a misapplication of the sociopolitical theories, the use of the terms creates political narratives (Roe

1994; Stone 1988) that have negative repercussions for gay and lesbian policy issues and activism. Narratives commonly used in describing issues are a force in themselves. These stories often resist change or modification even in the presence of contradictory empirical data because they continue to underwrite and stabilize assumptions in the face of high uncertainty, complexity, and polarization (Roe 1994). They illustrate not only how the religious right and other groups attempt to persuade but also how language gives meaning to social action.

The use of the terms "extremism" and "paranoid politics," both in the media and in academic journals, creates political narratives that significantly undercut potential support for pro-gay initiatives. This occurs because the use of the terms is an ideological apparatus that reinforces hegemonic political systems. Labeling the religious right in such a manner gives the socio-political theories behind the label legitimacy. It confirms the accuracy of the label and the theories in describing the type of activism engaged in by the religious right. Ultimately, it subverts the political power of gay men and lesbians by forcing them to operate within political theories that do not account for or address their specific agendas and circumstances.

Further, labeling the religious right "extremist" or "paranoid" may itself be considered an extremist and paranoid act. Those who label come to be understood as extremist and paranoid. This transference of extremism occurs because, with the act of labeling, the labeler becomes engaged in political discourse with the religious right. Since the discourse of the religious right carries the extremist label, all discourse that follows is defined by that label. It becomes intradiscursively dependent (Foucault 1991, 58). In essence the political contest is taken *to* the religious right and then is played on their terms. The response required is necessarily an equally extremist or paranoid defensive tactic. Thus, classifying the religious right as paranoid or extremist has two narrative implications. First, doing so accedes the theoretical legitimacy of the terms in applying to, and restricting the legitimacy of, the political actions of the religious right. Second, doing so results in similar acts that entail restrictions of legitimacy of the political actions of pro-homosexual activists.

The ramifications of reinforcing political notions of extremism while engaging in extremism are that they force the gay community and its supporters into stances that Ruthann Robson (1992) describes as "separatism" and "assimilation." Choosing to call the religious right "extremists" forces a response to the actions of the religious right that can be understood as similarly extremist, thus placing gays, lesbians, and their supporters outside acceptable political activism. Understanding the religious right to be paranoid or extremist leads to separatist groups such as ACT-UP and activism similar to that related by Sarah Schulman (1994) in her tales of the Lesbian Avengers. The labeling of the religious right as paranoid can require a homosexual-centered activism where gays will work with other gays and nongays are unwelcome.

While emotionally and perhaps even logically justifiable, this type of activism can essentialize and reify issues that impact homosexuals. In effect, it constructs "gay" issues as unique and different from the issues of "other" Americans. By placing the fight with the religious right outside the boundaries of normative political action we deny the policy issues of homosexuals legitimacy and membership within this system.

Additionally, we open the door to further abuse and inequality of treatment because, as Michael Walzer indicates, in a political system "the denial of membership is always the first of a long train of abuses" (1983, 62). The evidence indicates that recent engagement of the religious right in political battles outside normative political activism has opened the door to further abuse. For example, as indicated earlier, religious right affiliation is on the decline (Schneider 1998). However, in recent years there has been a dramatic increase in anti-gay activity (PFAW 1997), a flurry of anti-gay marriage bills in state legislatures, and Congressmen willing to bash gays and lesbians in the media (Trent Lott and James Inhofe in Gergen 1998). The contradictory evidence of the decline of the religious right and the increase in anti-gay activities reinforces the position that separatism leads to further abuse.

Resisting the religious right within existing, normative theories of political activism also has negative repercussions for gay policy issues. "Assimilation" requires the sublimation of gay and lesbian interests. It assumes that access to policy making will be granted and, once granted, change can occur from within existing hegemonic political structures. Kirk and Madsen's (1989) *After the Ball* is a treatise for assimilative activism. They claim that homosexuals are just like everyone else: "We look, feel, and act just as they do; we're hardworking, conscientious Americans with love lives exactly like their own" (379). By their logic, gay men and lesbians will be given the political access necessary to make policy changes if they will just act, look, and feel like the average American (whatever that may be).

With assimilative political activism homosexuals become simply an interest group with its requisite distribution of public goods, compromise, and instability of identity. As Theodore Lowi (1979) defines interest groups:

(1) Organized interests are homogeneous and easy to define. Any duly elected representative of any interest is taken as an accurate representation of each and every member. (2) Organized interests emerge in every sector of our lives and adequately represent most of those sectors, so that one organized group can be found effectively answering and checking some other organized group as it seeks to prosecute its claims against society. And (3) the role of government is one of insuring access to the most effectively organized, and of ratifying the agreements and adjustments worked out among the competing leaders. (51)

Political success depends on an interest's ability to organize and unify behind a single message of its group's desires, needs, and demands. Assimilative political activism requires homosexuals not only to think and behave within normative strictures but also to agree on issues, direction, and leadership. The danger of assimilation, then, is that it requires homogeneity both within the gay community and between the gay community and "other" Americans.

Conclusion

My primary purpose in this chapter has been to expose educators, researchers, and pro-gay activists to the possibility that taken-for-granted notions of "extremist" and "paranoid" politics may actually work against the interests of gay men and lesbians. My speculations are intended to encourage readers to think more critically about the "universality" of notions of political activism rather than to offer concrete recommendations. Nonetheless, I would argue that the act of labeling the religious right "paranoid" or "extremist" places gay activism within existing political theories. With such labeling we have in essence locked ourselves into two competing theories of activism, separatism and assimilation, neither of which serves gay and lesbian interests well.

When we choose to call the religious right "extremists" or "paranoid," we acknowledge the legitimacy of the theory those terms represent in explaining not only the activism of the religious right but also our own. If we characterize the religious right in those terms, the only avenue available to us is to engage in the normative political activism of interest groups that provides little help in addressing the policy issues of gay men and lesbians or, for that matter, the issues of any dominated group. The potential for political change depends, not on separatism nor on assimilation, but on forcing the hegemonic political system and its theorists to recognize alternative issues and forms of activism.

Notes

1   See Catherine A. Lugg (1998), Didi Herman (1997), Mortimer Ostow (1990), Grace Halsell (1986), Lowell D. Streiker (1984), and Gary K. Clabaugh (1974).

2   For alternatives to extremism and paranoid politics, see Steve Bruce (1988), Pamela Conover (1983), and Michael Wood and Michael Hughes (1984).

3   There is some dissention among theorists about the strength of U.S. political parties. Some scholars indicate that parties are strengthening and some indicate that the parties are in decline. Those studies that indicate parties are strengthening tend to define strength based on party-in-the-electorate characteristics (Crotty 1991, Longley 1992, Jackson 1992). Political parties as electorate organizations have been strengthening. Their election campaigns are more organized; they provide more resources to their candidates; and they engage in more types of election activity.

   The theorists who claim political parties are weakening base their conclusions on the party-in-the-government function (Brady 1990; Sibley 1990). The lack of party-in-the-government strength is visible in the relative proportion of congressional "party votes" (that is, when 90 percent of one party votes against 90 percent of the other party). Between 1960 and 1994, only 5 percent of Congressional roll call votes were party votes. The confusion in the literature over party resurgence is therefore due to the differing measures used to determine strength.

Works Cited

Bailey, Derrick S. 1955. *Homosexuality and the western Christian tradition.* New York: Longmans.

Brady, David W. 1990. Coalitions in the U. S. Congress. In *The parties respond: Changes in the American party system,* edited by L. Sandy Maisel. Boulder, Colorado: Westview Press.

Bruce, Steve. 1984. *Firm in the faith.* Brookfield, Vermont: Gower Publishing.

————— 1988. *The rise and fall of the new Christian right.* New York: Oxford University Press.

Cable News Network. 1990. Transcript of news broadcast, September 2.

Clabaugh, Gary K. 1974. *Thunder on the right: The protestant fundamentalists.* Chicago: Nelson Hall.

Conover, Pamela. 1983. The mobilization of the new right: A test of various explanations. *Western Political Quarterly* 36: 632–49.

Crotty, William J. 1991. Political parties: Issues and trends. In *Political science: Looking to the future.* Vol. 4. Evanston, Ill.: Northwestern University Press.

Foucault, Michel. 1991. Politics and the study of discourse. In *The Foucault effect: Studies in governmentality with two lectures by and an interview with Michel Foucault,* edited by Graham Burchell, Colin Gordon, and Peter Miller. Chicago: The University of Chicago Press.

Gerson, Michael J. 1998. Out of the political closet. *U.S. News & World Report,* July 27, 28.

Halsell, Grace. 1986. *Prophecy and politics: Militant evangelists on the road to nuclear war.* Westport, Conn.: Lawrence Hill.

Herman, Didi. 1997. *The antigay agenda: Orthodox vision and the Christian right.* Chicago: University of Chicago Press.

Herrnson, Paul A. 1994. The revitalization of national party organizations. In *The parties respond,* edited by L. Sandy Maisel. 2nd ed. Boulder, Colorado: Westview Press.

Hofstadter, Richard. 1965. *The paranoid style in American politics and other essays.* New York: Alfred A. Knopf.

Hunter, James D. 1991. *Culture wars.* New York: HarperCollins.

Jackson, John S. 1992. The party-as-organization: Party elites and party reforms in presidential nominations and conventions. In *Challengers to party government,* edited by John Kenneth White and Jerome M. Mileur. Carbondale: Southern Illinois University Press.

Lipset, Seymour M. and Earl Raab. 1970. *The politics of unreason: Right–wing extremism in America, 1790–1970.* New York: Harper & Row.

Longley, Lawrence D. 1992. The institutionalization of the national Democratic Party: A process stymied. *Western Political Scientist* 7: 9–15.

Lowi, Theodore. 1979. *The end of liberalism: The second republic of the United States,* 2nd edition. New York: W.W. Norton.

Lugg, Catherine A. 1998. The religious right and public education: The paranoid politics of homophobia. *Educational Policy* 12, no. 3: 267–83.

Niebuhr, Gustav. 1995. The religious right readies agenda for second 100 days. *New York Times,* May 16.

Ostow, Mortimer. 1990. The fundamentalist phenomenon: A psychological perspective. In *The fundamentalist phenomenon,* edited by Norman J. Cohen. Grand Rapids, Michigan: William B. Eerdmans Publishing Company.

Parsons, Talcott. 1954. *Essays in sociological theory.* Glencoe: The Free Press.

People for the American Way (PFAW). 1997. *Hostile climates: A state by state report on anti-gay activity.* Washington, D.C.: People for the American Way.

Robson, Ruthann. 1992. *Lesbian (out)law: Survival under the rule of law.* Ithaca, N.Y.: Firebrand Books.

Roe, Emery. 1994. *Narrative policy analysis: Theory and practice.* Durham, N.C.: Duke University Press.

Salter, Stephanie. 1998. Despite his antics, Pat Robertson proves he's no joke. *The Arizona Republic*, June 16, B5.

Schneider, William. 1998. And now, the Dobson and Bauer show! *The National Journal* 30, no. 31: 1838.

Shulman, Sarah. 1994. *My American history: Lesbian and gay life during the Reagan-Bush years.* New York: Routledge.

Sibley, Joel H. 1990. The rise and fall of American political parties, 1790–1990. In *The parties respond: Changes in the American party system*, edited by L. Sandy Maisel. Boulder, Colorado: Westview Press.

Smelser, Neil J. 1963. *The theory of collective behavior.* New York: The Free Press.

Smith, Tom W. 1992. Are conservative churches growing? *Review of Religious Research* 33, no. 4: 305–329.

Stone, Deborah. 1988. *Policy paradox and political reason.* New York: HarperCollins.

Streiker, Lowell D. 1984. *The gospel time bomb: Ultrafundamentalism and the future of America.* Buffalo, N.Y.: Prometheus.

Wood, Michael and Michael Hughes. 1984. The moral basis of moral reform: Status discontent vs. culture and socialization as explanations of anti-pornography social movement adherence. *American Sociological Review* 49: 89–99.

Zorova, Gregg. 1995. Flying right. *Los Angeles Times*, Sunday profile, E1.

Chapter 6

Another Queer Theory: Reading Complexity Theory as a Moral and Ethical Imperative[1]

Brent Davis
Dennis J. Sumara

For two years we participated in a study with eight other queer teachers into the complex relationship between subjectivity and pedagogy. Naming ourselves the Queer Teachers' Study Group, we endeavored to specify, for ourselves and for others, the phenomenological particularity of enacting pedagogy as queer subjects and, as well, the ongoing struggle to develop subjects with queer pedagogies.

During one of our day-long meetings, we found ourselves preoccupied by our conflicted relationship with our bodies and the various ways we struggled to adorn, drape, conceal, elaborate, and exoticize them. Emerging from a series of writing practices and readings dealing with "embodiment," the topic of clothing served to focus our attention on the ways in which cultural practices of concealment and identification shape biological bodies and cultural identities.

Because all of us identified as lesbian, gay, or transsexual, clothing presented a way for us to identify with or against mainstream beliefs about the lines that divide male from female, gay from straight, dyke from fag, butch from femme, and so on. As we discussed our often conflicted relationships with what we wear—and with the cultural identities and identifications clothing announces—it became evident that we were caught up in a queer set of practices in which it was unclear whether our bodies, psyches, sexualities, and experiences were shaped by clothing or whether we participated in that shaping through the costumes we chose to wear. Michael, for example, explained how he could never find clothing (men's or women's) that conformed to the shape of his body or to his internalized understanding of his gendered and sexualized identity. Maura explained how she deliberately chose attire that identified her as a dyke to other lesbians and, at the same time, protected her from predatory heterosexual males. Kelly explained how it was not until her transition from men's to women's garments that she felt comfortable in clothing that better fitted her sexually borderline physiology.

As our discussion evolved, it became increasingly difficult for any of us to speak about "clothing" without delving into the sexed, raced, and gendered identification practices and identity experiences that we had had and were having. This discourse revolving around clothing suggested that our experiences of living queer were far more complex than the depictions of "queerness" presented in popular culture, in academic theorizing, and even in the self-narrated depictions of our own lives. Moreover, in complex ways, our discussion of "clothing the body," as a particular cultural identification practice, rendered bare our own discomfort with the clothed "body of the teacher"—that is, with the professional personas we had all enacted in ways that separated them from our queer identities. Co-opting the term "drag"—which, for the most part, has been used in reference to men dressing as women—we came to understand that each of us continued to perform "teacher drag" in our classrooms, schools, and universities. Teacher drag had become for us a signifier for the robing and disrobing we felt must take place in order to re-complexify our teaching identities—that is, to acknowledge and announce our complicity in schooling practices we consider oppressive, particularly for those who identify as "other."

We begin with this query into the relationship between the queer teacher's pedagogical practices and the identity-identification of the queer teacher's body to signal the inadequacy of conventional theoretical and interpretive understandings of the relations of teaching. As well, we invoke images of the queer body-identity to point to the need to understand complexity as an everyday instance of "queerness"—as an understanding of the impossibility of coming to terms with the projects of "education," of "educational research," and of "identity politics" without a more full-*bodied* interpretation of the ways in which normalized, privileged discourses and practices have squeezed the queer body into the suit of the familiar, the figure, the father, the master.

In this article, we develop "complexity theory" as another queer theory and, particularly, use it to interrogate commonsense notions of development, education, research, and identity. We also query complexity theory itself, offering Cohen and Stewart's (1994) formulation of "complicity" as an interruption in the already mathematically sanitized and culturally privileged discourse of complexity theory currently working its way into educational research. These queries proceed phenomenologically and biologically at two sites: our own professional (research and teaching) practices and, more broadly, our own lives. In so proceeding, we aim to render strange and queer those academic discourses (including those of "complexity") that have banished the mark of the troublesome biological body in order to support an idealized epistemic body.

Theories of Complexity

Although its history has been brief, complexity theory has already attracted widespread interest among researchers and theorists in virtually every field of academic inquiry. Compatible with such discourses as radical hermeneutics, deep ecology, and the "new" sciences, complexity theory might appropriately be described as one facet of a multidisciplinary change of mind-sets—of the sort, we suspect, Kuhn (1962) had in mind when he coined the phrase "paradigm shift." Our society is, arguably, in the midst of a transformation of worldview, moving away from the reductionist project of modernism and toward the expansive play of postmodernism. Or, to put it differently, the once pervasive desire to interpret phenomena in terms of linear relationships, causal logic, and statistical reduction is giving way to an awareness that most, if not all, of what we experience in the universe is better understood in terms of the fluid, self-similar, recursive, and hazily bounded notions provided by chaos dynamics, fuzzy logic, and complexity theory.

Complexity theory is a field of inquiry that examines those phenomena that are self-organizing, adaptive, and dynamic—in brief, those phenomena that are alive or that we tend to describe with metaphors drawn from vibrant bodies, evolving organisms, and life processes. Examples include the cells, collectives of cells (for example, organs), collectives of organs (for example, human bodies), collectives of persons (for example, a classroom grouping), each of which has a sort of integrity that transcends its component systems. A complex system is more than the sum of its parts.

As Waldrop (1992) explains in an account of the emergence of the field, complexity theorists "are forging the first rigorous alternative to the kind of linear, reductionist thinking that has dominated science since the time of Newton" (13)—a timely undertaking, given that the reductionist project of scientism, especially as it had been taken up in the humanities, has already been widely rejected. Now more attentive to the personal, social, and planetary consequences of positivist thinking—yet still affording a particular privilege to the rationalist-empiricist argument—we are primed and ready for a mathematical alternative to that approach to inquiry that relies on rigid definition, that adheres to an unforgiving reason, and that demands verification through replication. Complexity theory inserts itself precisely here, speaking in a more tentative voice and translating the insights of poets, phenomenologists, and ecologists into the privileged tongue of science. Events are inextricable from one another; experience is irreducible; we are not converging on a unified and complete understanding of the universe.

In spite of its appeal, though, we in the humanities have good reason to be cautious about this framework, in part because it presents a risk of perpetuating the privilege of the "hard sciences" (and, correspondingly, eclipsing the *complex* insights of hermeneutics, cultural criticism, and other systems that predate the emergence of complexity theory). But more important, just like catastrophe theory of the early 1970s and chaos dynamics of the 1980s, complexity theory already appears to be incapable of living up to its early promise. In particular, complexivists are now being criticized for having missed the mark in their research by relying too heavily on overly simplistic models. Like those with the analytic and reductionist mind-set they have aimed to supplant, complexity theorists may have succumbed to the same sort of oversimplifying tendencies in their quest to simulate "real-world" phenomena.

Such are the criticisms beginning to arise, and they are in many ways justified. Complexity theory, for example, is founded on a distinction between systems that are *complex* and those that are merely *complicated*. The latter category includes such objects as clocks and computers—mechanisms that can be dismantled and reassembled, and whose behaviors can be understood by anyone with an adequate knowledge of their components. Complex systems, however, are more spontaneous, more adaptable, more self-defining, more unpredictable—in brief, more alive. They cannot be understood by merely examining their subsystems. The most exhaustive knowledge of livers, hearts, kidneys, and spleens does little to help make sense of the collective character of the embodied unity they collectively bring forth. But an attentiveness to that bodily unity—that is, in the current example, to an individual person—is patently inadequate as well. For an individual to be understood in any deep way also requires that he or she be studied within the complex biological and social systems in which the person comes to form and of which the person is part. Such complex phenomenal levels do not begin with the body biologic and end with the body politic: The dimensions of analysis can be extended from at least subcellular to the planetary, and perhaps beyond.

Complexity theory thus insists that living phenomena be regarded, simultaneously, as collectives, as unities, and as subsystems. In terms of current research into complex systems, this is where the problem arises. While embracing the contingencies of existence by refusing overly simplistic explanations, complexity theory has become almost totally reliant on a mechanical device that is merely complicated. Studies of complexity, for the most part, are conducted by means of *computer* simulation. Granted, the resulting simulations can be enormously complicated, generating unexpected and spectacular results, but the results are calculable (and, indeed, calculated) nonetheless. Being finite, they cannot, for example, model the sorts of recursive embeddedness and self-transcendence that are hallmarks of living systems.

The inadequacy of computer simulation arises from its lack of plasticity. Unlike the environment in which a living organism comes to form, the "environment" that the computer provides is as yet incapable of entering into a choreography with the unfolding simulation. As such, a reliance on such simulation would amount to committing an "error of types" by projecting the current conclusions of complexivists onto living systems. A naive understanding of complexity theory presents a danger of re-presenting human experience in terms of mechanical behaviors.

From Complexity to Complicity

Biologist Jack Cohen and mathematician Ian Stewart have added their voices to the emerging chorus of criticism. Complexivists themselves, Cohen and Stewart (1994) present their critiques as a starting place for the formulation of an alternative theoretical positioning. Noting the tendency of phenomena (or, at least, human experiences of phenomena) to range from the seemingly simple to the exceedingly complex, depending on one's vantage point (in other words, noting how we are implicated in the phenomena that we study), Cohen and Stewart bring the oppositional notions of "simplicity" and "complexity" into dialogue. Rather than allowing these to remain opposites, they propose two complementary notions, *simplexity* and *complicity* (a play of the words "simplicity" and "complexity"), with the goal of pushing complexity theorists beyond their current crisis.

The term "simplexity," they propose, could be used to refer to any human-contrived system of interpretation, however elaborate, intended to describe or simulate the universe, or some aspect of it. The defining feature of a simplex system is its dependency on initial conditions. In such systems, the *space of the possible* is fixed at the start. In terms of conventional theories of the cosmos, Newtonian mechanics is perhaps the most prominent example of simplexity. Comprised of a series of relatively simple rules, this particular mathematical model has helped us organize and predict our experiential world—so effectively, in fact, that Western societies tend to forget that this instance of simplexity is only one of many possible descriptive systems.

There are many other instances of simplex systems in current popular and academic discourse. Schooling itself is an example (as we develop later), as it tends to be founded on a small set of well-articulated, but troublesome, formal principles. The human body, as well, is overwhelmingly regarded as simplex, consistent with the system of modern (analytic) philosophy upon which medical science (and most of Western thought) rests. Founded on axioms announced by Descartes and derived through the rules of logic developed by Aristotle, Western bodies (physical and epistemic) are generally announced to be and perceived as simplexities.

These sorts of models, relatively easy to simulate and tending to eclipse the complicity of their authors, have occupied the imaginations of those engaged in simulation-based complexity theory research. Cohen and Stewart contrast these simplexities to complicit systems, ones that do not depend on initial conditions and cannot, therefore, be simulated by such mechanical devices as the modern computer. In cases of complicity—of which evolution and cognition are two important and intertwining examples—systems interact in ways that change one another, resulting in a growth in complexity from relatively simple beginnings. There is an opening of new possibilities, a continuous enlargement of the space of the possible.

This notion of "enlarging the space of the possible" is essential to understanding the difference between the projects of complicity and simplexity. Current inquiries into complexity (or, in Cohen and Stewart's terms, simplexity) might be interpreted in terms of pursuing the modernist ideal of progress—which, in effect, represents an effort to manage complexity, to train it to one's purpose, and to use it in the project of controlling one's situation. Enlarging the space of the possible is, in many ways, the antithesis of the ideal of progress. It insists that we are collectively moving toward increased complexity; hence, we are forever falling short of our desire to render the world manageable. The difference between the desire for progress and the recognition of ever-increasing complexity is thus a temporal one: Complexity, like modernism, points its desire toward the future; complicity is more focused on the contingencies of the immediate situation, acknowledging that the future depends on the present but is not determined by it.[2]

Cohen and Stewart's choice of the terms "simplexity" and "complicity" is more than a clever rhetorical device. "Complicity," in addition to sharing an etymological heritage with "complexity," evokes senses of being *implicated in* or *serving as an accomplice to* and thus announces a need to be attentive to one's own participation in events. It is a notion meant to prompt an awareness of what Varela, Thompson, and Rosch (1991) call the "fundamental circularity of being"—an idea they illustrate by pointing out that the universe changes with an event as mundane as a shifting thought. That thought is not merely in the universe, it is *part* of the universe. In other words, we are fully implicated in our world, and this notion extends well beyond the now commonplace understanding that perception is not innocent. It is not merely how we make sense of the cosmos—that is, how we assign it form through perception—that makes us complicit. More profoundly, we are knitted into a complex and dynamic choreography of being that, following Gregory Bateson (1979), we might call "knowing."

This is no small point. In our modern and Western arrogance, there is a pervasive belief that our systems of knowledge are the most accurate, the best representations of the "world out there," the closest to ultimate Truth. But the notion of complicity does not allow knowing and understanding to reside within individuals or within collectives. Rather, knowing is considered in terms of appropriate situated action—that is, as the ability to maintain viability within a dynamic context. Or, in Cohen and Stewart's terms, we tend to regard knowledge in simplex terms, but it is a complicit phenomenon. Given, therefore, the mounting evidence of our collective failure in this regard—the possibility, for example, that our society might have pushed the planet to the brink of disaster—the belief in the supremacy of modern thought is a matter that merits considerable and immediate re-cognition.

The formulation of complicity alongside the ecological-hermeneutic conception of fundamental circularity—all coupled with Bateson's conflation of knowledge, action, and identity—should prompt those interested in both complexity theory and schooling to consider the moral and ethical dimensions of the formal educational project, another complicit project commonly misperceived as a simplex one. Schooling has been the subject of modernist analyses that fragment participants, intentions, and actions to the extent that teaching and learning are pervasively cast as manageable, controllable, and mechanical processes. This confident image of schooling, supported by prescriptive curriculum manuals and the "how to" textbooks at the core of virtually every teacher education program, are problematized by the notion of complicity. Complicity makes it plain that each and every one of us is mired in the phenomenon of schooling: participating, implicated, guilty.

Complicity and Morality[3]

Formal education, it seems, is wont to robe itself in the rhetoric of benevolence and hopefulness—a self-characterization thoroughly debunked in the recent "critical" discourse. In fact, a vast literature now argues that far from presenting opportunity, far from serving as a key influence in a meritocracy, the school is implicated in the very structures it claims to interrupt.

In spite of such a damning critique, however, it has been difficult to challenge the idea that schooling is both important and inherently good— albeit as an agent of society, subject to corruption. Formal education continues to be clothed in a cultural mythology that asserts its own goodness and that points critics back to a fabled golden age when excellence and opportunity were its defining characteristics. It is thus that, in even the most scathing criticisms of conventional schooling, one inevitably finds reference to the importance of some sort of organized, collective intervention directed toward affecting mind-sets and their associated patterns of acting—that is, toward embracing some form of formal education. And while such proposals may vary from current enactments, the defining purpose remains basically the same: Modern schooling is essential for ensuring an informed citizenry.

In the face of this faith in the inherent goodness of schooling, what tends to remain under-addressed or unaddressed (but certainly not *undressed* or exposed) within much of contemporary educational discourse are the moral and ethical dimensions of the formal educational project. Moreover, when these issues do arise, "morals" and "ethics" tend to be used as though they were self-evident notions, founded on what have come to be regarded as essential truths logically derived from such modernist axioms as the primacy of the individual, the inevitability of competition, and the consequent need to protect one human from another.

"Moral" and "ethical" have become abstract ideas, unconnected to human relational experience—and thus, paradoxically, functioning to condition or shape human behavior. As Foucault (1980) has shown in his investigations of particular practices, prescribed and normalized patterns of behavior (including those seen as ethical and moral) emerge from specific historical events and sets of circumstances. The popular contemporary discourse of "morality" and "ethics" is, then, strangely ahistorical; it is a discourse "disembodied" from (that is, not evidently complicit in) its own past.

Complexity theory, of course, rejects the modernist axiomatic notions underlying this simplex system—and, hence, the resulting conclusions. Using Cohen and Stewart's framework, such conceptions of morality are analogous to Newtonian mechanics and other formal systems that combine rather simple premises into consistent, prescriptive, and normative worldviews. As with commonsense perspectives on knowledge, morals and ethics are assigned an existential status. They are regarded as part of the way things are—woven into the God-given natural order, as it were. In fact, this conception of morality seems to have become so much a part of common sense that it is difficult to consider alternatives. Any proposition that diverges much from this simplex model tends to be dismissed as relativistic, groundless, or godless.

But an alternative to the popular conception of morality does exist, one that has emerged with ecological, pragmatic, hermeneutic, and complexified awarenesses. As David Michael Levin (1989) explains:

> The two different ways of thinking about moral problems are (1) a competitive model, which gives primacy to the individual and relies on the supervenience of formal and abstract rules to achieve co-operation and consensus and (2) a cooperative model which gives primacy to relationships and relies on contextual narratives and dialogue—communication—to resolve moral problems. (221)

These two modes of describing and enacting relationships form, in effect, two contrasting ethics: The first, as Levin puts it, is an ethics of "universal rights and duties," founded on what is considered to be rational argumentation and unambiguous (although largely tacit) assumptions. One might call it a *modern* ethic: individualistic, oppositional, logical, hierarchical, and totalizing. As Mark Johnson (1993) elaborates, moral judgments in this framework are distinguished from other categories of reasoning (such as aesthetic, artistic, and imaginative) as they are aligned with mathematized, scientist thought: "'Moral' judgments . . . were supposed to involve the judging of particular cases as falling under a particular moral concept, and thereby governed by a specific moral rule" (207). That is to say, in this mode, moral concepts are assumed to be shared; moral reasoning consists of the straightforward application of moral laws in concrete instances.

The other mode is an "ethics of care, responsiveness, and responsibility" (Johnson, 207). Unlike the impositional and totalizing modernist ethic, this one attends more to the complexity of existence. It is an ethic, as Johnson explains, that arises from the fact that we are embodied beings—a notion that draws on an awareness that our individual bodies are complexly intertwined in transcendent collective forms. It is thus an ethic that brings together the individual and the collective. As Levin puts it, this ethic "is represented mainly by images of communicative and collaborative positions, and replaces images of hierarchy with images of webs, networks, and weavings" (221). It is, in other words, an ethics of complicity.

Or conversely, Cohen and Stewart's formulation of complicity might be read as a moral and ethical imperative when applied to all categories of intentional activity, including schooling and teaching. However, somewhat in contrast to the modernist ethic, complicity cautions that an attentiveness to intention is patently inadequate. In fact, the consequences and material products of our actions are more in need of interrogation than our purposes for acting. This need arises because every human action enlarges the space of the possible in ways that are simply unforeseeable but which, once unfolded, implicate the actor. Thus, it is not enough to focus on the process. Such conclusions should prompt a complete rethinking of the project of modern education, founded as it is on the premise that the process of moving through school—that is, the process of being exposed to a range of ideas with a particular cultural currency but of questionable pragmatic worth—is both important and necessary. Schooling has been cast, uncritically, as a practical activity.

Elaborating on this sort of phenomenon, Borgmann (1992) suggests that "practical" has become synonymous with "moral" in Western cultures, leading to a situation in which morality is more closely aligned with *conduct* than with the material products of such conduct. This severing of "doing" from "making," and the aligning of the former with moral virtue, can be traced from Aristotle, through Kant, to our present situation. Borgmann suggests that this segregation of the phenomenological from the material has been comforting for philosophers and the public because it enables the belief that, even though modern developments have decimated traditional, more ecologically sound productions, morality remains. While we may well face a planetary crisis, for example, our collective moral fiber remains intact.

This assumption, of course, means that although technology has become increasingly sophisticated and the fabric of society ever more complex, our moral aptitudes remain naive and simple. The privileged attention to the "making" encourages little attention to what has been made—to what is materially present, to the functioning of cultural objects that mediate and collect experience, to the physicality of our collective character. Borgmann suggests that a postmodern morality requires more attention to the consequences of action—to the way in which products are *complicit* in the complexity of human-and-world relations. As he puts it,

> What needs moral consideration in production is not so much the producing as the product. Insofar as production is a kind of doing, it is amenable to the application of conventional morality that has recently exfoliated on the branches of professional ethics, engineering ethics, business ethics, and risk assessment. What remains unexamined all the while is the power of products, of the material results of production, to shape our conduct profoundly. Any moral theory that thinks of the material setting of society as an essentially neutral stage is profoundly flawed and unhelpful; so, in fact, is most of modern and contemporary ethics. (110)

Echoing the phenomenological insights of Merleau-Ponty, Borgmann goes on to suggest that life is already full. Any change in the material structure of existence, then, is more than just an addition, it is an alteration of the complex fabric of relations. Introducing a novel into a classroom, for example, changes the patterns and modes of interaction among readers' family members. And so, the *moral* fabric of life in any community (family, school, neighborhood) is less affected by practices than by the material products that organize these practices—things, not activities. In examining complex systems it is thus important to note that the material objects that mediate practices are inextricable from the moral decisions invoked in their selection. As such, the study of morality must be more closely linked to the "cultural objects" that mediate everyday public life—including the texts and the tasks that frame life in schools.

All that we have announced in this section, of course, are sensibilities that have been discussed by educationists under the general heading of "critical discourses." Neo-Marxism has called for an attentiveness to power structures and hidden agendas, feminisms for attention to patriarchal discourse and implicit masculinist biases, postmodernism for attention to totalizing thinking and enacted dichotomies. For us, though, the notion of complicity adds something more. The significance of a complexified understanding of moral and ethical judgment—that is, the importance of an awareness of complicity—is that it refuses to allow complexity theory to slip into the perceived-to-be-neutral category our culture reserves for any discourse able to vest itself in the garments of mathematics. For us, complicity compels an acknowledgment by those who dwell in the sacrosanct, unquestioned center that they too are thoroughly implicated in the unfolding of our cultural world—with all its inequalities, injustices, and scabrous edges. Within the sciences, complicity replaces the disembodied eye of the scientist gaze with the complex body that perceives; within the humanities, complicity rejects the disembodied I of modern analytic thought in favor of a complex collective body united in its knowing and knowledge.

We have recently been struggling to bring this formulation into our own research, our teaching, and our lives. In an effort to speak to these matters—that is, to speak to our re-cognition of our separate and collective bodies—we turn now to brief discussions of two research efforts: first, a long-term collaborative action research project we have undertaken with a group of teachers, students, and parents in a small elementary school; the second, the Queer Teachers' Study Group we mentioned earlier.

Complicitous Research

> "This really is a complex book. . . . I want all of my kids to read it."

The parent of an 11-year-old uttered this statement during a meeting of community members and teachers in the staff room of a semi-rural elementary school. The meeting occurred during the early stages of an investigation that, as researchers, we had originally conceived in terms of a study of schooled mathematical and literary practices.

The project began as a series of meetings with all the teachers of a K–7 school. Initially intended as an inquiry into the processes of learning—or, more specifically, into the ways in which tacit conceptions of individual cognition and collective knowledge help to shape and are shaped by schooling activities—the study began with explorations of the participants' largely unarticulated beliefs about teaching and learning. The focal points of these discussions were actual learning experiences as, collectively and individually, we engaged in activities of reading, writing, and mathematical investigation.

One early meeting revolved around a shared reading of Lois Lowry's (1993) novel *The Giver*, an award-winning book written for adolescent audiences. As we sat to discuss our impressions of the book, one of the teachers (notably, the school's principal) announced that, while she enjoyed the read, the "novel was not suitable for use in this community." As it addressed such issues as prepubescent "stirrings" and the murder of those deemed physically or mentally inadequate, the consensus of the teachers was that the story would offend the sensibilities of parents. In brief, they believed the adult community members would be uncomfortable allowing a teacher to "risk" opening matters of sexuality and genocide among 11- and 12-year-olds.

That initial matter out of the way, the remainder of the animated two-hour session focused on the readings of the participants. As the meeting progressed, it became apparent that the novel spoke to a range of contemporary issues, among them social control, suppression of cultural difference, and a collective "forgetting" of the past. By the end, everyone agreed that the novel was provocative and well worth reading.

At this point we once again raised the topic of its appropriateness for use in the school. In light of the group's engaged discussion, and in an attitude of deliberate complicity, we suggested—to the agreement of all present—that a group of interested parents should be invited to read and respond to *The Giver* in a similar setting.

A few weeks later, the teachers and several parents met with us around the same table. To the surprise of those who had attended the previous meeting, none of the issues that had so concerned the teachers actually came up during this 90-minute interaction. On the contrary, as in the first discussion, the talk focused on an array of societal issues and on the superior quality of the text. In this spirit, the parents en masse insisted that the book be taught: "Our kids *need* to read this book."

When the teachers revealed their earlier concerns, the general reaction of the parents was surprise. "That stuff was pretty tame," was the way that one parent described the book's treatments of euthanasia and burgeoning sexuality. "And besides, these are things that the kids are thinking about anyway." On the basis of such sentiments, it was agreed that Dennis would co-teach a unit of study developed around *The Giver* in a grade 5/6 split classroom.

We need not discuss here the details of the unit, but the incident provides an example of what we perceive to be *complicitous research*—that is, research informed by and attentive to the complexities and contingencies of schooling and, more importantly, to the influences of researchers on the situations they study. Perhaps the most obvious quality of this series of events was the way in which the various interested groups came together into a collective project. As we discuss elsewhere (Sumara and Davis, in press), the reading of the novel became a community event, marked by conversations between students and their parents, among parents, among teachers, across groups—conversations that have since continued around the reading of other novels, writing practices, and mathematical investigations. These sorts of phenomena have spread beyond the particular community that includes the school. In fact, we recently learned that parents in other locations, prompted by the events in "our" school, have organized their own reading and study groups.

Accordingly, we suggest that, informed by complicity, the projects of both schooling and education change dramatically. No longer concerned principally with characterizing or announcing what *is*, research and teaching take on a deliberately transformative role, founded on the conviction that one's participation is always and already affecting the situation and lives of everyone else.

It bears mentioning that, on the surface, what we call "complicitous research" has much in common with the project of the critical pedagogy movement. We expect, in fact, that we will be accused of saying little that Paulo Freire (1971) failed to announce a quarter century ago when he described the impossibility of neutrality . . . or that Neil Postman and Charles Weingartner (1969) neglected to articulate in their characterization of teaching as a subversive activity. But a significant difference does exist. They founded their analyses on a conviction that the defining quality of human relationship is competition—as evidenced by the overarching concerns with domination, oppression, power structures, and subversion. Complexity theory, while accepting the role of competition in the unfolding of civilization, places a much greater emphasis on collectivity: on mutual affect, joint action, and co-emergence. Further, as we discuss in the next section, the concern in complicitous research is as much with the biological body as it is with the collective corpus—a point that almost goes without saying, since complexity theory casts the collective as a biological unit (and complicity adds that the collective is also a lived phenomenological unit). While such emphases acknowledge the important concerns raised by Freire and others, they prompt a greater attitude of considered participation than of aggressive subversion.

The significance of this difference became evident for us as we discussed the reactions of the parents with the teachers. Complexity theory—and more specifically, the notion of complicity—provided a means to explore the possibility that what happened was not a "breaking down of barriers," but a recognition that the (modernist) separations of school from home, teacher from student, and school from "real world" are mere rhetorical devices. Rather than erasing such distinctions, the events around the novel alerted all involved to their artificiality as relationships came to be understood as more intertwined, more fluid, more complex than had previously been supposed. In brief, we found ourselves able to discuss our actions and understandings in terms of how they knit us together into bodies which, just as happens when the subsystems of a physical body come together to form a unity, have their own sorts of transcendent integrities. We were, moreover, each complicit in these emergent integrities, these bodies of knowledge.

As the unit of study progressed, the recognition of such complex intertwinings widened. Gradually it became apparent that not only were the events in the staff room, the classroom, and the community interrelated, but they also had a self-similar character. That is to say, the same sort of evolutionary processes, the same sort of blurred boundaries we noted in our initial meeting with the parents (in terms of problematizing the borders that tended to be drawn between the projects of the school and the projects of the parents) became evident across varied phenomenal levels. In fact, the way in which individuals and collective unfolded from and were enfolded in one another became a significant topic of discussion among students, parents, teachers, and the community in general.

Such events and insights were hardly accidental. As researchers, our actions were driven by what we would call a moral-ethical impulse (following Levin, Johnson, and Borgmann), founded on an attentiveness to our own complicity in affecting events that ranged from emerging individual perceptions to evolving community sensibilities. We deliberately inserted ourselves into the space that Bruner (1986) calls "culture making" by recommending a novel, by explicitly implicating parents, and by introducing some of the notions of complexity theory as a means of making sense of unfolding events.

On this matter, we should note that the idea of complicity frees us from the simplistic criticism that we have no right to impose our own value judgments on other communities—that is, that our role as researchers is to study, not to affect, let alone attempt to transform. Complicity also alerts us to the fact that we are inevitably engaged in transformation: Each and every act, however benignly conceived, seeps beyond its intent as it enlarges the space of the possible. We are always already participating in culture making. What complicity adds is that we have a responsibility to consider, in tandem, our intentions and the events occasioned by our actions.

Once again, this insight has already been announced in the critical education discourse; that should not be surprising, given the roots of that movement in the work of critical hermeneutics (see Gallagher 1992). We are thus prompted to consider, all at once, past, present, and projected circumstances, constantly attentive both to intention and to ever-evolving consequence. Teachers and researchers are hardly causal agents (in the direct, linear sense of the term). But neither are they innocent or helpless with respect to the unforeseeable consequences of their acts. In setting aside the belief that our action can determine such phenomena as learning and collective knowledge, complexity and complicity compel us to recognize that they continue to depend on what we do. Modernist conceptions of authenticity, linear progress, and unbreachable gaps are thus replaced with postmodernist images of dispersed and fluid identities, complex choreographies, and inevitable participation.

An immediate consequence is that researchers cannot think of themselves as "operating in" educational settings, mining the desired data, and then severing all ties. Complicity compels us to recognize a different sort of investment. As demonstrated in the announced research, it requires a willingness and an effort to formulate one's place in the community and, reciprocally, to allow that community to become part of the research.

We are taking a deliberate ethical stance here, suggesting that educational research is not merely research that occurs in education settings, nor merely research that is focused on educational issues. Rather, educational research is research that seeks to educate. In effect, for us, complicitous research takes on many of the qualities of collaborative action research—including collaborative decision making, commitment to an extended effort, abandonment of attempts to control while being attentive to affect, and a willingness to live with the associated discomfort and ambiguity—all accompanied by a refusal to abdicate responsibilities associated with the differentiated role of the researcher. This model conflates the projects of research and education, both of which involve efforts to deliberately, but thoughtfully, affect the way things are—that is, to enlarge the space of the possible.

Moreover, the action research model depends on a deliberate attentiveness to the ways in which what we know are caught up in what we do and who we are. It is an approach to research founded on an attitude of complicity.

Complicitous Lives

On that note, we now turn to an issue that is not often raised in discussions of educational research. We would like to suggest that an awareness of complicity should prompt educational researchers to forgo the temptation to think of research as something that they do (generally for reasons—including tenure, funding, and acclaim—that render the actual research of secondary concern) and to consider what it means to live a life that includes research.

We offer the idea of complicity as more than an injunction to enact certain sensibilities while conducting academic inquiry. Complicity speaks to more than our manner of *behaving*, it is a statement about *being*. We can illustrate the import of this assertion by comparing the formal definitions of "morals" and "ethics." Although popularly considered synonymous (and, in fact, both deriving from terms meaning "custom" or "habit"), academic and legal scholars have pried them apart. Academically and legally speaking, "moral" and "ethical" both refer to codes of conduct, where morals take up matters of (inter)personal relationship and ethics have more to do with professional comportment. Hence, discussions of morals tend to deal with such fundamental(ist) issues as right and wrong and good and evil. The discourse around ethics tends to be framed more in terms of appropriate and inappropriate and professional and unprofessional. Morals are thus popularly believed to be preexistent, commonsensical, "out there," God-given. Ethics, in contrast, although acknowledged to be founded on morals, are more readily seen as authored and, hence, subject to revisions as roles and contexts evolve.

Our earlier decision to avoid this distinction and to treat the terms as interchangeable announced our conviction that any separation of issues of morality and ethics is purely artificial and founded on a prior separation of life inside the workplace and life outside it. As we understand it, complicity compels us to regard morals and ethics as conflated. With this collapsing of categories comes a recognition that we are as complicit in cultural mores as we are in the much more obviously authored ethical codes of professional organizations. Once again, we believe that complicity prohibits a distinction between matters of behavior (the realm of ethics) and matters of being (the realm of morals).

Accordingly, an understanding of complicity forces a decision with regard to how one approaches such matters as interaction, human agency, and implicatedness in the evolving universe. One must choose either to approach such issues with an attitude of *complacency* (thereby ignoring ethical import) or with an attitude of *consideration* (thus striving to become hermeneutically and ecologically mindful).

In our own lives, we attempt to do the latter and begin by refusing the simplistic-simplex separation of our work from our recreation. Drawing on the postmodern trope of "play"—understood, as Gadamer (1990) explains, as the proper possibility of movement—we resist even the attempt to enact a separation of leisure activity, research, teaching, and idleness. For us, in all its aspects, life is about creating a harmony among imposed categories, and we create this harmony in the complicit space of playing and being played.

Put differently, however much we might want to step outside contemporary civilization and blame its problems on another group or another era, we believe ourselves to be thoroughly complicit in the society in which we live. This is an understanding we endeavor to enact in the daily conditions of our lives. Specifically, for example, we draw no distinction between our theoretical practices and our daily living practices—and, in fact, attempt to continually create a dialectic between these. Put simply, theory, for us, is not merely something that we produce for academic purposes. Rather, theory gives direction to our lives in very explicit and specific ways. Upon moving to Vancouver several years ago, for example, because we were embarking on research into the relationship between gay and lesbian teacher identities and pedagogical practices, and aimed to do this through a longitudinal collaborative action research project, we theorized that our home needed to be located within an urban area densely populated by queer persons and, in addition, containing the schools where the teachers with whom we were working taught. As well, because we understood that our own phenomenal world needed to, in explicit ways, become entangled (complicit) with the worlds of our research collaborators, we understood the importance of implicating ourselves in the complex web of relationships of the lives of these teachers. Research for us, then, and the theories that guide our actions, are intricately entwined in the geographical and social topographies of our lives.

At the same time, the specific research practices that occur amid these daily living conditions are influential to the very practices and attendant personal identities that we perform. Reading and responding to queer works of fiction over a three-year period with our Queer Teachers' Study Group, for example, radically reshaped each of our understandings of our formerly lived identities and of our currently lived situations. As well, in important ways, this work provided new theoretical knowledge that we brought to bear on our own evolving identities and identifications. For example, while we began our study with queer teachers with a radical separatist mind-set, strongly believing that the way to interrupt ongoing practices of heteronormativity and homophobia was to deliberately perform our "queer" identities, our research-living practices over the past three years have taught us that these practices of self-disclosure, far from disintegrating categorical stereotypes of what constitutes gay and lesbian identities, function instead to reaffirm the heterosexual center by exoticizing "queer." Further, this exoticizing of the queer other serves not only to affirm and maintain heterosexual privilege, it continues to collect those who identify as "not heterosexual" into homogenizing categories that, by definition, function as simplex rather than complex systems. While all members of our Queer Teachers' Study Group believed that we would share fundamental (simplex-like) commonalties because of our self-identified "queerness," we found instead that, as Sedgwick (1990) suggests, "People are different from one another" (22). And, most importantly, we discovered that although we each collected ourselves into a particular categorical signifier (for example, "lesbian," "gay man," "transgendered") we were, in the end, not entirely sure what that meant. What constituted the quintessential lesbian? How could one perfect transsexuality? What does it mean when gays and lesbians are categorized by virtue of imagined sexual acts while heterosexuals are categorized by much more complex characteristics (such as participation in various familial and economic units and modes of production)?

As we moved into the third year of our project and our life within a queer community, we came to question the theoretical directive that shaped both our research and our living situations. Of greatest concern to us was the way in which we noticed the lived identities of ourselves and others as being strongly shaped by cultural stereotypes and mythologies of not-heterosexual identities. In the end, we came to understand that any study of "queer" identities must not begin with an excavation of the lived experiences of those who explicitly identify as queer, but with the difficult process of excavating and interpreting what we have come to call the "heterosexual closet." While much important work in gay and lesbian studies has functioned to legitimize the lived practices and experiences of not-heterosexual identities, it has at the same time worked to reify "heterosexuality" as a normative category according to which homosexual identities are defined and, of course, maligned.

This theoretical insight helped us to understand that, while we needed to have lived in gay and lesbian communities and worked with politically proactive gay and lesbian teachers to come to this knowing, the continued development of our research and theoretical work depends on a shift in the topographies of our complicitness. When faced with the challenge of moving our academic careers from the west coast of Canada to the Toronto area, we decided that rather than living within densely populated and diverse urban communities that are believed to be phenomenologically expansive—thus, providing ample opportunity for the development of many forms of identity—we would live, instead, in a more rural area where these diverse identities and experiences are *commonly believed* not to exist or to be supported. Rather than continuing to maintain, through our lives and research practices, that queer identities are things that we can readily identify and interpret, we theorized that queer identities were likely to be found in queer places—that is, in places where one would not expect to find them. And, following insights by novelist Barbara Gowdy (1996) and theorists such as Eve Sedgwick (1990)—who suggest that we ought to study the minutiae of differences among persons, not merely among categories of persons—we believe that living in a very rural, small-town setting might create conditions that make us complicit in our research, teaching, and other lived experiences in very different ways. Aligned with the belief that perception involves practices of discarding as much as practices of apprehending, we theorize that this deliberate shift in our phenomenal world will contribute to a needed re-perception and re-cognition of matters related to identity and pedagogy.

It is important to state, however, that this re-theorizing of what might constitute needed knowledge about heterosexual and not-heterosexual identities did not emerge only from the particularities of the community in which we lived and the research that we conducted with gay, lesbian, and transgendered teachers. Because our theoretical interests included questions about the development of the literary imagination in school settings, we participated in the research mentioned earlier around *The Giver* in a small town setting. It was the rather strange juxtaposition of this research with the Queer Teachers' Study Group that provoked us to wonder about the generally assumed homogeneity of rural populations. After all, despite all beliefs to the contrary, the various materials read and topics covered in the curriculum developed around *The Giver* for 11- and 12-year-olds was diverse, expansive, and, at times, most certainly queer.

Further, our own intimate involvement in the daily activities of this small school and small community, over a period of several months, helped us to understand that the group of persons collected in this area, far from agreeing on what constituted a "proper identity" or an "acceptable" lifestyle, differed as widely in their beliefs and practices as the members of our Queer Teachers' Study Group. In fact, although they first appeared to perform relatively homogenous identities, the past and currently lived experiences of the teachers, parents, and students with whom we worked were far from what might be expected of such a community. As we continued to integrate ourselves into the communities of practice developing in this school setting, it began to seem that the performed daily identities of its inhabitants were far more diverse than those we were experiencing living in the West End of Vancouver. Of course this diversity, this departure from the stereotypical normative heterosexualized identity, was not readily available for interpretation. It needed to emerge through our involvement with curriculum forms that compelled members of this community to reorganize perceptions in order to see and understand freshly. The *practice* of shared reading and response to a literary text created a form through which the transparency of our various shared and idiosyncratic experiences and beliefs were rendered available for interpretation. And, as Borgmann helped us to understand, it was by attending to what was *produced* through these practices (that is, to our oral and written responses) that enabled us to re-theorize the complexity of our evolving identities within this particular social topography.

For us, then, it is not so much the practice of theorizing that is significant to understanding complexity; it is continually interpreting the ways in which theory functions as a moral and ethical imperative in the lives of those who engage in theoretical practices. Understanding education as complicitous in the complex choreographies of sociality means that education is not merely that which we transpose onto the social topography, it is complexly and relationally intertwined with it. Most important, the identities that participate in these complex choreographies are not ones that are brought to them, nor are they ones that can be extracted from them. Rather, as Probyn (1996) suggests, identities are lived "on the surface" of everyday, remembered, and interpreted experience. The way one "thinks," then, is not so much a matter of collapsing one's past with one's present. Acts of cognition, including acts of theorizing and of educating, are always played out in the complex surface web of memory, landscape, social topography, and cultural forms. This complexity constitutes the ever-evolving place of education—a place where those who conduct educational research and who engage in the practice of educating are always already wholly complicit.

Concluding Remarks

As is likely evident from the preceding section, we hardly came to the ideas we present here by reading only in complexity theory. Far from it, our initial introduction came through our studies in hermeneutics, continental and pragmatist philosophies, deep ecology, the "new" sciences, literary criticism, and critical educational discourse. More recently, our studies of queer theories, psychoanalysis, and feminisms have broadened our thinking. For us, then, the initial appeal of complexity theory was less the ground it was breaking than the privileged tongue it speaks.

Constituted in the symbol systems of mathematics and the sciences, complexity theory arrives as an already privileged discourse. In fact, were it not for Cohen and Stewart's efforts to prevent it from being cast in terms of neutrality and objectivity, we would probably critique rather than embrace it. But the formulation of the notion of complicity takes the discourse into the realm of human agency. As researchers, for example, we are complicit in the systems that we study, as much and as often as we might wish to dissociate ourselves from what we regard as dubious educational practice. With complicity, the roles of educational researchers greatly complexify, for they are not innocent in the collective construing of the phenomena they study. Complicity prohibits a separation. Complicity is a moral and ethical imperative.

This understanding prompts us to find the resources to meet with students, parents, and teachers; to participate in teaching projects; to become involved in community events; and to avoid both those dichotomies that serve as popular targets for educational critique (for example, mind/body, thought/action, knower/known, teacher/learner, individual/collective, theory/practice) and the currently accepted critic/criticized dualism. Like the others, it dissolves in complicity.

Complicity thus prompts us to reconsider the unformulated ground, striving to afford less privilege to the formulated figure. This prompt is nothing short of an ethical imperative as it transforms and conflates the projects of research and education, pushing them both toward a hermeneutic attitude. We are admonished to understand—and to refuse to allow curriculum events to hang uninterpreted. This matter goes beyond how we approach our research: It is a statement about how we should live our lives.

Notes

1   The research reported in this paper was supported by the Social Sciences and Humanities Research Council of Canada, Grant #410-96-0686. The opinions expressed herein do not necessarily reflect the position, policy, or endorsement of the Council.

2   In further contrast with modernist thinking, and consistent with the postmodern sensibilities announced by Borgmann (1992), Lyotard (1984), and others, the notions of "enlarging the space of the possible" involves a recognition of the impossibility of neatly delineated boundaries. While Cohen and Stewart's choice of terminology might seem problematic in this regard (that is to say, the words "space" and "possible," when used in the current academic climate, might be misinterpreted as an effort to contain the fullness of experience), the notion acknowledges the shifting and co-implicated characters of the phenomenological and the biological.

3   For the time being, we are deliberately using "moral" and "morals" interchangeably with "ethical" and "ethics."

Works Cited

Bateson, Gregory. 1979. *Mind and nature: A necessary unity*. New York: E. P. Dutton.

Borgmann, Albert. 1992. *Crossing the postmodern divide*. Chicago: University of Chicago Press.

Bruner, Jerome. 1986. *Actual minds, possible worlds*. Cambridge, Mass.: Harvard University Press.

Cohen, Jack and Ian Stewart. 1994. *The collapse of chaos: Discovering simplicity in a complex world*. New York: Penguin.

Foucault, Michel. 1980. *Power/knowledge: Selected interviews and other writings, 1972–1977*. Brighton, UK: Harvester Press.

Freire, Paulo. 1971. *Pedagogy of the oppressed*. New York: Seaview.

Gadamer, Hans-Georg. 1990. *Truth and method*. 2nd ed. New York: Continuum.

Gallagher, Shaun. 1992. *Hermeneutics and education*. Albany, N.Y.: State University of New York Press.

Gowdy, Barbara. 1996. *Mister Sandman*. Toronto, Ont.: Somerville House.

Johnson, Mark. 1993. *Moral imagination: Implications of cognitive science for ethics*. Chicago: University of Chicago Press.

Kuhn, Thomas. 1962. *The structure of scientific revolutions*. Chicago: University of Chicago Press.

Levin, David M. 1989. *The listening self: Personal growth, social change and the closure of metaphysics*. London: Routledge.

Lowry, Lois. 1993. *The giver*. New York: Dell.

Lyotard, Jean-François. 1984. *The postmodern condition: A report on knowledge*. Minneapolis: University of Minnesota Press.

Postman, Neil and Charles Weingartner. 1969. *Teaching as a subversive activity*. New York: Delacorte Press.

Probyn, Elspeth. 1996. *Outside belongings*. New York: Routledge.

Sedgwick, Eve Kosofsky. 1990. *Epistemology of the closet.* Berkeley: University of California Press.

Sumara, Dennis and Brent Davis. In press. Unskinning curriculum. In *Curriculum: New identities for the field*, edited by William F. Pinar. New York: Garland Publishing.

Varela, Francisco, Evān Thompson, and Eleanor Rosch. 1991. *The embodied mind: Cognitive science and human experience.* Cambridge, Mass.: The MIT Press.

Waldrop, M. Mitchell. 1992. *Complexity: The emerging science at the edge of order and chaos.* New York: Simon & Schuster.

Chapter 7

Transgression and the Situated Body: Gender, Sex, and the Gay Male Teacher

Eric Rofes

I am a middle-aged white gay male educator who has taught at the pre-school, elementary school, and middle school levels. I have worked as a youth advocate, served on statewide panels addressing issues affecting children and youth, and published several books on topics of concern to kids. Currently I am completing a doctorate and teach education courses to undergraduate students at a large research university in the San Francisco Bay area and am active in school reform efforts.

I spend most of my work life grading papers, counseling students, preparing and teaching classes, and observing in classrooms. I attend conferences focused on contemporary school reform initiatives and engage in rowdy debates focused on school choice, equity, and multicultural educational practices. I am currently engaged in an ongoing study focused on historical constructions of childhood, urban youth identities, and the effects of charter schools on public education.

I live in the heart of the Castro, the primary gay neighborhood in San Francisco, considered by many to be the primary gay city in the United States. I have been active in gay liberation for almost twenty-five years, and have worked in gay community centers, AIDS organizations, and the lesbian and gay media. While I have certainly engaged in mainstream gay rights work, my primary interests have focused on aspects of gay liberation that chart directions far afield from mainstream, heteronormative cultures and social formations. I am not interested in a gay rights agenda that argues that lesbians and gay men are the same as heterosexuals, and therefore deserve equal rights. I am committed to a gay liberation agenda that argues that queer cultures have much to teach mainstream America about sex, gender, and equitable relationships.

While the gay movement in the 1990s has moved politically from the left to the center (and some would say to the right), I've maintained ongoing activism based in what some would characterize as the "left fringe" of gay liberation. Let others work for gay marriage; I am interested in developing, exploring, and affirming patterns of kinship that are not based on a nuclear family structure or a traditional, "committed," gendered dyad. While gender-nonconforming men and women have been shunted aside by a gay rights movement hungry for "respectable" leaders who have mass appeal because they do not threaten the status quo, I am fixated on the social and cultural power emerging from troubling, subverting, and violating gender norms. During a time when AIDS has served as a convenient excuse for social critics to declare an end to a "failed" sexual revolution, I continue to immerse myself in communities that value sex and I organize my social and sexual practices in ways which could be described as "nonmonogamous," "promiscuous," or, drawing on Whitman's poems, profoundly "democratic" in spirit.

Each day when I wake up, two people move in me: the teacher and the lover. I do not view these two aspects of my life as contradictory or paradoxical, though I know others might. During most of my career in education I have juggled two identities—the educator and the gay liberationist—and attempted to understand their intersections and explore the tensions that emerge from their simultaneity. For a long time I have suspected some people with whom I work in schools and on educational policy matters would find aspects of the way I enact my sexual identity problematic. I have also noticed that some colleagues in gay and lesbian movement work discount my work in schools or have no interest at all in my educational efforts.

At times, I feel split down the middle, ricocheting between extremes. I might check my answering machine at home on a Sunday afternoon to find a student calling with questions about white racial formations for the following day's midterm examination. The next message might be from my lover who is calling to inform me he will be late for dinner as he is meeting his boyfriend for a late-afternoon romp. I might do an Internet search under my name and turn up seemingly paradoxical listings: a selection of explicit sex writings from my latest book precedes a report from an education newspaper about my charter school research.

While life may *feel* schizophrenic to me at times, intellectually I believe my work in education and gay liberation emerges from the same source:

a commitment to creating sites that resist, undermine, and throw off insti-tutionalized forms of oppression that have become endemic to late–twen-tieth-century life in the United States. My interest in school reform is motivated by a desire to see urban schools become places that expand the critical consciousness of poor young people and provide them with tools for social and political change. My interest in undermining gender as a normalizing and oppressive construct emerges from my awareness of the continuing power of patriarchy to limit the life chances of girls, women, and gender-nonconforming boys. The struggle for sexual freedom—a prob-lematic term, I'll admit, when bandied about in post-AIDS America—for me, offers insights into the transformative possibilities of pleasure in an advanced capitalist system that has succeeded in commodifying and gain-ing monopoly over most forms of leisure, play, and pleasure (Bronski 1998).

Ultimately I believe my work as a teacher is about supporting students as they become agents of transgression and activists for social and politi-cal change. My mission as a teacher is best captured by bell hooks in the introduction to her book *Teaching to Transgress: Education as the Prac-tice of Freedom* (1994):

> The classroom remains the most radical space of possibility in the academy. . . .
> I add my voice to the collective call for renewal and rejuvenation in our teaching
> practices. . . . I celebrate teaching that enables transgressions—a movement against
> and beyond boundaries. It is that movement which makes education the practice
> of freedom. (12)

Yet I often feel an overwhelming hunger to learn from other educators who share similar values about how they construct their various identities and practices and how their work in schools and with children intersects with deeply held, but often transgressive, values. I am interested not only in teaching students to transgress, but also in finding ways to continue to engage myself in transgressive activism and social practices during midlife years when many previously radical friends are making compromises and embracing politically problematic social and economic practices. I hunger for a community of educators who live out our class, gender, race, and sex politics, not simply in our teaching or our academic publishing, but in our everyday lives.

I am most eager to learn from other gay male educators who may face similar barriers, fears, and points of controversy. Are there ways to situate ourselves in relationship to activities common to some contemporary gay cultures such as cybersex, drag, sex in parks, or participation in leather subcultures, without denying our own interest or participation, feeling shame, or being ejected from our profession? Are the only alternatives available to gay male teachers to remain chastely single and asexual, blissfully wedded to a monogamous long-term spouse, or maintain strict boundaries between our sexual communities, practices, and identities and our teaching? Can we begin a conversation about the challenges facing male educators who do not perform traditional masculinities, a conversation that ironically has been initiated not by gay male teachers ourselves or the groups which purport to represent us, but by the film *In & Out?* Or do we have to pretend that gay male educators as a class enact masculinity in only traditional ways and that none of us camp, lisp, utilize effeminate inflections, diction, or gestures, or cross our legs in class in the "wrong" way?

I do not deceive myself and pretend that I represent the vast majority of gay male teachers currently working with children in the United States. The liberationist project of the 1970s has long ago taken a backseat to assimilationist values in gay movement circles (Vaid 1995). While many men may share similar everyday stigmatized social practices and kinship formations (sexual activity that is not limited to a single, ongoing partner; gender performances that play with hypermasculinity, effeminacy, drag, and butch/femme dynamics; patterns of social relations that are centered around friendships and communities rather than a dyad or nuclear family), few maintain critical consciousness about these practices or place them in a politicized ideological framework. I want to talk with the ones who do.

I begin this paper by examining representations of gay male school teachers in discourses produced by gay men. My objective here is to illustrate how gay men represent ourselves in public discourse: what gets said, how it gets stated, and what gets silenced. I search in this literature for moments of transgression: when gay men perform identities and practices that are counter to hegemonic heteronormative constructs. Ultimately I search in the literature for answers to a series of questions I carry with me on a daily basis: What can gay male identities and cultures offer the field of education? How can my performativity as a gay male college teacher rupture traditional forces that keep in place an oppressive status quo? What is my responsibility to my liberationist politics in my work as an educator and what kinds of risks am I willing to take?

I next visit my classroom where a number of incidents have left me pondering, reflective, but with little clarity or resolution. I use this series of events to illustrate dilemmas I have faced and the imperfect ways I have responded. These examples appear, not because I seek to expose my own circumstance or to boldly bare my soul, but because I believe other educators of varying identities face similar challenges. Through recounting these incidents I aim to raise critical questions about the intersection of politics and teaching, identities and careers, self-care and courage.

Finally, drawing on the work of scholars of masculinities, I suggest places within discourses on gender, the body, and sexuality that offer opportunities for gay male teachers to more fully recognize our potential contributions to the field of education and to the lives of children. My intent here is neither to produce an idealized, utopian (and intimidating) vision of what is possible, nor to suggest that a singular path must be taken to more fully integrate our identities in ways that allow both the lover and the teacher within us to inform one another. Instead my aim is to offer one possibility among many for allowing gay male teacher identities to emerge free from a burden of stigma and shame and fully able to play a transformative role in the social change work of education.

The Discourse of Gay Male Teachers

First-person narratives by gay male teachers usually reveal the trade-offs lesbian, gay, bisexual, and transgendered (LGBT) people are forced to make as we gain entry into broader arenas within the public sphere. As the gay drive to assimilate accelerates, it may be useful to consider what aspects of queer lives and cultures are deemed acceptable in mainstream (read "nongay") circles and what are branded unacceptable and cast out. These questions might be pondered not only by gay teachers but by all openly LGBT people working outside specifically queered spaces. Likewise these questions may be appropriately considered by other marginalized groups seeking entry into the status quo, who are also expected to cut off parts of themselves before being embraced as part of the American family.

Fundamentally, this is a question about democratic participation in the public sphere. When we say we "value diversity," do we mean we seek to create sites where people of different genders, races, classes, and sexual identities can come together and *bring with them the social and cultural attributes that mark them as different, unusual, transgressive?* Or do we mean that we like the *concept* of diversity but, in practice, aim to whitewash, silence, de-sex, straighten out or overlook cultural differences? When white organizations seek to diversify, they frequently seek people of color who share their class, cultural, and ideological values.

They grab at the African American corporate attorney, the female CEO, the assimilated Cuban physician, and feel smug about their new diverse organization. They like the concept of diversity, but are circumspect about creating situations where people truly have to work across social and cultural differences.

Yet some of us believe that only by engaging in sustained work across authentic differences can social change occur (Pharr 1996; Reagon 1983). We believe that the historical struggles of distinct groups have produced unique social patterns and cultural responses that have much to offer the world. We seek a multiculturalism that goes beyond "heroes and holidays," stretches further than ethnic potluck suppers, and is rooted in an authentic confrontation with difference (Lee, Menkart, and Okazawa-Rey 1998). From this vantage point, some gay men usefully might serve to complicate hegemonic understandings of the ways in which kinship patterns are structured, sexuality is enacted, and gender is performed.

Yet the narratives of gay male teachers reveal that such contributions are not easily made. An analysis of stories of gay male teachers included in Kevin Jennings's 1994 volume *One Teacher in 10: Gay and Lesbian Educators Tell Their Stories* illustrates precisely the powerful challenges faced by gay male teachers who simply seek to survive in K–12 schools. With stories of verbal harassment, physical assault, threats of punitive action, or employment termination threaded throughout the volume simply because some teachers acknowledge themselves as gay, it seems impossible to imagine gay men having any breathing room in which they can assert transgressive aspects of gay male cultures. Not only are teachers—including queer teachers—a notoriously conservative lot (Lortie 1975), but the field of education is so intensely focused on social reproduction that pockets of resistance are few and far between (McLaren 1995). Add to these factors the very real threats that confront openly gay educators, and a risk-averse population is likely to be created. As John Pikala, an English and Latin teacher in Saint Paul, Minnesota, wrote in Jennings's volume:

> My theme has been of a person, wounded by abandonment, who is a reluctant risk taker. I guess it is no surprise that some of us gay people, since we often face threatening situations, are hesitant about taking the risk of coming out. Gay teachers in particular feel that they are vulnerable; teachers as a group are probably the most deeply closeted segment of the gay community. We fear that, should we come out, we will lose, if not our jobs, at least the support and respect of our colleagues, superiors, students, and community. (93)

This explains, in part, the failure of gay male teachers to position themselves in relation to sex in anything other than heteronormative ways. With so much at stake simply by coming out, they imagine (perhaps appropriately) the earth cracking open and swallowing them up if they talk about sexual or romantic lives outside of a traditional committed dyad. Eleven of the twenty-three gay male contributors to this book refer to their "partner," "lover," or "life partner" while the others, for the most part, are silent about their sex and relational lives. When a gay teacher maintains a relationship that approximates or serves as a conceptual equivalent of the heterosexualized construct of couple or nuclear family, the relationship gains entry into the text. The gay male teacher narratives in this book lack references to any other form of sexualized male exchanges and authentic gay male community–based patterns of flirtations, casual sex, open relationships, or multipartnerism. On the page, at least, gay male teachers are not part of the leather scene, do not engage in sex in parks or highway rest areas, and do not trick out at their local bars on a Saturday night.

I say Pikala's quote explains *in part* this tendency to silence transgressive acts because sexual shame may be another force that delimits and restricts discussions of sex. One is tempted to probe behind some of the statements by the gay male teachers in this book. A San Francisco high school teacher captures a common response of many queer educators when faced with discussions about gayness: "I don't think any teacher wants to initiate a conversation that leads to his or her students picturing them having sex, especially a type of sex which many still find revolting" (97).

A biology teacher in Cincinnati recounts the questions of his students in response to his impromptu coming out:

> For the next thirty minutes I related my story and answered questions from my students, so many questions. "When did you know you were gay?" . . . "Does the principal know? . . ." "How do you and your partner 'do it'? . . ." For the most part, the questions were an honest attempt to get some real answers. I was candid with them, but drew a line at privacy, my own and that of others. To questions of a sexual nature, I told them that those were personal, but that what goes on between two people of the same sex is not unlike a heterosexual couple. The important thing, I explained to them, is the love and caring that exists between the two individuals. (229–230)

Certainly many heterosexual students and faculty members continue to find gay male sex disgusting, but gay male teachers themselves may also harbor powerful feelings of revulsion toward their sexual practices. The French sociologist Pierre Bourdieu has suggested that disgust should be "unpacked." What many naturalize as "good taste" emerges out of powerful social, economic, and cultural processes:

> Tastes (i.e., manifested preferences) are the practical affirmation of an inevitable difference. It is no accident that, when they have to be justified, they are asserted purely negatively, by the refusal of other tastes. In matters of taste, more than anywhere else, all determination is negation, and tastes are perhaps first and foremost distates, disgust provoked by horror or visceral intolerance ("sick-making") of the tastes of others. . . . Aesthetic intolerance can be terribly violent. (Bourdieu 1984, 56)

When we insist that questions about sex acts remain privatized and support relegating them away from sites of public discourse, we may be buttressing an entire apparatus of social control that keeps in place patriarchy and heterosexism and makes disgust for male-to-male sex common. Some have argued that relegating sex to the private sphere is associated with many risks and that public sex functions in radical and liberating ways (Califia 1994; Dangerous Bedfellows 1996). Writing about gay men in particular, Michael Bronski (1996) has argued:

> [W]e are obsessed with sex. And it's a good thing. Sexuality and eroticism are extraordinarily powerful forces in all our lives and gay culture acknowledges and supports that. . . . Mainstream culture is predicated upon repressing or denying sexuality. . . . [G]ay culture, by its insistence on the importance of sexuality, challenges this. (11–12)

The drive by gay male teachers to privatize the social and sexual practices of our communities raises a number of critical questions about how gay men consider and understand our social formations and sexual practices. Are kinships patterns that centrally feature friendship networks or a sequence of three-to five-year-long primary relationships in which we give ourselves permission to have outside sex booby prizes foisted on us against our will by a homophobic culture culture? Or do we find meaning and pleasure in these arrangements? Are promiscuity and casual sex a pathetic but understandable gay male cultural response to widespread societal persecution and the failure to have access to the institution of marriage, or can they be seen as life-affirming practices of bonding and exchanges of pleasure, intimacy, and affection? Are our voices and gestures, inflections and movements that violate gender norms and expose us as queer, things we feel embarrassed about, even as we insist they have a right to exist without harassment or persecution, or do we understand them as critically important forms of resistance to gender performances that reproduce male supremacy and reinforce patriarchal power?

I implicate myself in these same silences and denials. My own writings about my work as a gay male sixth-grade teacher reflect the same tendency toward silencing heretical sex, gender, and kinship constructs as *One Teacher in 10*. In 1985, I published a book about my first teaching job, which I lost after two years when I came out of the closet. Reading my book *Socrates, Plato and Guys Like Me: Confessions of a Gay Schoolteacher* (1985) today, I am struck by my own reluctance to bring key aspects of gay culture and my emerging gay identity into the text. There are multiple allusions to visiting gay bars, but always for seemingly chaste purposes. I visit Provincetown for a weekend, but there's no indication of my disco and leather bar visits. The only relationship that I acknowledge in the book is with a Catholic priest. In real life, this relationship was quite sexual and allowed me to experiment with practices that were new for me, but the transformative nature of my relationship with "Tony Mosca" does not appear in the book. Instead I romanticize the relationship while I de-sex it:

> Loving a priest is not a picnic, but throughout the waning months of the year, I easily overlooked the problems. Sharing the Christmas holidays with Tony's clan was a special treat for me as I was learning to eat spicy Italian cooking and observe new ethnic customs. I envied the tacit acceptance of Tony's homosexuality by his family who—while never defining or categorizing or stating in words what was obvious—welcomed me as a son. And I was struck by the exhilaration of pulling blankets up over two big men on a cold winter evening and snuggling all night long. When Tony would tiptoe out at dawn to hurry to the seven o'clock mass, he'd kiss me on the forehead and set the alarm. I felt loved and cared for by another man—for the first time. (109)

The intense erotic connection I had with Tony is absent from the book, as are all the lessons he taught me about my body, desires, and spirituality. Likewise, throughout the book, I perform traditional masculinity as a teacher and, while this was usually the way I appeared in the classroom at this time, I certainly had moments where I was caught gesturing or inflecting in effeminate ways.

These silences about gender and sex appear in other books about lesbian and gay male teachers (Khayatt 1992; Kissen 1996). Why do we censor ourselves, and who benefits from the silences we create? When I reflect on the 28-year-old I was when I wrote this book, I cannot deny that my work in gay liberation at this precise time was powerfully transforming my understandings and relationships to sex and gender. Yet it seemed radical enough to be writing a book about being a homosexual teacher; including gender nonconformity or sexual liberation may have undermined my intended project. In my quest to show that I should be allowed to remain in the classroom as an openly gay teacher, I sacrificed parts of my identity that did not comfortably fit into the world's sense of what is appropriate conduct for a teacher.

I am struck these days by the continuing silences about sex and gender that continue to dominate discourses on gay male teachers. As a member of the Gay, Lesbian, and Straight Educators Network, I read monthly newsletters and see the programming at countless conferences for gay teachers. Yet I never see workshops for gay men who struggle to maintain integrity about the way we perform gender in the classroom, or read about resources for gay male teachers arrested during police raids on public sex areas. I currently subscribe to two e-mail lists that frequently present me with interesting juxtapositions: One is a list that provides daily articles about gay issues in K–12 schools and the other focuses on police crackdowns on public sex spaces throughout the nation.

In stories published about the entrapment of men in park lavatories or highway rest areas, when the men's names and occupations are listed—a continuing problematic policy of many newspapers—there is almost always a schoolteacher or two in the mix. Do our gay teacher groups feel a responsibility to assist these teachers exposed to public scandal and potential job loss? Or is this aspect of these men's lives considered "conduct unbecoming," and relegated elsewhere?

Two Classroom Predicaments

Enacting Masculinity

At various times in my college teaching career I have become almost paralyzed with uncertainty about what to wear, how to speak, how to walk, how to sit, how to move. I alternately neurotically obsess on these questions or repress them fully. I sometimes find myself spending as much time struggling over questions of appearance, voice, and movement as I do over the content of a day's lesson. I have occasionally opened my clothing closet on a morning when I am teaching to find issues of whiteness, class status, gender performance, and sexual identity enactment unleashed in a manner that threatens to overwhelm me and make me late for work.

When I am teaching "Education 188: Gay and Lesbian Issues in Schools," I am hyperaware of how I represent myself as a gay man to my students. I wonder how my queer students would like to see me perform gender and what my heterosexually identified students take away from their time with me. Should I look and act like a stereotypical fag or should I provide an alternative vision of gay manhood? Is it okay to use camp, wit, and biting irony, or should I eschew the affectations of fagdom and provide an alternate vision? Is it okay to cross my legs, move my hands, raise my eyebrows? Can I call my gay students "honey"? Is it okay for me to refer to male colleagues as "girlfriends"? What image should I project when I walk across the room?

I feel as if biology has situated me in a somewhat privileged position to grapple with these questions. I possess key attributes that resonate with traditional masculinity in American culture: I am 6'4", have facial and body hair, and am built like a linebacker. I have taken what genetics has offered and made decisions that affix my position within masculine norms: I have a thick beard, speak in a deep voice, wear my hair in a crew cut, and work out at a gym. I can easily perform a white ethnic masculinity common among working-class and lower-middle-class men. At times I look more like a stevedore than a schoolteacher.

Yet I am acutely aware that the masculinities I perform are cut through with political issues that can trigger a range of problematic responses. I may put on a performance of machismo, playing the big tough butch man at a local leather bar on a Saturday night as a sexual strategy signaling a range of possible erotic activities and roles to the men I desire. Yet that same Village People macho man might make me seem intimidating and unapproachable to my undergraduate students and suggest an affirming of patriarchal norms that I actually seek to undermine. In one-on-one counseling situations with gay male students I may cross my legs, affect a gentler voice, and make expressive hand gestures in an attempt to dissipate any sense of threats students may feel from me. Yet the same display of femme energy might alienate many of my heterosexual students or confirm stereotypes. It also might undercut my ability as a teacher to structure the classroom, present expectations, and enforce standards for classroom discourse and student work. Should I resist affirming stereotypes that let these students know some gay men are sometimes effeminate?

When I first began to teach college, I found that the energy I project has a powerful influence on the response of students. I attempted to initiate empowering student-focused conversations utilizing my best critical pedagogy skills. Students worked with me to frame questions and organize classroom time. We planned format and process in order to maximize participation. Yet when time for discussion came, few students would participate. It sometimes felt as if I were pulling nails out of walls to get the vast majority of students to check in as part of the conversation.

One of the students—a women's studies major—was kind enough to come up to me after one of my early failures at facilitating and encouraging a lively, engaged conversation. "The class is intimidated by you," she said matter-of-factly, shaking her head. "You say all the right things and clearly understand how these discussions are supposed to happen. Yet your energy—it's all wrong. It sends a very different message than the words you actually speak. You give off profoundly mixed signals."

I turned to colleagues for advice—lesbian colleagues, actually—who talked to me about gender performances in the classroom. They enlightened me about putting both my "butch energies" to work in my pedagogy and also my "femme energies." At first I did not know what they meant, but I listened intently, took a lot of notes, and mulled their comments over in my mind for quite a while. I realized that they were asking me to apply a valuable lesson I had learned early on in my career as a gay activist to my undergraduate teaching.

I have chaired many public forums, tense community meetings, crisis-sparked town hall discussions where people of divergent groups come together for debate, conflict, and resolution. When facilitating these events, I have learned to draw on different masculinities at different times. My butch energy is useful in setting limits, confronting participants who violate collectively made discussion rules, and keeping the group on task. It comes from a place within me seeking to control, direct, and order and, while the gestures, inflections, and movements that accompany it may or may not look traditionally masculine, the energy definitely taps into that particular source within me.

My femme energy is employed to open up access, invite participation, cut through and deflate tension. It employs humor, self-deprecation, campiness, and gentler qualities. I have become adept at recognizing when my femme energy will bring me things that my butch energy won't; I have some ability to dance between the two in a subtle but intricate performance of diversely gendered energies.

Hence I deliberately and self-consciously have carried my butch/femme energies into my classroom pedagogy. My women's studies student proved to be correct: If I introduce a class discussion gently, with openness and playfulness, and leave space for silences, humor, and the flexibility needed to accommodate last-minute student-initiated changes, my students respond enthusiastically. When I default to my butch energies due to fear, disorganization, or mindlessness, the students usually are silent, frozen, sometimes even withholding.

I began to consider anew the male teachers I'd known who had been explicitly effeminate, including music and drama teachers I'd had during my own high school years and one social studies teacher whose hands danced before him uncontrollably whenever something truly excited him. His enthusiasm proved infectious to us and we students would become caught up in whatever passion he was creating in the classroom at that moment. Only after class, behind his back, would we mock him, call him names, and ridicule his style of teaching. Was this simply a case of his teaching methods successfully capturing the interest of his students or was there something we truly loved about his campy gestures and queeny voice? Did these instances—moments of authentic pedagogical magic— allow teacher and students together to collectively break out of constricted gender roles and, for at least a few minutes, violate patriarchal dicta?

Educators have started to write about how sexist and heterosexist practices in classrooms harm gender-nonconforming children, including boys and young men (Boldt 1997; Sedgwick 1993; Thorne 1993). Mairtin Mac an Ghaill (1994) has described schooling as a "masculinizing agency" and discussed the "way in which dominant definitions of masculinity are affirmed within schools, where ideologies, discourses, representations and material practices systematically privilege boys and men" (4). R. W. Connell (1995) has argued that "a degendering strategy, an attempt to dismantle hegemonic masculinity, is unavoidable; a degendered rights-based politics of social justice cannot proceed without it" (232). He argues that schools must play a critical role in a move toward these politics:

> The importance of education of masculinity politics follows from the onto-formativity of gender practices, the fact that our enactments of masculinity and femininity bring a social reality into being. Education is often discussed as if it involved only information, teachers tipping measured doses of facts into the pupils' heads; but that is just part of the process. At a deeper level, education is the formation of capacities for practice. (239)

Clearly gay male teachers have a great deal at stake in developing a "degendering strategy." Yet we are wrong if we pretend that our mere presence in the classroom is counterhegemonic. Being transgressive because we are openly gay, yet compliant because we affirm traditional masculinities, may do little to alter the sex/gender system that wreaks havoc in our everyday lives.

Sex, the Body, and the Classroom

It's frightening to think about the relationship between one's sex life and one's classroom, or one's embodied identities as a teacher and a lover. Many gay men maintain sharp divides between the two, insisting one's sex life is personal, private, and has no bearing on one's students. Yet the erotic circulates in any classroom and is often harnessed as a source of power that drives teaching pedagogies.

Like gay-identified men working in other mainstream cultural institutions (religious organizations, the health care industry, the political arena), gay male teachers are offered only two options: Take a lover and perform with him a type of coupledom that approximates heteronormative patterns, or desexualize ourselves, stifle our erotic energies, and disprove the stereotypes of the sex-obsessed homosexual. Gay male teacher identities rarely allow men room to construct personas that do not suppress the erotic, yet also do not become leering, harassing letches who are inappropriate in a workplace. I worry that our performances within these narrow options present our gay male students—and others—with examples of gay identities that are neither helpful to them nor relevant to their lives and the difficult choices they must face in integrating sexual identity, sexual orientation, and sexual energies into their personhood.

What possibilities exist for the creation of new kinds of gay male identity that acknowledge the value some of us place on the erotic and the ways in which it enters not only our classrooms and teaching practices, but the classrooms and practices of all effective educators? Is it possible to be seen by students as a sexual being without pandering to stereotypes or imposing one's comfort with sex on students who maintain different values? Will I ever be able to find a way to support students as they struggle with their own sexual concerns without stifling my own struggles and silencing my own stories? And how can teachers from any vulnerable marginalized population even consider such questions without undermining their jobs and putting their careers at risk?

I have faced a range of issues about sex, the body, and erotic desires during the three spring semesters in which I've taught my gay studies class:

- What do I do when I find in my mailbox on Valentine's Day a single long-stemmed rose that a staff member insists was placed there by "an unknown male undergraduate" who tried to deliver it surreptitiously?

- How do I respond when a student asks me if I'll be dropping by the Bondage a Go-Go sex club on Wednesday night?
- When the weather gets warm and I'm feeling good about my body, is it ever okay to wear a Lacoste shirt to class that shows my big arms? What about a tank top or simply a sleeveless vest?
- What should I do when I'm cleaning up after a workout in the university recreation center's showers and two of my undergraduate gay male students walk in and proceed to shoot quick glances in my direction as I quickly finish showering and toweling off?
- How do I react when I recognize a former or current student at a bathhouse, sex club, or while I am in a chat room on AOL?

The only conversations in this arena of which I've been a part have focused on the ethics of college teacher/student liaisons. I answered that question years ago for myself—deciding I did not need the risk and the headaches such interactions could bring—so perhaps this has allowed this other series of questions to emerge for me. If I believe that there are many diverse and ethical ways for people to structure their social and sexual practices, isn't it important to affirm various options within the classroom? Is it possible to affirm one pattern of sexual organization without undercutting others? What responsibility do gay male teachers who enjoy and intellectually support casual, nonmonogamous sexual relations have to our gay male students?

My students know that I have a lover and live with him in San Francisco. This is introduced, appropriately to my mind, during the first class when I explain why I ask them not to call me at home after 9 p.m. Several have met Crispin either when we have run into students on the street or at gay community festivals and street fairs, or when he has dropped in at our class potluck suppers. I am always acutely self-conscious of how I interact with my lover when students are around: I want to be "appropriate" but neither fully stifle the attraction and physicality between us nor elevate the erotic element of the relationship over others. When he visits me in class, I give him a peck of a kiss when I first see him, and I am conscious that I do not want to stifle touching his arm or holding his hand briefly. If I run into students on the street when we are wearing tank tops or leather armbands, I become quite self-conscious but I do not avoid greeting them nor feel ashamed to be seen or known to participate in gay male sexual cultures.

Last year, one of my students drew an analogy in class that used my relationship with Crispin in a way that revealed that the student believed we were in a monogamous relationship. I cannot recollect the precise context for this incident, but it was something similar to a discussion I have recently had with my students about the president's alleged affair with Monica Lewinsky. During a heated discussion on this topic, one student asked me, "How would you feel if Crispin were to have an affair with some other guy?"

In fact, I know how I would feel because our relationship is not sexually exclusive and we regularly discuss our feelings about each other's "extra-marital" liaisons. But how do I answer this question when it comes from undergraduate students who assume being in a couple is automatically equated with monogamy?

When a student, Brenda, first raised a similar question in class and displayed her assumptions about the nature of our relationship and the boundaries about sex we had constructed, I paused for a moment and considered my response. It seemed like an important teachable moment had arrived, but one fraught with risks of all kinds. Through my mind raced a number of scenarios: the dean confronting me with evidence that I had flaunted my sexual promiscuity to my students; a lawsuit where a group of students sue me for sexually harassing them by responding to Brenda's statement with anything other than "my sex live is my personal private business"; the newspaper headlines declaring, "He Teaches at the University, but at Night He Wallows in the Sexual Gutters of the Gay City." I paused before responding, then I downshifted energy and spoke directly to Brenda. "This might sound strange for you to hear but I feel as if I should correct an assumption that seems to lie behind your state-ment," I said calmly. "You seem to believe Crispin and I have structured our relationship in a manner that parallels traditional monogamous het-erosexual relationships. Many couples—of all sexual orientations—choose other ways of organizing their relationship. It has been documented that gay men in particular often maintain what are known as open relation-ships. I just wanted you to know that your assumption doesn't fit our relationship design because we do not maintain monogamy in our rela-tionship or believe we should control what our partner does with his body and his time. Open relationships surely have their challenges, but we've found it works best for us."

When I finished, there was total silence in the room. A few hands slowly were raised, additional students put forward some questions, I of-fered responses, and then we returned to the lesson at hand. I felt con-flicted between wanting to fully exploit a teachable moment and wanting to place what I felt were appropriate boundaries on the discussion. Over the next few weeks, I heard from several students that they'd appreciated my candor and the respect with which I held them indicated by my disclosure. From that point forward, I felt the class became an intimate site for teaching and learning and that the rigid role of teacher had flexed in a way that promoted the critical pedagogy of the class.

I have had other encounters with my undergraduates that have challenged my commitment to including sex and the body in my teaching as something more than a distanced, depersonalized intellectual exercise. When I have run into students at San Francisco's Folsom Street Fair, an annual event celebrating the leather and fetish communities, and we've all been dressed in sexualized clothing, I have felt it important when I see them next in class to acknowledge the encounter before class in a casual, informal manner. Here I aim to show that participation in such activities is neither embarrassing nor a "big deal." One lesbian student once referenced her interest in sadomasochism in a personal reflective paper, indicating that her middle school students could deal with her lesbian identity but not her sexual interests. I felt it was appropriate and valuable to affirm her situation by sharing an incident from my own years as a middle school teacher, when students on the playground who were playing with handcuffs jokingly asked me if I'd ever seen a pair. I indicated that I owned my own set of handcuffs and left it at that.

As I recall these encounters, I realize that my aim is not to get into trouble or earn a reputation as a particularly transgressive or radical educator. Instead I believe that the stigmatizing, silencing, scapegoating, and attacks that commonly surround the appearance of sex in the classroom are social practices that produce a populace that experiences sex and desire in a manner best characterized by confusion, frustration, pain, and abuse. If critical pedagogy is about collectively gaining a deep understanding of how social and political forces interact with all of our everyday lives and help to produce our identities, social practices, and communities, then silencing, avoiding, or depersonalizing/ disembodying sex may function powerfully to affirm and reify a dangerous and oppressive status quo.

Conclusion

Jonathan Silin (1997) has argued that "Americans are alternately expansive and silent about the place of sexuality in the early childhood classroom" (214). The intense obsession with sex and schooling and the profound silences associated with it are part of an ideology that is effective at, as James Sears (1992) has aptly stated, "reproducing the body politic"

(15). Keeping sex private and silencing discussion of desire, bodies, and erotic practices in classroom discourse effectively ensures the continued marshaling of sex as a form of social control. As Sears states:

> Sexuality, then, is more a construct of ideology and culture than it is a collection of information about biology and the body; power and control are central to our modern understanding of sexuality and ourselves as sexual beings. . . . How we define and express our sexuality has significant political implications. . . . There is, then, an integral relationship between the learning of human reproduction and reproduction of social relations. Understandings of gendered and sexual arrangements, teenage pregnancy, and child sexual abuse further illustrate this relationship. (18–19)

All teachers teach a great deal about sex, whether we acknowledge it or not. What we say and what we don't say, what is voiced and what is silenced, create knowledges for our students that contain tremendous implications. Gay male teachers, whose bodies, desires, and practices may transgress heteronormative constructs and patriarchal paradigms, could be a source of startling new learnings. This paper represents an initial attempt to trouble the comfortable notions of gay male teacher that circulate within liberal educational discourse. I have attempted to examine ways in which gay male identities and cultures might be useful in our pedagogical practices.

For too long, gay men have understandably fought a narrow battle, seeking admittance into the classroom as openly gay educators. Likewise, queer students of all genders and sexualities have worked to achieve a relative degree of safety in public schools throughout the United States. All too often, as we've made these efforts, we've made compromises and sacrifices that have gone unspoken and unacknowledged. We've gained a limited entry into the classroom by denying authentic differences between many gay men's relationships to gender roles, sexual cultures, and kinship arrangements and those of the heteronormative hegemony.

This paper is a call to dialogue about the sacrifices we have made and the implications they have for democratic education and social change.

Works Cited

Boldt, Gail. 1997. Sexist and heterosexist responses to gender bending. In *Making a place for pleasure in early childhood education*, edited by Joseph J. Tobin. New Haven: Yale University Press.

Bourdieu, Pierre. 1984. *Distinction: A social critique of the judgment of taste*. Cambridge, Mass.: Harvard University Press.

Bronski, Michael, ed. 1996. *Flashpoint: Gay male sexual writing*. New York: Masquerade Books.

Bronski, Michael. 1998. *The pleasure principle: Sex, backlash, and the struggle for gay freedom*. New York: St. Martin's.

Califia, Pat. 1994. *Public sex: The culture of radical sex*. San Francisco: Cleis.

Connell, R. W. 1995. *Masculinities*. Berkeley: University of California Press.

Dangerous Bedfellows, ed. 1996. Introduction. In *Policing public sex*. Boston: South End Press.

hooks, bell. 1994. *Teaching to transgress: Education as the practice of freedom*. New York: Routledge.

Jennings, Kevin, ed. 1994. *One teacher in 10: Gay and lesbian educators tell their stories*. Boston: Alyson.

Khayatt, Madiha D. 1992. *Lesbian teachers: An invisible presence*. Albany: SUNY Press.

Kissen, Rita. 1996. *The last closet: The real lives of lesbian and gay teachers*. Portsmouth, NH: Heinemann.

Lee, Enid, Deborah Menkart, and Margo Okazawa-Rey, eds. 1998. *Beyond heroes and holidays: A practical guide to K–12 anti-racist, multicultural education and staff development*. Washington: Network of Educators on the Americas.

Lortie, D. 1975. *Schoolteacher: A sociological study*. Chicago: University of Chicago Press.

Mac an Ghaill, Mairtin. 1994. *The making of men: Masculinities, sexualities, and schooling.* Buckingham, UK: Open University Press.

McLaren, Peter. 1995. *Critical pedagogy and predatory culture.* New York: Routledge.

Pharr, Suzanne. 1996. *In the time of the right: Reflections on liberation.* Berkeley: Chardon Press.

Reagon, Bernice. 1983. Coalition politics: Turning the century. In *Home girls: A black feminist anthology,* edited by Barbara Smith. New York: Kitchen Table.

Rofes, Eric. 1985. *Socrates, Plato and guys like me: Confessions of a gay schoolteacher.* Boston: Alyson.

Sears, James T. 1992. Dilemmas and possibilities of sexuality education: Reproducing the body politic. In *Sexuality and the curriculum: The politics and practices of sexuality education,* edited by James T. Sears. New York: Teachers College Press.

Sedgwick, Eve Kosofsky. 1993. How to bring your kids up gay. In *Fear of a queer planet: Queer politics and social theory,* edited by Michael Warner. Minneapolis: University of Minnesota Press.

Silin, Jonathan. 1997. The pervert in the classroom. In *Making a place for pleasure in early childhood education,* edited by Joseph J. Tobin. New Haven: Yale University Press.

Thorne, Barrie. 1993. *Gender play: Girls and boys at school.* New Brunswick: Rutgers University Press.

Vaid, Uvashi. 1995. *Virtual equality: The mainstreaming of gay and lesbian liberation.* New York: Anchor/Doubleday.

PART TWO

THINKING CULTURE

Chapter 8

From the Closet to the Corral: Neo-stereotyping in *In & Out*

Shirley R. Steinberg

Weekly manicures, style consciousness, limp wrists, Judy Garland albums, Rogers and Hammerstein overtures, neatness, swishing, and a love of poetry do a queer make. As we end a century of filmmaking, Hollywood writers create signifiers that define queerness to viewers. These signifiers serve to create and reinscribe a pedagogy that includes stereotyping, homophobia, and the desexualization of homosexuality. When viewers use critical media literacy they become informed and are able to discriminate between films that serve to liberate queerness as opposed to those films that reinscribe heterosexism. As we incorporate a pedagogical look at the curriculum that cinema presents, disturbing patterns emerge in films that appear to be queer friendly on the first read.

Gay filmmaker Paul Rudnick (*Jeffrey, In & Out, Addams Family Values*), for example, is keenly aware that he is writing scripts for a public that is traditionally homophobic. His intent is to introduce mainstream audiences to gayness as an alternative lifestyle that in no way can harm their comfortable, heterosexual lives—to make gayness palatable and "not so bad." Using his own gayness as capital, Rudnick's film *In & Out* claims a legitimacy and self-consciousness that is intended to disarm even the most disapproving viewer. Instead of declaring "We're here, we're queer, get over it," as Rudnick did more comfortably in *Jeffrey,* the script quietly whispers the message: "We're here, we're queer, and we are endearing enough to overlook our one flaw—we're queer." I contend that many films designed to soften the blow (pun intended) of homosexuality serve to recover homophobic stereotypes and actually harm Hollywood attempts to normalize queerness and create tolerance. Rudnick's intent, while noble, turns into more fodder that straight viewers must sludge through in order

to make sense of the queer way of knowing. Consequently, a film such as
In & Out becomes a hegemonic device that serves to reinscribe hatred
and a fear of homosexuality.

    In & Out may be defined as a liberal film, even an emancipatory film
by those who ignore the critical underpinnings involved in creating a film
for a mainstream audience—underpinnings that lay tacit frameworks of
prejudice that feed into the attitudes of many viewers. Despite its attempt
to normalize queerness, Rudnick's film is an example of a pedagogy gone
awry. In this chapter I will discuss the 1997 film *In & Out* and the negative effects the film creates in the attempt to liberalize queerness. This
popular film was well received throughout North America and now enjoys
a wide video distribution. Written by Paul Rudnick, the film stars Kevin
Kline, Joan Cusack, and Matt Dillon. The packaging blurb accompanying
the video introduces us to the film:

> Welcome to Greenleaf, a picture-postcard Indiana town where the high school is
> the proud focus of attention and "alternative lifestyle" means you bowl on alter-
> nate Tuesdays. But on the night of the Oscars telecast, the town's—and the world's—
> center of attention is Greenleaf teacher Howard Brackett. A former student who's
> now a superstar actor tells an audience of millions that Howard is gay. Poor
> Howard. He's outted when he didn't know he was in!
>
>   Kevin Kline plays stunned Howard, scrambling to go forth with his wedding to
> devoted Emily (Joan Cusack) and doing his frantic best to assert his manliness.
> With clever dialogue, antic situations and a stellar cast that includes Matt Dillon,
> Tom Selleck, Debbie Reynolds and Bob Newhart, *In & Out* is out-and-out fun!

The comedic tone of the film and its dialogue and zany antics clearly
follow Rudnick's agenda, which is to soften queerness into acceptability.
In his efforts to do this, however, he re-stereotypes characters and we
leave no smarter and no more enlightened than we entered.

    The film carries an illusion that it is emancipatory and empowering,
indeed a film that would encourage an acceptance of diverse lifestyles;
Rudnick's film, in fact, serves in a counterhegemonic position to reinscribe
a neo-homophobia that is liberal in nature. This neo-homophobia becomes the sexual counterpart of political and economic neo-liberalism. I
am using the concept of neo-liberalism as an acceptance of diversity within
the globalized economy—an acceptance of diversity as long as one can
continue to exploit the diverse "other" in the economic context of society.
Thus, we can economically exploit homosexuals along with other traditionally excluded groups. Homosexuality has become Hollywood's new-
est commodity, wrapped in an acceptable fashion: desexualized, warm
and fuzzy—the marketing of otherness for its appeal and its exoticism.

Rudnick's treatment of queerness in *In & Out* is flawed because he uses character "flaws" attributed to gayness to enhance his queer characters and to disarm any fears or expectations the audience may have. Instead of enlightenment, we leave the theater with a vivid redescription of what queerness is—that is, what the heterosexual world wants queerness to be. In the way that *Moonstruck* reinscribed Italianness and that *Goodbye Columbus* reinscribed Jewishness, *In & Out* defines gayness as a condition that includes a litany of characteristics. After Greenleaf's famous alumnus Cameron Drake dedicates his Oscar to Mr. Brackett, "who is gay," students and colleagues start to review "the signs" that they had earlier ignored. When Mr. Brackett enters his class, the students query: "Is it true?" Brackett replies, "Of course not." At this point the class visibly relaxes and the students "figure out" the reasons Howard was assumed to be gay:

> "Look at you, you're an English teacher. You like poetry and odes and
>   sonnets."
> "You are kind of prissy."
> "You're smart and well-dressed and really clean."
> "It doesn't look good."
> "You've got the drama club and you've got that bicycle."
> "You've been engaged for three years."
> "Add it up and of course the guy thinks you're gay."
> "He was in that movie, so his brain is already going that way."
> "He remembers you, smart, clean, totally decent human being, and
>   that equals gay."

Relieved that there is a logical explanation for this mislabeling, Brackett goes to explain to the press that he is not gay. As he leaves the room a student reminds him to "watch the wrist." The audience laughs.

The video blurb's description tells us that "poor Howard" has to deal with this condition. We are never told why Howard is poor and why he must defend himself. Are we just to assume that when one is outed, they are to be pitied? Is queerness a condition? An illness? Is an apology expected? The blurb goes on to describe Howard trying to "assert his manliness"; the text of the film tells us exactly what manliness *isn't*. As it is defined, or rather undefined in Howard's discussion with the students, a man is not: one who likes poetry, odes or sonnets, one who is prissy or smart, or one who is well-dressed and really clean. A man doesn't sponsor the drama club and doesn't ride a bicycle in *that* fashion.

The theme of manliness dominates the film: Howard is pushed into a frantic pace as he demands that people see him as manly. He plays a tape called *Be a Man: Exploring Your Masculinity*. The narrator instructs him to dress like a man, be in control, and to take charge. Howard must pull out his shirttail and be messy, adjust his genitals with a rough gesture, and talk tough—"hot damn, yo." Above all, he must "avoid rhythm, grace and pleasure. Men do not dance, they work, they drink, they have bad backs. Whatever you do, do not dance." The test begins when the tape begins to play "I Will Survive" by Gloria Gaynor; Howard resists the music for the first few beats. We see him begin to weaken only seconds later and he disco dances with fervor throughout the house. The tape concludes and the narrator declares him a "pussy boy" for giving in and dancing to the music.

At this point in the film, Howard is the *only* person who doesn't realize he is gay. The audience is thoroughly convinced, naturally, because we have been given all the signs. During the rest of the show we will anticipate his own self-discovery and the completion of his outing. When he finally renames himself as gay, we are relieved and comfortable with his life choice. In fact, in one of the final scenes, when Howard is fired for being gay, each student in the auditorium declares that he or she too, is gay, and then each townsperson stands up and proudly declares his or her gayness. "We are all the same, and if Howard is gay, then I am gay." Somehow I am reminded of the student in my school who had cancer. She started wearing a baseball cap to school; consequently, the school allowed all the students to wear baseball caps. While the student certainly felt comforted that she was not alone in wearing a cap, she still was the only one with cancer. Similarly, Howard is still the only one who is gay.

Missing in this discourse of gayness and outing is an essential ingredient. Other than a closed mouth kiss by a gay newscaster (played by Tom Selleck), gayness is never associated with sex. Although it is a sexual lifestyle, gayness is never associated in the film with many of the attributes that add up to being gay. The signifiers defined by the students—neatness, limp wrists, etc.—paint a one-dimensional picture of gayness that excludes sex and sexuality. Actually, one could argue that the only unquestionable signifier of gayness is that one has sex (or wants to have sex) with someone of the same gender. Why then, is Rudnick so careful not to allow his gay character to have sex? I contend that the sexual act would be crossing the heterosexual line of decency, the line that defines what gayness really might be. I am not essentializing homosexuality as only being about sexual practices and preferences, but indeed, to ignore sexual aspects is to blind oneself to much of the essence of being gay. In the same sense, Howard is full of "gay attributes," full to overflowing; but he never has sex. In fact, he never discusses sex or implies that he understands that being gay means having sex with men.

Is this film then compromising with straight audiences? Are straight viewers being asked to just "give a little"? Let homosexuals swish and decorate, be flamboyant and style hair, and in exchange, *In & Out* will have characters that entertain and do not fuck—or fuck *with* heterosexist sensibility. Gay characters then become gay caricatures, court jesters brought in to the court of heterosexuals for viewing pleasure—kings and queens of fools. Disney "liberated" a similar character, an "other," in *The Hunchback of Notre Dame*—one of Quasimodo's most empowering events was centered around his being crowned the "King of Fools." This title brought him out of his shy shell, and the townspeople and the audience were relieved at the sense of socialized justice in the hunchback's newfound fame. Of course, he was still ugly and disfigured and never found the love of a mate, but the audience became part of the redefinition of his otherness, in that even a hunchback with a disfigured face has a place in the world and we are able to love him for *who he is* (although not sexually).

Gay television characters are treated in the same way. Story lines for gays and lesbians lie in their ability to coordinate, accessorize, and get laughs. The gay sidekick has replaced Gabby Hayes (to Roy Rogers), Tonto (to the Lone Ranger) and Danny Glover (to Mel Gibson) as the foil to the straight straight-man/woman's character. As audiences cry for the plots to "bring us our fools," gay and lesbian characters adopt many of the same characteristics identified by Howard's English students. Homosexuality is okay if it is funny, identifiable, and, above all, desexualized. In a blackface of the nineties, a gay man replaces Mr. Bojangles as a neutered entertainer. As long as he kept his place, Mr. Bojangles was no sexual threat to Shirley Temple; nonsexual gay and lesbian characters, indeed, are no sexual threat to our sons and daughters. Rudnick's films help viewers to accept outing from the closet, but corral queerness into a containable space with definable attributes and no sex. When queerness is contained in this virtual space, it is never a threat to our American, Christian values. The "greatest" country on earth remains untouched—and, in a way, more tolerant.

The last thing any marginalized person needs is tolerance. Political wimpiness in the liberal agenda tokenizes any marginalization and relegates it to second-class citizenry for all time. When we are tolerated, we are never at an equal level with the tolerator. Tolerance implies that the tolerator is condescending to accept those being tolerated in spite of their "problems." I don't want to teach for tolerance, I want to teach for equality. Anything less is unacceptable. Along with eating tacos to understand our Chicano brothers and sisters, lighting a menorah to remember the Jews, and drinking green shakes on St. Patrick's day for Irish awareness, movies that highlight gay characters without being gay are not liberating anyone.

In *In & Out* there is never an attempt to problematize the essentialization of "authentic gayness." It is taken for granted that all gay men are effeminate, artistic, and identifiable by unmanliness; they are unworthy of the description manly. The power of patriarchy is recovered from the threats of the gay rights movement and its feminist supporters in a remasculinized, albeit more tolerant, form. Although it takes one step forward toward acceptance, a film like *In & Out* unfortunately takes two more steps back.

In his earlier film, *Jeffrey*, Rudnick tells the story of a gay man who loves sex. Unable to live with the uncertainties and fears of AIDS, he vows to give up sex. Jeffrey resents the constraints that AIDS has drawn around sexual relationships and dreams of a life unencumbered with the disease: "Sometimes I just have to be a gay man with a cock." He mourns the fact that bodies can now harbor death and claims that "bodies are built with the capacity of joy." Rudnick's gay characters here are full, not stereotypically "faggy," and they do not fit within any particular category. The fact that gay men have sex with other men is never hidden or ignored. Gayness is out and about. *Jeffrey* played in select theaters for a few weeks and quickly was released on video. *In & Out,* on the other hand, was a smashing success and even gathered Academy Award nominations. In a film that addresses the sexuality of gay men, Rudnick defies the audience to take exception to the film's content. Two years later, his film *In & Out* hides gayness with a paranoid, one-dimensional character that discovers his own sexuality in spite of his penchant for disco dancing.

There is one point in the film when we begin to think that a turn has been taken and that being gay will finally be identified with having sex: After everyone in town declares themselves gay the scene changes to a church and Tom Selleck's gay character and Howard are busily adjusting their tuxs and bow ties. The air is full of festival and it is obvious that there is going to be a wedding. I remember feeling relieved that finally love and sex would be dealt with in the film. It was apparent that the men (Selleck and Klein) were going to marry. However, the next scene jolted me back into reality as I realized that at the altar are Howard's mother and father, renewing their wedding vows—we are faked out again. The one point in the film that could legitimate gayness as a sexual and loving lifestyle buries itself in an embarrassed and weak conclusion that leaves us empty. Heterosexism is reinscribed and strengthened.

We haven't "come a long way, baby," and I am concerned that the public support and acknowledgment for a film such as *In & Out* perpetuates an intolerant tolerance that serves *only to redefine* in an acceptable fashion what queerness *should be*—if we have to put up with it at all. Shame on you, Paul Rudnick; backtracking into padded closets only serves to reconstruct a new barrier. Films such as *In & Out* are now corralling queerness into a fenced arena, leaving the audience to laugh along with the funny queers, always bracketing the plot with the unseen label: it's okay; we can deal with it, just keep your pants on and your tongues in your mouth—*don't go there*, we don't want too much information.

Chapter 9

Terms of Identity:
Ellen's Intertextual Coming Out

Nancy Lesko

In the spring of 1997, the cultural waves moved with the season's media event: Ellen Degeneres's character was coming out on the ABC television sitcom *Ellen*. The event was widely heralded as a breakthrough, a first for television: The lead character in a network show openly acknowledged her homosexuality (Handy 1997). The coming out was doubled: The lead character in the show, Ellen Morgan, admitted to herself and others that she was gay; and in linked magazine stories and television interviews the actress, Ellen Degeneres, acknowledged that she, too, was gay.

This lesbian prominence on prime time television can be viewed as a major victory of the gay and lesbian movement. Cultural theorist Arthur Kroker claims that nothing happens in our society unless it happens on television (Lipsitz 1997). Public visibility is understood as a first step toward public acceptance and toward the "mainstreaming" of gays and lesbians in various sociocultural niches. When gay and lesbians are visible in the media, another step has been taken toward their visibility and acceptance as a "natural" part of social life. Rosemary Hennessy summarizes this position nicely:

> Cultural visibility can prepare the ground for gay civil rights protection and affir-
> mative images of lesbians and gays in the mainstream media . . . can be empow-
> ering for those of us who have lived most of our lives with no validation at all from
> the dominant culture. (1994–95, 31–32)

From this position, Ellen's television coming out was demonstrable progress, worthy of celebration.

But as Joshua Gamson suggests, the desire of homosexuals and bi-sexuals to be recognized and validated has been stronger than the desire to do careful analyses of "*the dynamics of becoming visible*" [emphasis added]. Gamson foreshadows another dynamic: "Cultural visibility, especially when it is taking place through commerce, is not a direct route to liberation; in fact, it can easily lead elsewhere" (1998, 12). Danae Clark adds that in the urgency to consider the agency of spectators and the empowerment of activists, "we risk losing sight of the interrelation between reading practices and the political economy of media institutions" (1993, 195). Similarly, Larry Gross recognizes that the media and the market are not outside historically constructed perspectives:

> When groups or perspectives do attain visibility, the manner of that representation will itself reflect the biases and interests of those elites who define the public agenda. And those elites are mostly white, mostly middle-aged, mostly male, mostly middle- and upper-middle-class, and (at least in public) entirely heterosexual. (Gross 1994, 143)

Gamson asks whether the path to media visibility is open equally to all gays and lesbians. Do those homosexuals with less status, that is, working-class queers, bisexuals, transgendered, those in noncommitted relationships, or those who violate middle class norms of taste, get to speak as much? Or do the more normalized gays and lesbians have greater access to broadcast and print media? Analyzing daytime talk shows, Gamson concludes that "acceptable" gays and lesbians have been more visible: "[W]here bisexuality functions primarily as a stand-in for promiscuity and is therefore denigrated, monogamous sexuality gets the high ground, taking monogamous *homosexuality* along for the ride" (1998, 22). Similarly, lesbians who remain within traditional lines of feminine gender conformity, who "look like women," are deemed more acceptable by talk show audiences. Their credibility translates into greater visibility, and they are perceived by many within the gay and lesbian movement as better spokespersons for homosexuality.

Preferences for "better representations" of homosexuals also operate among talk show viewers. Gamson's interviews with viewers confirm that Oprah is seen as a classier, more middle-class show; middle-class viewers dislike and avoid "sensationalistic" and "exploitative" guests. Oprah "gets a better class of people" who neither spit nor swear nor "display their sexual selves in public" (Gamson 1998, 27–28). Viewers, both liberal and conservative, are more accepting of those who do not flaunt their sexual preference in what is seen as vulgar ways.

This work is useful in distinguishing different kinds of visibility related to monogamous/non-monogamous states and class backgrounds of homosexuals on television talk shows. Gender-nonconforming homosexuals and nonmonogamous homosexuals are not welcomed by either liberal or conservative middle-class viewers. Gamson concludes his examination of lesbian, gay, bisexual, and transgender visibility on talk shows by extrapolating to theories of the relationships between public and private identities. In order for the work of social change to occur, a sense of collective identity is both personally and politically critical: "Identity requires stable, recognizable social categories" (1998, 34). But, he warns, "Fixed identity categories are both the bases for oppression and the basis for political power" (35). These understandings of the vexed relationships between identities, politics, and visibility prompt a rethinking of identity in the next section.

Identities as Duties and Obligations

I want to unite, decidedly nonmonogamously, Gamson's work on the dynamics of becoming publicly visible with Cindy Patton's (1993) efforts on queerly politicized "identities." Patton understands postmodern politicized identities as distinctive from the Civil Rights—era idea of an essentialized identity as the basis for political action. Civil Rights activism was based on the fact that Blacks are identifiably distinctive persons who have been segregated and denied equality of opportunity on the basis of skin color and made claims for adjudication of social, economic, and legal equality on that basis. Patton argues that this kind of political activism is grounded on a clearly distinguishable identity or what has now been called an essentialized identity. Similarly, feminists have claimed rights on the basis of being women, and gays and lesbians have followed the same mode of action. However, Patton argues that these approaches to linking politics with an essentialized, or core, identity have been made antiquated by the contemporary identity politics of groups as diverse as the New Right and Queer Nation, both of which ground their identity on what they *do*, not on who they *are*. Both claim that their members and ideas are everywhere. Thus, Patton is arguing that we need to rethink the connections between politics and identity. The new identities are linked to postmodern forms of governmentality—techniques, strategies, and procedures that promise to regulate individuals and groups in relation to authoritative criteria (Barry, Osborne, and Rose 1996)—but forms in which transcendent essence has been supplanted.

Patton reads the New Right identity as linking an epistemological superiority to a moral duty, and she concludes that identities are based

upon duties and obligations (or responsibilities), not on ascribed characteristics. After examining the New Right strategies of misreading gays,
she writes: "[W]hat is at stake is not the content of identities but the
modes for staging politics through identity." She continues: "Instead of
understanding identity in an ego-psychological or developmental framework, I will argue that identity discourse is a strategy in a field of power in
which the so-called identity movements attempt to alter the conditions for
constituting the political subject" (1993, 145). Patton reads identities as
performative acts with strong ethical dimensions:

> [I]dentities suture those who take them up to specific moral duties. Identities
> carry with them a requirement to act, which is felt as "what a person like me
> does." There is a pragmatic, temporal aspect to identities, whether we believe in
> them or not: the requirement to *act* implicit in even transient identities means
> those who inhabit them feel they must do something and do it now. (1993, 147)

Patton proposes to treat identities as "rhetorical closures" that are linked
with strategies, alliances, and re-alliances and affect the staging of political claims (147). She emphasizes repeatedly that identity "is a matter of
duties and ethics, not of being" (148).

Thus, Patton's work urges a closer look at the terms by which a queer
identity is asserted, paying attention to the duties and responsibilities
attendant on particular subject positions. If "the achievement of identities
is precisely the staking out of duties and alliances in a field of power"
(174), what duties and alliances are staked out in the April 30, 1997,
coming out episode of *Ellen*?

Intertextually Coming Out

Media attention is formatted according to intertextual, or crossover, markets: books, talk shows, news shows, sitcoms, news magazines, newspapers, and popular culture magazines (Lipsitz 1997). Ellen Morgan's and
Ellen Degeneres's coming out was just such a cross-marketing event: a
Time magazine cover, two *20/20* evening television interviews, an *Oprah*
afternoon talk show, and the prime time sitcom itself, as well as numerous
articles in the *New York Times*. In addition to these venues, other print
and broadcast media followed the story actively. For one example, the
Indianapolis, Indiana evening news on April 30 opened with reports of
the sitcom and cross-marketed events. I assume that this was not an
anomaly—that media attention is strategic, expensive, and successful. As

Lipsitz reminds us, "Nearly everything on television is an advertisement for some form of entertainment or product available in another medium" (1997, 9). This powerful cross-over approach to marketing means that whatever *happens* on television does indeed happen to all of us (in its reiterations in so many different social sites).

What are the terms of identity in which Ellen intertextually came out? I focus upon the episode of *Ellen* in which she announced that she is gay, the two hour-long *20/20* interviews flanking the sitcom episode, the appearance of Ellen Degeneres with Anne Heche, her lover, on *Oprah*, and print media stories in the *New York Times* and *Time* magazine. I am pursuing the politics of Ellen's coming out by interrogating the terms of her appearances across these various social sites.

Given the queerness of these cross-marketed events, Ellen asserted her lesbian identity in terms that were very familiar, nonsexual, personalized, and commodified. Specifically, I view her intertextual coming out as largely from the positions of:

- a shunned, misunderstood daughter
- a woman with personal problems (she worries about her weight, is afraid no one will like her, could not find herself, doesn't click with anyone, lacks self-confidence, etc.)
- a commodity, a Hollywood star
- a consumer
- liberated by her honesty about her sexuality

I will draw upon two video clips to illustrate and explore these aspects of the intertextual coming out. My argument is that in the intertextual commodification of *Ellen* we find an intense emphasis on liberation and consumption, lesbian identity as a set of personal problems, and lesbian identity largely overwritten by heterovisuality. Thus, Ellen's terms of identity seem largely contained within consumption, monogamous and invisible sexuality, and a middle-class emphasis on a therapeutized self.

Two useful scenes from *Ellen* immediately follow Ellen Morgan's verbal announcement to Susan (the woman she is attracted to, played by Laura Dern) that she is gay. It was a humorous scene in the airport in which Ellen Morgan accidentally spoke her coming out announcement into a loudspeaker. How did Ellen Morgan proceed with her new identity? The next scene is a dream sequence followed by a scene with Ellen at her therapist's office. These two scenes aptly portray the themes of consumption and personal problems.

Scenes from *Ellen* (at the supermarket and in the therapist's office)

The Supermarket Dream and the Therapist's Office

The supermarket scene is intriguingly constructed and very funny. On the one hand it expresses the seeming excessive visibility of coming out: All the employees and signs in this small market shout "lesbian" at Ellen, who floats through the aisles. Each melon, granola bar, and employee reiterates "lesbian." The store manager, played by Billy Bob Thornton (who identifies himself by clearing his throat à la his character in *Slingblade*)[1] tells Ellen that there's a special price on melons for lesbians that week. The sacker offers to help Ellen load her packages into her "gay car." Every commodity is shockingly related to Ellen's newly announced sexuality. Granola bars are hawked (by a nerdy Demi Moore) as good for people "on the go or in the closet." Ellen's gayness reverberates in every fruit and item she buys. In this supermarket scene and in the therapy session, commodities define Ellen.[2] She is both a consumer of commodities and a commodity herself. And she is surrounded by other Hollywood commodities; Demi Moore, Laura Dern, Billy Bob Thornton, and k.d. lang people her supermarket. The cross-marketing of Ellen involves the drawing upon numerous television and film stars who bring their appeal and recognition to *Ellen*.

In the next scene, Ellen relates this dream to her therapist (played by Oprah Winfrey) in the context of a therapy session, that is, as a person with a series of personal problems. She reels off the litany of her personal problems to her therapist: She has never clicked with anyone; she has never thought she would have a "normal life." In therapist mode, Oprah asks, "What's a normal life?" Ellen Morgan replies: "The same thing everybody wants: a house with a picket fence, a dog, a cat, Sunday barbecues, someone to love, someone who loves me, someone I can build a life with. I just want to be happy." The life she wants is defined as "what everyone wants"—a relationship imaged in a house and pets. In this scene, we again see the cross-marketing of stars; Oprah is the most influential black woman in television and has the power to make commodities such as books overnight sensations via her Book Club and to make their authors into millionaires. Her role on daytime television is to listen to people, a better class of people; and the extension of her television persona into Ellen Morgan's therapist was easy. At the same time, the substance of the therapy session focused on commodities. The happy life for Ellen Morgan is "universal"—a house, a picket fence, pets, and Sunday barbecues. She wants, of course, also to have someone to share this life with—in other words, she wants a monogamous relationship.

In an analysis of the media portraits of the O. J. Simpson trial, George Lipsitz argues that three main themes organize television discourse in the United States:

1. the primacy of products as the center of social life
2. the stimulation and management of appetites
3. alarm about the family in jeopardy

In short, Lipsitz finds that television "limits social life to a series of personal problems and acts of consumption" (1997, 26) and that relationships are established and maintained through the acquiring of commodities. Stories that break this frame cannot receive much attention. Ellen's coming out conforms to the cross-over marketing strategy and to the substantive focus on a series of personal problems and acts of consumption.

Robyn Wiegman notes that Ellen's coming out by consuming and by being consumed is not anomalous: "The commodification of the lesbian as a category of identity is often what passes, inside and outside the lesbian community, for evidence of political progress" (1994, 3). In short, might it be possible that the national consumption of Ellen Morgan and Ellen Degeneres's coming out passes for gay and lesbian progress? Similarly, Ellen Morgan's definition of a good life, a liberated life, is also grounded in consumption. She fits the analysis put forward by Gamson. She is the discrete lesbian: she speaks of love and relationships, not sex. She aims to be "happy," not shocking. She wants to be in her own house behind the picket fence, not in parades or otherwise in the faces of straight people.[3]

"What Do You Do?"

Oprah Winfrey was a principal player in the intertextual coming out of Ellen. As already noted, she played Ellen's therapist on the sitcom episode. She also devoted, in the best cross-marketing fashion, most of her afternoon show on April 30th to Ellen Degeneres. Ellen's lover, Anne Heche, also appeared on the program. Ellen answered Oprah's questions, covering some of the same personal history as she did in the 20/20 interviews with Diane Sawyer that aired as bookends to the Ellen sitcom episode. Ellen also answered questions from the studio audience, questions posed by an older white man and a middle-aged white woman who clearly held anti-gay positions, although the studio audience appeared to be overwhelmingly sympathetic.

The portion of this media event that I am most interested in occurred near the end of the segment with Ellen and Anne. Oprah asked them: "Everyone out there is wondering—if you're not swinging from the chandeliers, what do you *do*?" By television standards, a marked, long silence followed. No one spoke. I assume that no one spoke, in part, because the question was being finished in peoples' heads: What do you do . . . *in bed*? And that question could not be answered on the "better class" talk oeuvre of Oprah. Given Ellen Degeneres's quick intelligence honed as a stand-up comedian, she was silent for a long moment. Then, the terms of identity were stated.

Anne: Absolutely nothing! Our lives are so boring! (She smiles and leans toward Oprah as she speaks).
Ellen: We hide from the press. We can't go anywhere; getting off the plane was just a nightmare. I don't know. We didn't plan this. We're just happy.
Anne: We celebrate a lot. We play a lot. We talk a lot.
Oprah: Do you watch videos? Go shopping?
Anne and Ellen: We do all those normal things.
Ellen: We shop a lot. We shop *a lot*.
Anne: We shop a lot. We laugh a lot. And thank God every day that we have each other and are so happy. We do a lot of gratitude.
Ellen: Yeah.
Anne: A lot of thank you, thank you, thank you, God, for giving me this in my life.
         (She raises her arms to illustrate gratitude.)

Earlier in the program both Ellen and Anne discussed how liberating coming out and being together has been, and Ellen stated that "No one can hurt me now," with references to having been hurt by parents, a

Anne and Ellen on *Oprah*

brother, other comedians, and by the fears of what others would think of her. Despite the triumphant tone of those claims, the answers to Oprah's question, "What do you do?" were not so earth-shattering: We shop a lot; watch videos; hide from reporters. Anne's answer included a strong twelve-step-program emphasis on gratitude. Oprah's question jolted the guests and viewers of her show, and her question curiously echoed Patton's theorizing of identity: It's what you do, not who you are. What Anne and Ellen do established them as wealthy consumers, as a monogamous couple, as regular people who have problems and want to be happy. In the cross-market taming of homosexuality and in the presentation of Ellen as an individual with personal problems, the public visibility of identity is diminished.

In my view, the normalizing of Ellen was closely followed by her commodification. Being gay and being out of the closet were talked about as freeing, as living in truth and love, but the consumption of commodities and the commodifying of oneself were strong. Ellen Degeneres admitted this in *Time*: "I didn't do it [coming out] to make a political statement. I did it selfishly for myself, and because I thought it was a great thing for the show, which desperately needed a point of view" (Handy 1997, 86). The terms for political engagement, the duties and ethics of Ellen's coming out seem to focus upon personal happiness and marketing success. The allies in Ellen's terms of identity will be those who can also consume her version of happiness (that is, middle- and upper-middle-class viewers) and those who are commodities themselves.

Ellen Morgan and Ellen Degeneres both have had personal problems. In the highlighting of this term of their identity, the intertextual coming out positioned Ellen primarily as daughter and friend and diminished her as woman-identified lover, as homosexual, as lesbian. Writing of Tonya Harding, Nancy Kerrigan, and the 1994 Winter Olympics, Robyn Wiegman and Lynda Zwinger write about "heterovisuality":

> [T]he potential continuity between female homosociality and female homosexuality is disavowed through an intense insistence on a heterosexualized femininity, on one hand, and through *the cultivation of individual narratives of performance and personality on the other.* (Wiegman and Zwinger, 1995, 109; emphasis added)

The individual narrative of personality and personal problems of both Ellens tended toward a heterovisual performative identity despite the commodification of both actress and character as "lesbian." Although the occasion was grounded on their homosexuality, the lesbian-ness of their appearance was managed through the heterovisual lens. Through the *20/ 20* interviews about her family life, and interviews with Degeneres's mother, father, and brother, she was more memorably positioned as "daughter" and "sister" than as lesbian lover or activist. This highlighting of personality and personal problems offered mainstream audiences a glimpse into private lives, but a sanitized, neutralized glimpse. It was also a profoundly *normalized* representation of Ellen. Women connected with women appeared infrequently in the cross-marketed media events. Thus, although Ellen's coming out was marketed, both homosocial and homosexual connections among women were largely suppressed.

My emphasis has been that the terms of Ellen's coming out were nestled comfortably with commodities, monogamous relationships, and the therapeutic solving of personal problems. Although she came out, Ellen's intertextual politics didn't take us very far. Unlike theorist Michael Warner (1993), who sees queerness as an intervention in all categories of normalization, the terms of Ellen's queerness may have made us laugh, but questioned little else. The duties and responsibilities, the terms of Ellen's queer identity, were located around a struggle for authentic self through therapy, monogamous pairing, and consumption.

This analysis leads to a decidedly unsympathetic response to an additional layer of personal problems. The cross-marketing of Ellen's coming out became another problem that she discussed on *Oprah*. Although Ellen did only three cross-marketing events, the *Time* cover story, *20/20* interviews, and *Oprah*, she complained that "the media has gone crazy with it." Indeed. Ellen Degeneres's complaints about the media overreaction are hard to accept when she has cross-marketed herself in this way, but it adds to the story as yet one more personal problem.

Conclusion

The terms of Ellen's identity seemed overwhelmingly private—personal ease, personal relationship, personal consumption, and personal stardom. Although she was acting in the public realm, Ellen Morgan's and Ellen Degeneres's duties extended no further than the picket fence around her Beverly Hills home (portrayed in the *20/20* segment). Lauren Berlant (1997) suggests that there is an "iconic" citizen who is white, middle class and a family member—Ellen's coming out fit into this "iconic" citizen mode, despite her being gay. Her coming out focused attention on private behavior, which has become the barometer for citizenship. Only in the *last sentence* of the second *20/20* show did Ellen offer her hope that her coming out would help teenagers across the country to live their lives as gays and lesbians and to come out to their parents, too. Although seeming to articulate responsibilities toward a broader segment of the population, this comment remained within the realm of private life and the family. Ellen's "points of purchase," points of identification that allow viewers to make sense of cultural forms in ways that are meaningful or pleasurable to them (Fiske 1988), were likely to be on the level of personal problems, wanting a "normal" life with a loved one and friends, and wanting affluence in order to consume.

I have utilized a highly visible cultural event to raise questions about the supposed immediate and obvious effects on the public realm of private and privatized actions that are *publicly performed and consumed*. The market structuring of television narrative to emphasize personal problems, heterovisuality, and normalizing through the acquisition of commodities means that privately spoken truths can have a negligible impact on the public. The conventions of television privatize difference, re-embedding Ellen in her family, in her series of personal problems, and in her happy monogamous relationship. When considering television events in relation to social change, understanding the complex relationships between portraits of private lives that are publicly narrated and consumed continue to be both queer responsibilities and pleasures.[4]

Notes

1   Earlier in the coming out episode, Ellen Morgan and Susan have a playful exchange in which they impersonate the throat-clearing of *Slingblade's* main character, too.

2   I am aware of the multiple levels of this dream sequence and its psychoanalytic possibilities. My analysis must be seen as partial.

3   Some of the questions that Ellen Degeneres fielded on *Oprah* were around this issue of an excessive focus on homosexuality and sexuality.

4   This closing echoes Donna Haraway's (1991) words that our interpretive work needs to be both pleasurable and responsible to those we seek to describe and understand.

Works Cited

Barry, Andrew, Thomas Osborne, and Nikolas S. Rose, eds. 1996. *Fou-cault and political reason*. Chicago: University of Chicago Press.

Berlant, Lauren. 1997. *The queen of America goes to Washington City*. Durham, N.C.: Duke University Press.

Clark, Danae. 1993. Commodity lesbianism. In *The lesbian and gay studies reader*, edited by Henry Abelove, Michèle Aina Barale, and David M. Halperin. New York: Routledge.

Degeneres, Ellen and Anne Heche. 1997. Interview by Oprah Winfrey. *Oprah!* Harpo Productions, April 30.

Fiske, John. 1988. Critical response: Meaningful moments. *Critical Studies in Mass Communication* 5: 247.

Gamson, Joshua. 1998. Publicity traps: Television talk shows and les-bian, gay, bisexual, and transgender visibility. *Sexualities* 1, no.1: 11–41.

Gross, Larry. 1994. What is wrong with this picture? Lesbian women and gay men on television. In *Queer words, queer images: Com-munication and the construction of homosexuality*, edited by R. Jeffrey Ringer. New York: New York University Press.

Handy, Bruce. 1997. Roll over, Ward Cleaver. *Time*, April 14, 78–86.

Haraway, Donna. 1991. *Simians, cyborgs, and women: The reinven-tion of nature*. New York: Routledge.

Hennessey, Rosemary. 1994–95. Queer visibility in commodity culture. *Cultural Critique* 29: 31–75.

Lipsitz, George. 1997. The greatest story ever sold: Marketing and the O. J. Simpson trial. In *Birth of a nation 'hood: Gaze, script, and spectacle in the O.J. Simpson case*, edited by Toni Morrison. New York: Pantheon Books.

Patton, Cindy. 1993. Tremble, hetero swine! In *Fear of a queer planet: Queer politics and social theory*, edited by Michael Warner. Min-neapolis: University of Minnesota Press.

Touchstone Television. 1997. *Ellen (Coming out*, 30 April).

Warner, Michael. 1993. Introduction. In *Fear of a queer planet: Queer politics and social theory*, edited by Michael Warner. Minneapolis: University of Minnesota Press.

Wiegman, Robyn. 1994. Introduction: Mapping the lesbian postmodern. In *The Lesbian Postmodern*, edited by Laura Doan. New York: Columbia University Press.

Wiegman, Robyn and Lynda Zwinger. 1995. Tonya's bad boot, or, go figure. In *Women on ice: Feminist essays on the Tonya Harding/ Nancy Kerrigan spectacle*, edited by Cynthia Baughman. New York: Routledge.

Chapter 10

School Uniforms, Baggy Pants, Barbie Dolls, and Business Suit Cultures on School Boards: A Feminqueering

Glorianne M. Leck

School Boards and the Policies They Construct

Clothing is very much a social artifact—a form of communication.
—Nathan Joseph, 1986

School board policy makers have typically held power as representative members of the successful middle and professional class. Their gender display and work costume—the slacks or skirt, blazer or suit jacket, and tie or ruffles—seem designed to reveal their performance of "right" attitudes toward work, competition, gender, sexuality, nationalism, self-restraint, and religious conformity.

School boards that have voted to endorse school uniform policies appear to believe that by changing the image of the children attending the school they can change the social and academic environment. Their assumption is that requiring students to wear specific costumes of clothing will reduce inappropriate displays of sexuality in the school setting and will reduce the often extreme social consequences of adolescent fashion competition.

Results of studies done by Behling and Williams indicate that "persons are perceived to have a variety of personality traits depending on their physical appearance." Further, it appears clothing alone can create the perceptions of an individual's value. Individuals who dress in harmony with cultural norms are viewed more positively. In this sense "suits are 'good' and ragged jeans and worn out T-shirts are not" (Behling 1991, 11).

I believe school boards have made school uniform decisions without thorough studies of the context, meaning, and development of adolescent fashion wars, nor have they examined the distribution of negative consequences of these policies. Just as aspirin may mask a headache, school uniforms may mask necessary displays of social status differences and cultural norms. Masking may appear to level the playing field, but those educators committed to working with social inequities are likely to find that the mask of a school uniform actually impedes their efforts.

I suspect that because board members are political beings who operate on a corrective rather than a preventative plane, they are choosing to work with the symptoms of our social problems. We are all too familiar with the way corporate executives go about changing the "image" of a failed airline or a floundering corporation. The strategy of changing the image has become a favored way to manipulate public opinion. Therefore, it is no surprise that the school boards whose members reflect business and professional culture would choose to change the image of the schools for which they are responsible.

Predictably, the responses of school boards reflect their own economic interests, their economic privilege, their sexual identities, their class orientation, and an interactive conformity with their own sociohistorical perspective and context. Board statements that celebrate the value of diversity and the importance of individual rights are quickly rendered insincere or appear eclipsed by school uniform policy actions. It certainly appears to be the case that school uniform policies fly in the face of current emphases on diversity in the education of teaching professionals. Any call for "same treatment" and uniformity certainly appears to run counter to important conclusions that have been drawn from current research on how to improve teaching and learning.

Introduction and Positionality

The colonization of the life world means that life activities formerly subject to traditional norms, spontaneous action, or collective decision become commodified or are brought under the control of state institutions, and thus become normalized, universalized, and standardized.
　　　　　　　　　　　　　　　　　　　　　　—Kathy Ferguson, 1984

Somewhat near the end of the list in *The Manual on School Uniforms* issued by the U.S. government—and thus more in the background than in the foreground—is a note to school boards about having consideration for the family of the child in poverty. Item #7 of the eight-item list of government suggestions to school policy makers is: "Assist families that need financial help." The manual goes on to suggest ways of making prescribed school uniforms available to families who may not be able to afford them (3–6).

Interestingly enough, an assumption and an argument often given to the parents who are struggling financially is that school uniforms will reduce the cost of their children's clothing and reduce the parents' embarrassment about not being able to provide their children with clothes that are competitively fashionable. That message makes me pause. Recycling of hand-me-downs and purchases of used clothes from yard sales, Goodwill, and the Salvation Army are well-established practices among the urban and rural poor who haven't appeared particularly embarrassed about their resourcefulness or the principle of recycling. The school board policy of "concern" sends the additional message that one ought to be able to buy "new" clothes and fund one's children's fashion needs or be embarrassed. The government manual seems to include an afterthought of providing for the "less privileged." That sends a message that, in itself, reminds us of the policy's inherent reflection of hierarchy, arrogance, and a general lack of consideration for social diversity. Clearly it is a display of insensitivity to those who are not sharing in a *buy new* consumer culture.

In the school board minutes and reports that I have examined and in the government manual on school uniforms there is no mention of the need of oppressed groups—other than religious groups—to display counter or resistant social identities. Obviously, nonconforming social, sexual, or class identity disclosures are ignored, devalued and deliberately curtailed when a school board mandates a school costume. Here the illusion of sameness (uniformity) is associated with equality. Iris Young has carefully described in her very important work on *Justice and the Politics of Difference* that "cultural imperialism consists in a group's being invisible at the same time that it is being marked out and stereotyped" (Young 1990, 123). The image of uniformity may be fully intended to mask the material reality of what may actually be an increasing distance between economic classes within or among the schools in the United States.

Making difference invisible seems to be an obvious purpose of the school uniform policy. Behling reports that in her studies males and females were not rated differently in perceived academic potential when they were both dressed in the uniform-style blazer. She notes that females can dress for success by wearing a more masculine style of clothing (1994, 728).

Most notably, in school uniform policy there is no regard for the educator's need to look squarely in the face of the cultural, class, sexualized, gendered, and racialized features of the children they are intending to serve. It seems that as we professional educators are learning to seek more data to help us understand our own biases and the children we are attempting to serve, the school boards are retreating to uniformity as a strategy for reducing conflict and developing "same treatment."

It cannot be denied that fashion is and has been a major symbol system that we all use to display our cultural and identity frameworks. In the words of J. C. Flugel, the now classic contributor to our knowledge about fashion,

> Man, it has often been said, is a social animal. He needs the company of his fellows and is delicately reactive to their presence and behavior. And yet as the sense of vision is concerned, civilized man has little opportunity of directly observing the bodies of his companions. Apart from face and hands—which, it is true, are the most socially expressive parts of our anatomy, and to which we have learnt to devote an especially alert attention—what we actually see and react to are not the bodies, but the clothes. (1950, 15)

For educators, clothing cues can assist in our understanding of the construction of learning style, individual notions of resistance to the dominant culture, the trying on and symbolizing of identities, and/or the degree of willingness an individual student has to relinquish or conform to her or his family's cultural framework. And while so-called school uniforms are really work costumes and, fortunately, not strictly prescribed uniforms, they do deny important social interactive opportunities and they do mask social cues.[1]

The school uniform policies are, generally speaking, a paternalistic model of reform that blames the children for fanatic consumerism and then treats them as if they were paper dolls to be dressed by adults. Students are not and have not been passive recipients of culture. Their interactions with the symbols of clothing culture are rich and personally expressive. The paternalistic notion that children are at the bottom of the pecking order and should learn their place flies in the face of the rich contributions that young creator/consumers have been making to popular culture. More importantly, the reassertion of hierarchy threatens to diminish some of their decision-making responsibilities and decrease their cultural power. The success of uniform policies rests upon the assumption that parents of students, and the wearers themselves, will consent to downplay personal taste and displays of their positions in life that are tied to class, gender, sexual orientation, or racialization (Joseph 1986, 145). If it comes to pass that school uniform policies are not resisted by school-children and by parents who have a heightened political consciousness, I will be terribly surprised and very concerned.

While policy makers appear to be blaming the children and trying to cover up and therefore deflate "their" consumer behavior, they are also dodging the discussion of the role of fashion, not only as a social communication system, but as a consequence of unbridled capitalist marketing. Perhaps the children are the canaries. Perhaps they have given us a first warning about an out-of-control emphasis on marketing and consumerism that has promoted fierce competition for expressions of both deviance and conformity. What would young people's clothing symbol systems be if they were not driven by direct marketing to youth, corporate promotion of impulse buying, planned obsolescence, consumer competition, and the promise of greater wealth and increased erotic power?

It is my sense that schools have been a primary, if not *the* primary, setting within which children and youth have traditionally experimented with their social roles. Clothing has served as the medium for trying out and performing social roles. "Public" schools are where many young people have found themselves away from the supervision of their parents and parent surrogates and have found an opportunity to try out their own individualized social skills. Writing in *The International Quarterly* in 1904, sociologist Georg Simmel noted that "Fashion is the imitation of a given example and satisfies the demand for social adaptation; it leads the individual upon the road which all travel. . . . At the same time it satisfies in no less degree the need of differentiation, the tendency toward dissimilarity, the desire for change and contrast" (133). As Simmel has indicated and most of us remember, we used fashion as a way of displaying and marketing identities and values to our peer group and to adults in authority positions. Sometimes we tried conforming to the styles, sometimes we resisted and were dubbed the nonconformists, and sometimes we created the new styles to display our intention to move beyond the prescribed.

Operating as it does within a patriarchal heteronormativity, the practice of dressing to attract and maintain a single sexual partner has, in the industrial era, been a major responsibility prescribed for those gendered as feminine. Fashion itself has centered on competition to display the seductive qualities and the features of social and sexual power of masculine, feminine, and transgendered roles. My own experience may serve as an example to make this point. In the 1950s I personally resisted being a clotheshorse (that is what we, not yet feminists, called another woman who was consuming the latest clothing fads and keeping up with the fashions of the time). It is obvious to me—with hindsight—that my fashion statement was mulish and competitive, but held as much political significance as did the statement of the so-called clotheshorses.[2] While my dress of resistance was about my internal conflicts with identity, social roles, class, and values, it was also rich with symbolism, and I am sure it served my teachers and some of my peer group in understanding, if not condoning, my struggles (Steele 1985).

My adolescence was, like that of many others, a confusing one. I was expected to dress to attract young men. My mother and my peers worked tirelessly to try to feminize my appearance to make me presentable to boys and to teach me to at least appear somewhat submissive, that is, available for sexual selection. What those caring, but presumptuous, heterosexists did not know was that I was in love with my best friend. My best friend was beautiful, sensual, nurturing, gendered feminine, popular with the boys, and not a male. I couldn't let that friend know that I was in love with her. I also couldn't let the boys get too serious about me while I joined my best friend on those miserable double dates. I remember all too well the importance of clothing signifiers that were meant to deter men from viewing me as sexually available to them. I wanted my clothes to deheterosexualize my sexuality and gender display.

Even today, as a crone and an elder, I know the value of my buzz cut and dangling earrings. I know the power games involved in knowing ways to dress myself if I wish to garner respect from those who might otherwise dismiss me. I alter my appearance to avoid being dismissed by young people on the streets, politicians, businesspeople, and competitive young masculinized academics, many of whom dislike feminists, elders, tenured professors, old women, white women, and dykes. Clothes continue to do much to communicate the performance of my sexual, gender, and erotic orientation and my resistance to heteronormativity. It is from these reflections on my own marginalized perspective that I am drawn to examine who benefits from mandated uniformity and whether someone gives up significantly more than someone else in this rush to change the image of school-age youth through the imposition of paper-doll clothes called school uniforms.

What Problems Are School Uniforms
Supposed to Resolve?

The primary meaning of public is what is open and accessible. The public is in principle not exclusionary. While general in that sense, this conception of a public does not imply homogeneity or the adoption of some general or universal standpoint. Indeed, in open and accessible public spaces and forums, one should expect to encounter and hear from those who are different, whose social perspectives, experience, and affiliations are different. To promote a politics of inclusion, then, participatory democrats must promote the ideal of a heterogeneous public, in which persons stand forth with their differences acknowledged and respected. —Iris Young 1990, 119

We know that school settings can be and have been vicious and sometimes devastating social (and for that matter intellectual, spiritual, and physical) environments for some children. We also know that, historically speaking, schools have been a safer place to work out differences with one's peer group than have the streets, the woods, the parks, and nonsupervised house parties. Public schools have played a particularly important role in allowing children to be exposed to cultural diversity and to be granted some relief from the complete parochial indoctrination of their families.

Horace Mann, in defining the role of the public schools, clearly articulated the need for a common political education for all citizens in a democratic society. The extension of that principle has allowed public schools to provide children with a safe, reflective space and a context in which to explore their individual identities and beliefs. To continue to meet those objectives schools must be "safe" environments for discourse. Safety is obviously a very important issue for school managers. So what is the connection that school boards see between the safety of our public school students and the clothing they are wearing at school? What, for them, constitutes danger?

In conversations and interviews I have conducted, I have heard a concern expressed repeatedly by parents, school personnel, and school board members as they have talked about the "sloppy look," baggy pants, lack of "properness" among young women, gang wear, and violence among today's young people. As I explored concerns underlying these remarks, I detected that there was a great concern about the sexually ambiguous, the sexually active, the poor, and most often about the resistance expressed by "black male adolescents." These were viewed as contagions that might corrupt more obedient and academically focused students.

There was great consternation over those individuals and groups who would resist industrial capitalism's insistence on a work ethic. People asked me: "Why would someone not show respect for all the blessings bestowed on us by this rich nation?" Their attitudes reflected such indignities as: How dare anyone resist the tried and true religious values! How can we tolerate the challenge to heterosexual norms, let alone the erosion of public/private divisions of sexual behavior? How dare we suggest an equal value for feminine-gendered culture? What is with this ambiguity of sexual identities and these public displays of erotic preference? How dare anyone challenge the privilege of inherited wealth and power that is earned and should go to the children of those who earned it? Taxpayers and school board members were obviously asking, Who dares to knock on the door of traditional and modern paradigmatic epistemologies?

Values Mocked and Values Smocked

What happened was this. As soon as our friends saw us all dressed up in our warm clothes, though used and castoff they were, they began saying how crazy we was to have worn them. And that's when I began to notice that all the people in the black line had dressed themselves in tatters. Even people what had good things at home, and I knew some of them did. . . . So I was standing there hoping that the white folks what gave out the food wouldn't notice that I was dressed nice. . . . I had come to ask for what was mine, not to beg. So I wasn't going to act like a beggar. Well, I want you to know that that little slip of a woman, all big blue eyes and yellow hair (said). . . . "You don't need nothing to eat from the way you all dressed up." . . . I said, "my children is hungry."   —Alice Walker, 1995, 192–194

When we examine the symbolic representation of school uniforms in a contemporary context we need to ask each other what values and cultural expressions are being mocked and what cultural values are being smocked?

Prudence Glynn discusses the "place" and "meaning" of the three-piece suit in her *Skin to Skin: Eroticism in Dress*. The three-piece suit "is the dress of old men who prefer to mask their bodies and have the cheque-books to impose their will on generations of the poor. It is the dress of jealousy. . . . It has a neuter quality which can be described as emasculation" (1982, 58). Glynn indicates that with the presence of the suit, masculine sexiness shifts from the body to manifestations of economic and social power. Might it be the case that school board members, replete with their success and patriarchal identities, have come to believe that the school uniform will shift the young person's attention from sexual puberty to academic prowess? Do they seriously expect adolescents, especially those identified as oppressed, to relinquish their concerns about identity and sexuality when they, unlike men in suits, have no job (nor much hope thereof), no power, and no sanctioned sexual arrangement? Can we expect young people to divide their lives into spheres of public and private when they haven't yet explored an adult public identity or established their own homes, economies, and sexual preferences?[3]

Consider the context in the United States of long-standing negative racializations of particular groups. Consider how "black" men have been historically set apart from other oppressed groups and stereotyped. Racialized by skin color and set apart by gender, men racialized as "black" have long borne the burden of being perceived as lacking in economic ambition and as having a proclivity for sexual or reproductive power. Juxtapose that history of prejudice with the anger expressed by powerful school board members and parents as they talked about young "black" men in baggy pants. As a "black" male teacher testified to me in 1997, "The baggy pants are *the* symbol of resistance." Young black males in inner-city impoverished and economically quarantined neighborhoods have every reason to believe they will never wear business suits nor will they have access to the rank, wealth and institutionally legitimized power that those "suits" represent. Baggy pants have come to symbolize for many oppressed groups a display of opposition to the tight and tied uniform of the racially and socially privileged "white" male business class.

My interviews revealed that law enforcement officials and school administrators responsible for discipline most often equated gang members with baggy-pants clothing. They expressed great concern about how gang members used baggy pants to conceal weapons. It was clear that baggy pants were to be feared and their presence constituted a good reason for which one should support the call for school uniforms. A significant number of these spokespeople had had military experience, and they were convinced that uniforms promote discipline. They were not at all bothered by the idea that uniforms promoted hierarchy and a kind of militarism. They obviously saw little, if any, differentiation between the social conditions necessary for creating learning environments and the urgency and precision demanded to redirect individuals into being a part of a killing machine.[4] The common ground they saw was "having control over these young people."

In my urban neighborhood, long before the local school board introduced its school uniform policy, feminists, women in poverty, and people who identified as racialized minorities referred to people in power as "the suits." And just as Behling's research has suggested, so too the literature that appeared in the wake of the latest wave of feminism revealed that women were advised by fashion designers to "wear suits" if they (we) were to "dress for success." Similarly, following the reading of *The Autobiography of Malcolm X*, or the viewing of Spike Lee's film *Malcolm X*, there has often come a point in classroom discussions when the zoot suit phenomenon would be deconstructed. The discussants see the young

Malcolm X and his cohorts, who were attempting to "look good" in their flashy suits, as foolish exaggerations of a suit culture of which they could never be a part.[5]

The school uniform as it is currently fashioned in the U.S. pays a certain homage to the suit, both the business suit and the military uniform. The suit style acknowledges the dominant presence of the business and professional class and their ability to control schools. Just as in the industrial era, the "suit" again symbolizes the power arrangements of patriarchy, the superior character of rationality, the patrilineal inheritance of rank and privilege, the responsibility and benevolence of wealth, and the disciplined de-sexing of the public sphere. Understandably, then, the suit creates an image of power, and from that, an image of resistance has been, can be, and will be constructed. So what will happen in the public school where clothing, for example, baggy pants and the performance of fashion—gendered ware—have previously served as a peaceful means of resistance and as a medium for "value vogueing"? Does repression of clothing as a social symbol system simply move the battle to places where adolescent interactions are less supervised or less likely to be observed by adult members of the community?

I can, one year after the introduction of school uniform requirements in my midwestern, old industrial, inner-city neighborhood, look out the window and see a preponderance of baggy pants, and/or one-strap-unfastened overalls, and/or large-legged, low-slung baggy shorts as the predominant adolescent street costume. This has understandably become a pronounced costume of gang members, gang wannabes, and gang-mirror clothing styles among most of the young men and some of the young women who live here. Belonging to a gang in an economically quarantined neighborhood seems to be one of the choices that serves as an alternative to being owned by those seemingly aloof and indifferent men in suits. Men in suits, such as employers, are few and far between, and when they do offer an occasional job, they demonstrate no allegiance to the individual or his/her special needs.

When interviewing school students around the immediate neighborhood and at a "rally for school uniforms" held in the fall of 1997, young black males in loose-fitting sweat suits consistently told this graying and short-haired white woman in cotton slacks and a loose blouse that they hated the idea of uniforms. To quote one of the young men, "It ain't me. I ain't comfortable in anything but my jeans." And another: "Why should I have to be uncomfortable all day at school?" I consistently heard from the young women and the young men, "Why do we have to wear dress shoes? What's so bad about sneakers? They're comfortable."

Business suits are very much with us as corporate work and formal wear. Even middle-class men have reached further into their own liberation and they, like their sisters and wives, have begun to explore comfort and more colorful clothing expressions as part of their earned leisure from work (Glynn 1982, 60). Whether it be leisure from work, resistance to regimen, freedom from the scrutiny of the bosses, or expression of personal identity, the right to express it in clothing is an established practice. Each of those expressions is at issue for young people. The need to "say something" dissonant may be of particular importance for those who haven't inherited wealth. It certainly is a major concern for those who have little hope of attaining the ranks of the economically powerful eunuchs in corporate business suits. The particular young people I interviewed couched the issue of fashion in terms of personal expressions of identity and of a right to comfort. There was clearly a theme, which was, "If schooling, with its messages promoting delayed gratification, isn't going to give me access to wealth and social privilege, then at least don't expect me to deny the pleasures and concepts of my body."

Local expressions and displays of apparel indicate that suits are seen as something to be resisted by young people who find themselves in impoverished and/or negatively racialized circumstances. At the ages of fourteen, fifteen, and sixteen, the young men I interviewed were not hopeful of, nor were they aspiring to ever wear, a business suit. Many had even given up on the more familiar route from the streets into the military uniform. And as reporter Elizabeth Brackett noted from an interview with Chicago school principal Charles Mingo, "Some students feel uniforms carry a negative message. With one of three young black men in jail, anything that smacks of prison is not welcome, that includes school uniforms" (Brackett 1996). Survival in their present circumstances, on their streets, with their gangs, and in their homes was an immediate and much greater pressure for the young people I interviewed. Physical pleasure was their hedge on despair. School uniforms appeared to be repressive and had no representative symbolism of safety or achievement for these racially and economically marginalized young people. Spend an afternoon outside a school in an economically depressed neighborhood and watch how immediately upon departure from the school building, children, particularly black male children, will pull out their tucked-in shirts and roll up one of their pant legs. It is a statement signaling a new turf and a different set of rules. Rule number one: "I'm not one of them! I ain't crossing over; don't mistake this costume as me!"

Clothing that displays resistance to the suits, a preference for comfort and leisure, membership in a racialized group, a giving up of hope for a meaningful life, and/or gang membership is very subtle and rich with local meanings. Fearful outsiders may mistakenly see baggy pants or "wannabe" fashion as indicative of an individual's membership in a gang. But fashion is too contagious and dynamic to hold a singular meaning for very long. Efforts to squelch the role of fashion as a signifier used by gangs is not only ignorant of community needs, but also shortsighted, because it interferes with the entire code by which community members signify their involvement in or resistance to assimilation. Scholars such as bell hooks have written extensively about the negative effects of forced assimilation on racialized minorities. Assimilation at its very core is dehumanizing. She writes:

> Embedded in the logic of assimilation is the white-supremacist assumption that blackness must be eradicated so that a new self, in this case, a white self, can come into being. Of course, since we who are black can never be white, this very often promotes and fosters serious psychological stress and even severe mental illness. My concern about the process of assimilation has deepened as I hear black students express pain and hurt, as I observe them suffer in ways that not only inhibit their ability to perform academically, but threaten their very existence. (1989, 67)

Boards have tried to persuade the public that the introduction of school uniforms serves as a way to get rid of gang symbols and therefore of the presence of gang violence in schools. In that attempt to get rid of one problem, these policies seem to reintroduce the most intense kind of assimilation strategies, throwing us again into an inversion of "separate but equal." Here we have the logical extension of forced school integration: You will be treated the same and because of the historical circumstances of privilege, you will therefore remain unequal. Equality of opportunity to attend school or to wear the same clothes while attending school is not the same as having an equal opportunity to succeed in getting educated and to become an equal in the social-political-economic dialogue of values.[6]

How then do school boards solicit cooperation with "outsider" groups of resistant parents and students? That is to say, what do school uniforms mean if your point of view as a parent is that, "Gangs are good protection against cops" and/or "Academic achievement don't mean shit if you don't have connections!" The most frequently used strategy has been to try to make people believe that uniformity would serve their self-interests. The line I heard being used on resistant parents was that school uniforms would save them money and help prevent hassles with their own kids. That reasoning for buying into the school uniform "thing" was reflected back to me as I interviewed parents.

Adults attending the local rally and fashion show for school uniforms expressed relief from having to listen to their kids pleading with them to buy the latest fad in fashion. In some instances they saw it as deflecting violent confrontations away from themselves. There was a very clear sense that uniforms could mean they might be able to avoid conflict with their children and avoid some of the high costs of trying to keep their children in fashion. I found that most parents that I interviewed, especially single mothers with financial constraints and some apprehension about their own children's level of violence, were excited about the change and about the help they were getting from the "paternalistic" school board. They saw the board as helping them with what they perceived to be a threatening family and economic problem. Parents generally seemed persuaded that if their children dressed as well as the other children they would be treated better and receive more opportunities.

In the particular area where most of my interviews were conducted and predictably, given the settings I was able to access, the parents were striving to get their children into more stable economic conditions. For those particular parents, the crush of their own struggles suggests that being owned by a corporation might actually be better than suffering the indignities of a punitive and receding welfare system. They talked a lot about the struggles associated with being among the working poor. They had their own struggles with social conformity, race discrimination, respectability, and economic security; and single mothers who were heads of households saw their children in school uniforms both as an answer to their own economic constraints and as a way to move their "fatherless" stigmatized family into the middle class and the "suit" culture.

It was characteristic of my 1950s lower-middle-class and European ethnic privilege that I could anticipate real opportunity to move beyond the economic level that my parents had achieved. Today, forty years later, I do not hear poor children, black or white, believing and therefore striving to overcome the poverty and working-class or poor conditions of their families of origin. That difference in perception revealed in the fading hopes of the parents and the cynicism of the children is remarkable. Keeping hope alive is a major struggle for parents, community advocates, and teachers of children in poverty.[7] In a recent television presentation of the opening of a new parochial/charter/choice school, a spokesman pointed to the children all holding hands in prayer and wearing their brand-new school uniforms. He announced, "School uniforms, discipline, and prayers will give them the hope they need in order to succeed."

The "they are watching us" (Hawthorne) effect created by school change, charter schools, and media attention does seem to create a temporary image of a community and caring. However, we must consider the prospects that that kind of hype will endure. We also need to assess the possible consequences to children after current school board members or the founders of the charter or choice schools disappear with their humanitarian awards, their recognition banquets, and their personal profits.

Current employment profiles show an increasing number of minimum wage jobs with no benefits. With an ongoing clustering of welfare and working-class poor people in the same schools and neighborhoods, there aren't a lot of available models of individuals with job success that would bring hope to children in poor urban communities. Children who are housed and schooled in impoverished and abandoned communities have little if any opportunity to get to know someone with real social capital with which to support them in their efforts to move into better economic opportunities. Prayer and the lottery appear to be the leading currencies of hope.

For those who live in an environment of deprivation—a cycle of poverty—with a peer-group emphasis on immediate physical gratification, the long, hard work of career ladders seems impossible. Acquiring a good job often involves a long and consistent struggle for grades, the borrowing of money to invest in a college education, and a strenuous job search. Obliteration of pain, grandiose schemes of making a quick fortune (gambling, selling drugs, etc.), and survival supplant the goals of hanging in for the long haul, hard work, and earned rank. The consistent reinforcers don't appear to be there for the long-term strategies that would support deferred gratification.

Clothing is a system of and for communication. It is a medium through which meaning is conveyed.[8] The attempt to wrap everyone in the same clothes does even more to hide the expressions of resistance and identity that teachers and parents need if they are to provide "safety" for the children. Just as street-smart kids may have stolen those Nike Pumper sneakers in order to show wealth and power over their peers, I have no doubt that children who are street smart (meaning they are not rule-based learners, but are readers of context) will "wear" their uniforms and find ways to perform alternative meanings with them. I am just as sure that children who believe that they are going to have the same opportunity for success as children of privilege will not survive in the streets and in the social power systems that dominate outside their school. Only if they learn to read the social contexts of racism, sexism, opportunism, and distribution of wealth will they have any real and significant chance to challenge the contributing factors in their circumstances.

Will school uniform policies reduce the violence of those who feel they must cheat, steal, or kill in order to survive and/or excel in a system of have and have-nots? The image of uniformity and same treatment would have us cover up the worlds of gut-wrenching survivalism. It is necessary to note that at this political time in the United States, the tug of war between those who believe their very survival to be at risk and those in the suit culture is quite intense. Whether it be outbursts of young people in urban poverty, breadwinners in rural poverty, native peoples in despair over their lost cultures, racialized or religious minorities in struggles for their rights, people in so-called cults, people in so-called gangs, workers in dead-end jobs, women and children in abusive situations, workers in fear of losing their jobs, or young people feeling trapped in schools—no matter who the agents are—acts of members of such groups (shootings, bombings, and political struggles) are constantly portrayed as isolated incidents and as a surprise to the nation.

In a recent reflective reminder to its audiences, the Public Broadcasting System ran a special television program called *Affluenza*, in which Scott Simon described how personal crises such as divorce or being diagnosed with cancer actually serve to increase the demand for individual spending (which in turn increases the gross national product). There was an attempt in the *Affluenza* documentary project to reveal how the economy thrives on new markets and thus how disaster and the constant changing of social reform projects create opportunity for bursts of economic growth. Change and the manufacture of social crises for which solutions must be sought actually serve the interests of the business economy and reduce individual wealth.

Do school uniforms constitute a burgeoning new clothing market? Have school uniforms increased the cost of clothing for a household? After considering that thought I began to wonder just how much this school uniform matter could play into the corporate market grab going on between the Pat Robertson/James Dobson Christian Coalition/Focus on the Family factions and their polarization with Disney and ABC/NBC/CBS. While the former market products and salvation with arguments for "wholesome" patriarchal heterosexual family life, sexual repression, and

10 percent tithing to their corporate-affiliated churches, the latter market romance and sexiness and emphasize credit purchases as an investment in dreams of being rich and heroic. Both groups have well-organized strategies for marketing social images to the nation's children. Indeed, it wasn't long after my initial interviews that I began to hear the mothers say, "I thought the uniforms were going to solve the problem of conflict with my child, but now I am finding that I have to contend with the same conflicts, and I have to buy two wardrobes instead of one." Cha-ching!

School uniform policies may appear to work for school boards; the very event of requiring uniforms may create the temporary phenomenon of community involvement and parent/school cooperation. But what of the matter of improving access to success? Even if students achieved better grades, would that seriously affect differently placed social, racial, and sexual groups, not to mention the social status of educators themselves? What serves as a "just" assessment of such board policies?

Dressing Gender

A woman's concern for the aestheticization of her body was seen as a sign of her unreasonableness, her potential weakness in contrast to the rationality of men. The argument for austerity in dress and the return to more neutral forms not only valorizes what is seen as characteristic of men (their rationality), but there is the possibility that an anti-fashion sentiment feeds into an already existing discourse of woman's superficiality, duplicity, and the threat that her sexuality poses to men.   —Kim Sawchuk, 1987, 68

It is young, racially privileged, middle-class males who buy into traditional characteristics of masculinity who have the least to change or give up under the uniform mandates.[9] Young, racially privileged, middle-class women may find the uniforms familiar but confusing (Barnes and Eicher 1992). The young women I interviewed were in urban settings, most of them were not middle class, and many of them were racialized into a minority identity. They said they were okay with the uniform "thang." These young women consistently expressed, "At least I won't have to worry about what I have to wear." "Now I can get up ten minutes later and know all I have to do is put on my uniform." Further inquiry revealed that the response I heard was a gendered one. The expression of relief from daily fashion decisions referred to the burden they feel of having to perform and compete for sexual attention through clothes.

Their words led me to ask, What signifiers will be substituted for messages previously delivered through clothes? How and where will gender performance and sexual orientation be staged? Will sexual availability and actual sexual performance emerge more directly without the interventions often provided by clothing symbolisms? What is to happen in the evenings and on weekends? Will what is worn on dates and at parties become an even more intense performance in sexual costume? Will wearing uniforms during the weekdays up the ante for social positioning in the evenings and on the weekends?

Consumer culture has successfully marketed Barbie dolls to a majority of American families who have female children. The Barbie message that girls have received since they were very young is that clothes convey meaning, place, and possibilities for success (Lurie 1981; Wilson 1985). Barbie, along with other dolls, including paper dolls, taught girls to "try on" roles. Central to Barbie has been her success as a heterosexual woman who could attract males (Rand 1995). It is after feminist consciousness-raising and feminist political actions that Barbie's clothes appear to have moved beyond just modeling for how to get a man. Now Barbie dolls also model for vocations and vacations. The important point is that today's young woman has seen Barbie, her accessories, and her clothes as a conveyor of social-sexual status messages. While we pause to inquire about what Mattel will do with Barbie in her consumer culture school uniform, it is already clear that accessories have become the major market for adolescent females in communities where school uniforms have been mandated. In a report in the *New York Times* on February 19, 1998, reporter William Hamilton describes through various interviews with school children in uniforms the degree to which they are anxiously working to modify and make unique their uniform fashions. Sewing in additional seams, redesigning buttons, and selecting cuff lengths are some of the uniform alterations that he mentions. In contrast, most of the young women that I interviewed who were yet to purchase—let alone wear—their school uniforms, told me that they did not intend to bother to modify their uniforms. As they saw it, they could now spend more time on their clothes on the weekends and in the evenings. To them, the school uniforms appeared as a promise that they could be more neutral in gender while they were at school.

Even if they could escape the marketing of accessories and the pressure to compete for the attention of young men while at school, could they or we expect to see an improved condition for the liberation and equal opportunity for young women? Even if we were not aware of what is already happening in other communities where uniforms have been in place for a while, would we expect the promise of the neutralization of gender to truly represent an improved condition for the liberation and equal opportunity for all young women? Might we notice that this policy represents a major patriarchal reinstitution of anti-feminine-associated values? Ironically, while being expected to cover up or deemphasize matters of their demeaned gender identity, these young women were going to be studying a gendered—but disguised as objective—masculinist-patriarchal-heterosexist and racialized school curriculum.

I wish to suggest, as one who claims voice as *a* feminist and *a* queer, that in the effort by school boards to neutralize the clothing displays of female children and to de-sex the clothing displays of nonheterosexually inclined and differently gendered children there is a denial of the historical and individual conditions of each one of us. As Shane Phelan suggests, it is time for contemporary political theorists (and I assume political activists) to examine how expressive activity can itself be political activity and how sexual minorities, in particular, may need to move away from using the Fourteenth Amendment's promise of protecting persons and rely more heavily on the First Amendment's prospect for protecting our expressive activity (Currah 1997, 247).[10]

Add to that Jane Roland Martin's concern in *Reclaiming a Conversation*, where she notes that schools were originally designed, in the United States, for young boys and young men. Schools and their curricular emphasis taught and continue to teach patriarchal ideology and the valuing of tasks that require features of masculinity over tasks that require features of femininity and work assigned to women. As Martin explains, in its origins, coeducation in the United States only allowed females to be added to schools, but no change occurred in those schooling institutions that enhance the value placed on tasks previously assigned to women. As outsiders, girls were expected to feel fortunate and be glad to learn all the same things that boys had been taught. Boys only had to put up with the presence of these bothersome second-class citizens, and they did not have to learn about the discrimination created by patriarchal hierarchies, nor the state of oppression existing for those assigned what were considered insignificant and devalued tasks.

Many of us who concern ourselves with diversity know that patriarchal dominance has intended for us to believe that knowledge is neutral; that state-prescribed school curricula are universally needed; that fact is free of value; and that learning is free of racializing, masculinizing, and genderizing social hierarchies. I see in school uniforms an overt act of re-mystifying rationalism and its roots in patriarchy and European cultural values. By cutting off and thus denying explicit and familiar possibilities of free performance of symbolic resistance, school boards attempt to make invisible the historical features of racialized, class-based, gender-based, sexual, erotic, and cultural differences. In uniforms, diversity is disguised, made more invisible, and thus more legitimately ignored. Although teacher educators are promoting the study of diversity and multiculturalism in all the theoretical contexts of our work, the school uniform and its insidious brother the national proficiency exam are demanding that professional teachers ignore the cultural features that would serve to maximize the opportunities for success for nonwhite, nonmale, and nonprivileged students. Again the voices of the "queer" and the disenfranchised are to be silenced. Uniformity of and conformity to a system pretends now to afford opportunity, not for equal consideration or equal opportunity for success, but for *same treatment*.

Paulo Freire has tried to persuade us—and so I shall join in his message to say—that modernist models of expert and hierarchical problem-solving such as we see in school boards and government agencies are inadequate and counter to pluralistic public dialogue (Freire 1970). Problems articulated from the narrow perspectives of persons elected to school boards tend to ignore the need for diversity and genuine community dialogue. The solutions are not flowing from authentic problem-posing and dialogue within the multiple cultural frameworks of the many who are the bearers of a problem's consequences. In the matter of school uniforms, the issue is shifted from a focus on economic, racial, cultural, and gender inequities (as perpetuated by deep ideological structure) to a temporary policy of control over the image of the nation's children (Young 1990).

To look at an institution through the experiential understandings of my life as an outsider/insider and as one whose privilege and disposition have allowed me to choose not to be an invisible outsider, I bring my concerns to the dialogue about a school policy that ignores and makes invisible its consequences for the most disenfranchised. I share the sentiments of Kim Sawchuck as she announces that "postmodern thought realizes the full ability of capital to capitalize on every alternative discourse, every act of charity, every emotion and sentiment. Therefore it forces one to adopt the strategy of guerrilla warfare, of insurgency, interference and destabilization, rather than the archaic model of revolution that is a part of the language of classical Marxism" (1987, 74). In sharing that sentiment I encourage other queer theorists to continue the work that must be done to prick the illusion of fairness by policy makers who serve their own power base by abusing our children.

Notes

1   I will conform to using the term "school uniforms" because that is the way the school costume is referred to in the U.S. government documents. But as a matter of clarification there is in the history of costuming and fashion a differentiation made between the notions of a uniform and the concept of a work costume. The point of the uniform has typically been to create a total feel of uniformity and "oneness" of common purpose, that is, a military unit or a high school band. Each person, in a uniform, needs to be seen as necessary and mutually dependent on the others in order for the group to construct a unit of operation. Work costume varies from a uniform in that it serves as an identifying symbol for a particular type of job to be performed. Its purpose is to let us know who is doing what work.

    A work costume facilitates a work ethic and a sense of job identity. School costumes are meant to tell us that this young person is attending a school and often by the color or style of blazer, blouse, or shirt we can tell which school he or she attends. Certainly a part of costuming children for a work role is meant to encourage their dedication to the "job" they are to be performing (Joseph 1986).

2   The reference to "horse" had the connotation of a burden to bear, but it also played on the notion of a "dumb animal" who obediently provided physical services and companionship to her master upon his demand. Competition among women for the attention of men has been part of the set-up of internalized oppression for and among women.

3   I use the notion of preference, not as a substitute for sexual orientation, but rather as a reference to the particulars of erotic choice and sexual-body aesthetic attractions.

4   Space does not allow, but the topic of Junior ROTC in inner-city schools is very relevant to the school uniform issue.

5   It should be noted that the zoot suit and the Lindy (and swing dancing in general) are making a reappearance in the culture clubs around urban communities. I wonder if the openness to "school uniforms," the resistance to business suit culture, the fashion of flashy suits, and very physical partner-oriented dancing have any significant interconnections.

6   On September 1, 1998, the Ohio Supreme Court in a 5–2 decision repudiated an earlier decision by common pleas judge Linton Lewis Jr. Lewis had ruled in a school funding case that education is a fundamental right guaranteed under the Ohio Constitution and the equal protection clause. That ruling placed the state under an obligation to justify any inequities in funding. The Supreme Court's interpretation is that the state needs only to guarantee "adequate educational opportunity." Discrepancies between and among schools and school districts need

not be explained or justified unless one of the schools falls below the lowest level of "adequate funding." Under such a decision, separate need not even be equal.

7   I must credit my concerns over the matter of hope to my work with Jesse Jackson's ideas, with children in my neighborhood, and with racialized dialogues in my political community.

8   The more conformity that is demanded by the school board policies, the more subtlety of cueing may be expected from the children who feel constrained by the rules. "The first type of subtle cues is those intentionally directed toward limited audiences, for example, those used by marginal groups such as homosexuals in the days of the closet. . . . Other subtle cues are unintentional and consist of instances when we give ourselves away, for example the perpetual warfare between criminal and police. . . . Street criminals are detected by their frequent touching of trouser waistbands to reassure themselves of the presence of a revolver, a lack of shoe laces which is a carryover of prison habits, and in 1950, the wearing of sneakers then dubbed 'felony' shoes" (Joseph 1986, 52).

9   Masculinity is a feature of value related to patriarchy. Patriarchy is defined as a system in which whatever men do is more highly valued than what women do. Such a system is fluid and adapts to whatever men decide should be most important to do. It accents differences in human beings based on gender identity. Humans are systemically gendered into two sex-identified social groups, each gendered for roles and power relations. Individuals may violate their genderization and express themselves through competing gender values. When women are masculinized they are often rewarded or at least tolerated for some masculine features because that serves and perpetuates the notion that masculine is worthy of imitation. When men are feminized they are usually punished. This too is a dynamic of power and of maintaining the patriarchal value system. Feminine attitudes or behaviors exhibited by men are challenged because they are tied to same-sex sexual orientation that may be stigmatized behavior. Homophobia is an attitude or behavior that deters or intends to deter an individual from resisting full participation in patriarchal values and reproductive strategies by engaging in same-sex activity.

10   Currah cites Shane Phelan from remarks she made in the March 1995 meeting of the Western Political Science Association in Portland, Oregon.

Works Cited

Barnes, Ruth and Joanne B. Eicher. 1992. *Dress and gender: Making and meaning in cultural contexts.* Oxford: Berg Publishing.

Behling, Dorothy. 1994. School uniforms and person perception. *Perceptual and Motor Skills* 79: 723-729.

Brackett, Elizabeth. 1996. Uniform look. A transcript of *The News Hour with Jim Lehrer,* April 17. http://www.pbs.org/newshour/bb/education/uniform_4-17.html

Currah, Paisley. 1997. Politics, practices, publics: Identity and queer rights. In *Playing with fire,* edited by Shane Phelan. New York: Routledge.

Ferguson, Kathy. 1984. *The feminist case against bureaucracy.* Philadelphia: Temple University Press.

Flugel, John C. 1950. *The psychology of clothes.* London: Hogarth Press.

Freire, Paulo. 1970. *Pedagogy of the oppressed.* New York: Herder and Herden.

Glynn, Prudence. 1982. *Skin to skin.* New York: Oxford University Press.

Hamilton, William L. 1998. The school uniform as fashion statement. *The New York Times,* February 19, A19.

hooks, bell. 1989. *Talking back.* Boston: South End Press.

Joseph, Nathan. 1986. *Uniforms and nonuniforms.* New York: Greenwood Press.

LaPoint, Velma, Lillian O. Holloman, and Sylvia I. Alleyne. 1992. *NASSP Bulletin* October, 20-26.

Lurie, Alison. 1981. *The language of clothes.* New York: Random House.

Martin, Jane Roland. 1985. *Reclaiming a conversation.* New Haven: Yale University Press.

Rand, Erica. 1995. *Barbie's queer accessories.* Durham, N.C.: Duke University Press.

Sawchuk, Kim. 1987. A tale of inscription/fashion statements. In *Body invaders: Panic sex in America,* edited by Arthur and Marilouise Kroker. Montreal: New World Perspectives.

Simmel, Georg. 1904. Fashion. *The International Quarterly* 10: 130–55.

Steele, Valerie. 1985. *Fashion and eroticism: Ideals of feminine beauty from the Victorian era to the jazz age.* New York: Oxford University Press.

United States Department of Education. 1996. *Manual on school uniforms.* Government document on Internet: http://www.ed.gov/updates/uniforms.html

Walker, Alice. 1995. The revenge of Hannah Kemhuff. In *Skin deep: Black women and white women write about race,* edited by Marita Golden and Susan Richards Shreve. New York: Doubleday.

Wilson, Elizabeth. 1985. *Adorned in dreams: Fashion and modernity.* Berkeley: University of California Press.

Young, Iris. 1990. *Justice and the politics of difference.* Princeton, N.J.: Princeton University Press.

Chapter 11

Choosing Alternatives to the Well of Loneliness

Rob Linné

I picked up *Rubyfruit Jungle* from a friend in 1973 and felt the world shift around me. Rita Mae Brown wasn't just a lesbian novelist, and her book wasn't just a reassuring romance. Molly Bolt was a completely new way to imagine myself. Goddamn and Hello, I shouted, and went home to reinvent my imagination again.
                                                                —Dorothy Allison

Scratch the surface of most coming out narratives and you'll find a story about literacy, about learning how to read between the lines. Many lesbians and gays tell stories of hearing something in a film or reading something in a book that piqued their early interests in things queer. Such thoughts or ideas tend to set the proto-dyke or fag off on a search for other texts or images that might tell her or him more about what queerness is and if it may be possible to embrace the idea rather than always running away from it. For many, the first reading of a queer book or film marks a pivotal turning point in their life histories. Queer fictional characters are the first gays many people come to "know" and they serve as important role models and guides to new ways of being. Books, films, or other media become gateways through which individuals with queer desires enter the social spaces of queer life and culture.

> I couldn't believe my eyes when I read the back cover. The blurb shouted out to me: "A gay coming-of-age tale for the 80's." I had to have the book, but I couldn't let any one see me buy it in my town, so I stuffed it in my jacket and walked out. I became a thief that day which I'm not that proud of, but it enabled me to become a fag later that summer.[1]
>   I first saw the film Personal Best on cable. When the two women actually kissed I felt like this movie was made for me. I watched it every other time it came on HBO when my parents weren't around.

I learned how to live as a Chicano from my family and everybody on my block. I didn't need a how-to book. But I didn't know any out jotos in the neighborhood so I learned how to be gay by watching Torch Song Trilogy over and over before heading to the library in downtown Laredo.

Even in the post-Ellen era queer representations remain difficult to find, usually hidden beyond the margins of mainstream sensibilities and off limits to young people. Although the typical 16-year-old is daily bombarded with images of straight sexuality—on television, in films, inside teen magazines, on billboards, and in adolescent literature—he or she has to make an effort to catch a glimpse of queer sexuality in the mainstream media and arts. Realistic, positive queer images are even more difficult to find. When young people do find texts that include queer characters, too often the plots or characterizations only reproduce limiting or negative stereotypes. Mainstream film representations often portray queer characters as either dangerous predators or ineffectual victims (Russo 1987). Gay characters on television are usually relegated to the comedic foil of the straight man at best, the outrageous clown at worst (Hemphill 1995). The rare young adult novel that makes it onto the shelves at the suburban Barnes & Noble is likely to reproduce stereotypes or negative images as well.

Writers and publishers of young adult literature *problem novels* seem to have a difficult time resolving the "problem" of what to do with young queer characters. Often they just kill them.

I wanted Tom and Ward to love each other, to live happily ever after, and that was the way I ended it. But the publishers would not let me do this. In their words, this would be showing a homosexual relationship as a happy ending and this might be dangerous to young people teetering on the brink. One editor wanted me to kill Tom in a car accident! At least I held out for friendship at the end, one which might or might not develop into something more, depending on the reader's imagination.   —Lynn Hall, author of adolescent novel *Sticks and Stones*

Whenever a young person experiments with same-sex love or takes the first steps toward coming out in a young adult novel I'm reading, I hear the faint sounds of the ominous music that cues a movie audience when somebody is about to die. For example, when Barry makes Hal promise, "If I die first you dance on my grave" in the seminal young adult novel *Dance on My Grave* (1982), the compact turns into a self-fulfilling prophecy as Barry, Hal's first love, does indeed die in a motorcycle crash. The plot of *Happy Endings Are All Alike* (1978) seems to be heading toward a romantic climax for the protagonists Janet and Peggy, yet Janet worries about their situation. "It always seems as if when something great happens, then something lousy happens soon after." Her intuition proves prescient as violence soon disrupts the emerging relationship of yet another would-be queer couple in a young adult novel. Cart's (1997) survey of this subgenre in adolescent literature outlines the disturbing trend of young gay characters being punished with violence and even death. The first four gay-themed young adult novels to be published killed either the gay protagonist or the person he or she loved, usually in a car accident. Over the twenty years since these early novels, the death tolls have continued to rise; only the means of death have changed. Current plots include more suicides and AIDS deaths than car or motorcycle deaths. But the message remains the same: If you try gay sex something very scary may happen to you.

If the young gay characters manage to survive, they often seem destined to futures of loneliness and sadness. Young adult novels tend to leave gay protagonists alone and isolated at the end of the story, thus reinforcing the image of queer as helpless victim. Although rejection and isolation background many queer life stories, the river of pathos running through most gay-themed adolescent novels suggests that a life of desperation is all that awaits fags and dykes. Reconnecting with families of origin, reconfiguring home cultures, or completely reinventing the concept of family are not presented as options in most coming of age/coming out books.

> I was excited to find The Well of Loneliness, but after I finished it I felt a little queasy. Did I really want to go there?
>   Tommy Stands Alone was an exhilarating read for me; mostly it scared me though. I thought to myself, "Fuck that noise," and jumped back into the closet for another year or so.

Another strategy writers and publishers use to handle the "dangerous" topic of queers in adolescent books is to obscure queer sexuality. Since Judy Blume's *Forever* was published in 1975, young adult novels have been anything but reticent to explore youthful sexuality and other previously taboo topics. Young people can now find more explicitly sexual materials in the fiction section of their school libraries than they can on the average night of cable television. However, queer sexuality remains puritanically concealed in most young adult novels. When queer sexuality *is* hinted at, the trope of the adolescent homosexual "incident" or "experiment" is used to ensure that the possibility of heterosexuality is never absent.

Fuoss (1994) contends that the *containment* of homosexuality as an isolatable sexual behavior maintains the notion that it can be managed, policed, and ultimately reversed. Fuoss's survey of the limited instances of same-sex intimacy in adolescent literature indicates that most are portrayed as isolated incidences caused by external exigencies rather than interiorized queer desires. For example, in Donovan's *I'll Get There, It Better Be Worth the Trip* (1969), the sexual incident between the two boys follows closely after life transitions leave both boys feeling extremely lonely and needy. The sexualities of the characters remain ambiguous, presumably just "phases" they have struggled through, or "choices" they reconsider by the end of the novel. In the thirteen texts Fuoss examines, he traces the trajectory of sexual identity that twenty-one "sexually suspect" characters follow. Of the twenty-one characters who either question their sexuality, engage in a homosexual act, or claim a gay identity, only eleven remain self-identified gay characters at the end of their respective novels. This trope presumably diffuses homophobic tensions in the readers by intimating that a return to "normalcy" is always possible.

> *I had just about convinced my older sister that my love for Eloy was serious, not just a teen infatuation. But after reading* The Man Without a Face, *I began to question myself. Maybe I should just try harder to be more straight.*

A rule publishers of young adult literature attempt to enforce when producing texts with gay voices is the *mainstreaming* of queer characters. While the demographics of young adult fiction in general do not match proportionally with the ethnic or class demographics of America, the casts of gay-friendly young adult books tend to be overwhelmingly monocultural—White, middle class, suburban, and male. Jenkins's (1993) content analysis of sixty young adult books with gay characters found only *three* that portray people of color, all of them African Americans. Five of the sixty include working-class protagonists. Only sixteen of sixty novels portray lesbians while forty-four portray gay males. This trend grew more pronounced over the years as 39 percent of the novels written before 1984 included lesbian characters, while only 14 percent included gay females after 1984. Gender role-playing is enforced as well. Many writers for adolescent audiences seem to go out of their way to show gay male characters participating in "male activities" like hockey or auto repair. Writers also highlight the feminine sides of their gay female characters. While there is a multiplicity of gendered stances gay people choose for themselves in real life—some gays are accomplished athletes, others are talented artists—the insistence that gays in fiction conform to strict gender roles seems to be more a symptom of homophobia in the publishing industry than an effort to reduce stereotypes of gays as femmes or butches.

> I'm sorry but I just didn't see myself in the lily-white prep girls of Nancy on My Mind. When a girlfriend finally passed me a copy of The Color Purple, I wore the pages out. Shug Avery is my diva.

Bruner (1986) contends that "the function of literature as art is to open us to dilemmas, to the hypothetical, to the range of possible worlds that a text can refer to" (159). Young adult literature that includes queer characters can inspire young people to see other ways of acting in the world than the straight and narrow. However, young adult novels that limit the range of experiences and characterizations of gay people to a few tired clichés do not expand the view of sexual identities far enough and may in fact simply reproduce old stereotypes and fears. Teachers and librarians who work to include gay voices in their curricula and on their bookshelves need to scrutinize the gay-themed texts they choose for their students in order to offer the young people in their schools a realistic, wide-ranging view of queers and queer culture. I suggest educators pay special attention in choosing (1) books that illustrate gay empowerment as well as gay victimization; (2) stories that openly explore gay sexuality rather than hiding it as something shameful; and (3) novels that include a multiplicity of character types. Fortunately, a few current writers and publishers are breaking free of the old rules regarding gays in fiction and are creating interesting and surprising gay characters and queer story lines.

> "Tito!" Alex screamed. He ran forward as a line of flames licked across the bus roof like a snaking, red tongue. The peeling paint around the rusty stovepipe began to smoke. Alex pounded on the locked door, but it wouldn't budge, "Tito! Ken! Are you in there?" The air was suddenly too hot and thick to breathe. The fire lit the chaparral all around him, blackening it within seconds. "Tito!" Alex called again. The back of the bus erupted in flames. Alex grabbed Tito's T-shirt from the line and held it over his nose and mouth, fubbing his singed face. He fled with the fire at his back, not daring to turn around for fear the sight of it would make him fall into its path. He repeated Tito's name with every pounding step. Tito couldn't die. Not now.
> —From Blue Coyote

At this point in the suspenseful narrative of Blue Coyote (1997), Tito appears to be another queer kid suffering a violent death at the hands of straight writers and publishers, and the odds of escaping death are not very good for his "questioning" friend Alex either. However, both survive the disaster and seem to thrive in the aftermath of both the brush fire and their respective coming out ordeals. The plot and characterizations the author offers readers of this book exemplify the emerging trend in adolescent fiction to foreground the other side of queer victimization: queer empowerment. Alex and Tito do face hardships while navigating new terrain as young gays—Tito is physically assaulted by his father and kicked out of his home—but the two surfing buddies live to catch more waves together. Both characters are in fact strengthened by the rites of coming out, Alex especially. As a closeted teen, Alex is unsure of himself and a loner at school. After he defines himself as queer, he gains a sense of clarity and confidence in his ability to write his own life story. Alex takes control of his life and demonstrates his new independence by tattooing a blue coyote on his shoulder. The coyote symbolizes to the young man his newly acquired sense of freedom and wisdom.

Alex's journey to self-actualization, however, is not an individualistic one. Countering the many young adult novels that intimate gay youth are on their own, *Blue Coyote* illustrates how young lesbians and gays can seek out others to help with the project of constructing sexual identity. Tito and Alex depend on each other as well as other gays (especially the older and wiser Jimbo), other surfers, gay-hearted straights, and those family members who continue to support and love them.

> It wasn't until I was on the plane again, flying back to the Hamptons, that I began to look at things in another light. Seeing Alex confirmed what I'd suspected all along: I hadn't undergone some miraculous change. What had happened to me could only have happened with Huguette, could only have come about as it did. We were "firsts" for each other, without ever intending to be. The big difference was, I had Alex in my life and she had no one.   —From *"Hello," I Lied*

M. E. Kerr's *"Hello," I Lied* (1997) subverts the containment of gay identities by portraying a young male character who is quite happy with his sexuality despite some of the problems, such as gay-bashing, he must endure. Lang's brief romance with a young female friend represents a heterosexual "phase" or "incident" he passes through that does not really change his strong identification as a gay male.

In *Coffee Will Make You Black*, the American Library Association's *Book of the Year* in 1994, April Sinclair tells a coming-of-age story set on Chicago's South Side during the Civil Rights movement. Jean "Stevie" Stevenson, the young protagonist, is at first more concerned with her social life than the words of Martin Luther King Jr. But with Dr. King's assassination and the riots that burn through her neighborhood, Stevie's social reality is called into question. Running parallel to Stevie's political consciousness-raising is the plot line of her sexual awakening. As these two stories play out, interesting similarities and differences become evident in the experiences of ethnic and sexual minorities. Both groups are misrepresented by inaccurate portrayals in the media and arts, yet those on the margins still search those fields for rare sightings of people like themselves. In the 1960s, seeing a Black character on television was an event in a Black household:

> Me and Mama were all quiet; all you could hear was the snapping of our beans. "Somebody colored's on TV!" Kevin yelled from the living room. "Well, I sho' hope it ain't that Stepin Fetchit fellow again," I heard Grandma say as I followed behind her and Mama.   —From *Coffee Will Make You Black*

With help from her family and community, Stevie resists White hegemonic culture. She embraces the notion that "Black is Beautiful," stops straightening her hair, and tosses out her skin bleaches. These changes are more than superficial; they reflect deep changes in the way she embraces her unique culture. Stevie also turns to others—specifically, a caring school nurse—to help reach an understanding of her sexuality. During the course of this book, and the sequel *Ain't Gonna Be the Same Fool Twice,* Stevie grows into a strong Black woman who knows the importance of relationships and community.

Complex characters like Alex, Tito, Lang, and Stevie exemplify the good choices available for young readers because their characters are realistic, they reflect the diversity of our culture, and they are allowed to be both sexual and romantic. The following list of books includes other texts that can help young people imagine myriad ways to be queer (or queerly straight) in today's world.

Note

1 Any unattributed, italicized block quotations represent ethnographic fictions similar to those William Tierney (1997) employs in *Academic Outlaws: Queer Theory and Cultural Studies in the Academy*. These fictions are based on narrative research currently in progress as well as informal observations made volunteering at Out Youth Austin.

A Selected List of Further Readings

Books

Bauer, Marion, ed. *Am I blue? Coming out from the silence.* HarperCollins, 1994. Anthology of short stories by popular young adult authors.

Block, Francesca. *Weetzie Bat.* Harper & Row, 1989. A unique collage of a novel suitable for reluctant readers; incorporates gay characters easily into the milieu.

Block, Francesca. *Baby be bop.* HarperCollins, 1995. A continuation of the Weetzie Bat series. A light-hearted gay romance told in Block's fascinating Southern California magical realist style.

Block, Francesca. *Girl goddess #9.* Joanna Cotler Books, 1996. An engaging collection of short stories about nine fierce *girl goddesses*— some straight, some gay.

Chambers, Aidan. *Dance on my grave.* Harper & Row, 1982. A variety of literary styles tell a powerful story surrounding the relationship between two young men. Despite the clichéd death of one of the lovers, this is a classic.

Chase, Clifford, ed. *Queer 13: Lesbian and gay writers recall seventh grade.* William Morrow and Company, 1999. Many of the fashions have come back around—bell bottoms and disco beats—while many of the dynamics of junior never changed much, from sadistic gym teachers to unrequited first loves.

Crutcher, Chris. *Ironman.* Greenwillow, 1995. Another engaging novel by Crutcher set in the world of high school jocks with a subplot revolving around the main character's discovery that his coach is gay.

Eichberg, Rob. *Coming out: An act of love.* Dutton, 1990. Coming out letters from young people, as well as letters from parents.

Flagg, Fannie. *Fried green tomatoes at the Whistle Stop Café.* McGraw Hill, 1987. A humorous southern gothic with lesbian subtext.

Garden, Nancy. *Annie on my mind.* Farrar Straus & Giroux, 1982. Perhaps the best-known young adult book with lesbian protagonists.

Garden, Nancy. *Lark in the morning.* Farrar Straus & Giroux, 1991. A schoolgirl assists two young runaways.

Heron, Ann, ed. *Two teenagers in twenty: Writings by gay and lesbian youth.* Alyson Publications, 1994. Brief personal narratives written by gay youth.

Kerr, M. E. *Deliver us from Evie.* HarperCollins, 1994. A farm family struggles to understand their colorful daughter.

Ketchum, Liza. *Blue coyote.* Simon & Schuster, 1997. Ketchum explains the impetus for this sequel to her best-seller: "I wrote *Blue Coyote* in response to readers of *Twelve Days in August,* who asked: 'What about Alex? When will you tell his story?'"

Manrique, Jaime. *Latin moon in Manhattan.* St. Martin's Press, 1992. A young writer struggling in New York City cannot escape his Latino heritage.

Murrow, Liza. *Twelve days in August.* Holiday House, 1993. A soccer player questions his homophobia when a new member of his team is mistreated.

Simon, Ken. *Pizza face: Or the hero of suburbia.* Grove Weidenfeld, 1991. Most adolescents can relate to this protagonist and his pain of growing up unpopular.

Singer, Bennett, ed. *Growing up gay/growing up lesbian: A literary anthology.* New Press, 1994. Includes a wide range of literary styles, from the polished prose of James Baldwin to the street rap of The Disposable Heroes of HipHoprisy.

Ure, Jean. *The other side of the fence.* Delacorte, 1986. Two runaways— a straight girl and a gay boy—are changed by life on the streets.

Van Dijk, Lutz. *Damned strong love.* Henry Holt & Company, 1995. True story about a Polish adolescent and his lover who is a soldier in the occupying German forces.

Walker, Alice. *The color purple.* Pocket Books, 1982. Historic fiction set in a southern Black community.

Walker, Kate. *Peter.* Houghton Mifflin, 1993. An Australian teen struggles with his peer group's construction of maleness.

Walker, Paul Robert. *The method*. Harcourt Brace, 1990. A humorous "drama" set in an intensive acting class; focused on a straight boy but features a number of interestingly drawn gay characters and a tender coming out scene.

Wielder, Diana. *Bad boy*. Delacorte Press, 1992. A hockey league provides the backdrop for an examination of friendship and homophobia.

Wong, Norman. *Cultural revolutions*. Persea Books, 1994. Eleven loosely linked stories about a Chinese American family in Honolulu; centered on the "number one son" and his growing awareness that he is a *mahoo*.

Woodson, Jacqueline. *The house you pass on the way*. Delacorte, 1997. Staggerlee is a young African American girl who thinks she may have found "someone to whisper her life to" in her new streetwise friend.

Magazines

Oasis. (http://www.oasismag.com/) A deftly produced online zine written for and about gay youth.

Popcorn Q. (www.planetout.com/pno/kiosk/popcornq) A place to explore queers on film.

Queer Arts Resource. (www.queer-arts.org) An interactive Web site focused on works with queer voices.

XY. A magazine aimed at a young gay male audience that includes more cultural commentary and political edge than most teen magazines.

Films

Avnet, Jon. (Director). (1992). *Fried green tomatoes*. Based on a humorous southern gothic novel; the lesbian subtext is buried even deeper than in the novel for the film audience.

Epstein, Robert and Jeffrey Friedman. (Directors). (1995). *The celluloid closet*. A history of lesbian and gay portrayals in film that would serve well as an introduction to cultural studies in the classroom.

MacDonald, Heather. (Director). (1996). *Beautiful thing*. A coming-of-age romance set in a British housing project.

Maggenti, Maria. (Director). (1995). *The incredibly true adventures of two girls in love*. One of the few films focused on youthful lesbian love.

Works Cited

Allison, D. 1994. *Skin: Talking about sex, class, and literature.* Ithaca, NY: Firebrand Books.

Bruner, J. 1986. *Actual minds, possible worlds.* Cambridge, Mass.: Harvard University Press.

Cart, M. 1997. Honoring their stories too: Literature for gay and lesbian teens. *The-ALAN Review* 25, no. 1: 40–46.

Fuoss, K. 1994. A portrait of the adolescent as a young gay: The politics of male homosexuality in young adult fiction. In *Queer words, queer images: Communication and the construction of homosexuality,* edited by R. Ringer. New York: Routledge.

Hemphill, E. 1995. In living color: Toms, coons, mammies, faggots, and bucks. In *Out in culture: Gay, lesbian, and queer essays on popular culture,* edited by C. Creekmur and A. Doty. Durham, N.C.: Duke University Press.

Jenkins, C. 1993. Young adult novels with gay/lesbian characters and themes 1969-1992: A historical reading of content, gender, and narrative distance. *Journal of Youth Services in the Library* 7: 43–45.

Russo, V. 1987. *The celluloid closet: Homosexuality in the movies.* New York: Harper & Row.

Tierney, W. G. 1997. *Academic outlaws: Queer theory and cultural studies in the academy.* Thousand Oaks, CA: Sage Publications.

Chapter 12

Nurturing Images, Whispering Walls: Identity Intersections and Empowerment in the Academic Workplace

Townsand Price-Spratlen

> The season was always Christmas with you there and . . . you did not neglect to bring at least *three gifts*. You gave me a *language* to dwell in, a gift so perfect it seems my own invention. The second gift was your *courage*, [that] of one who could go as a stranger in the village and transform the distances between people into intimacy with the whole world. The third gift was . . . your *tenderness*—a tenderness so delicate I thought it could not last, but last it did and envelop me it did.
> —Toni Morrison, "Life in His Language"

Three gifts. Language. Courage. Tenderness. With these three terms, Toni Morrison emphasizes the gifts she gained from James Baldwin's writings. In doing so, she succinctly presents three critical components of a healthy learning environment, one that consistently and proactively contributes to the dialectics between knowledge and ignorance and between public and private spaces. This is true whether describing (as she is) a reader's relationship with an author, a teacher's relationship with students in a classroom, or any of the many other formal and informal learning environments that exist. Current discussions on pedagogy, social science, and the nature of subjective identity tend to overlook the academic workplace as a central site of identity reification (Miller and Rose 1995). One such semi-formal, semi-private workplace that is too often minimized is the office of a college professor. To help broaden our understandings of this particular site, what follows is a visual autoethnography of my academic workplace.

Images and Interaction

A faculty member's office is a political space of multiple dialectics. It is a space where, for both the occupant and visitors, the interplay of knowledge and ignorance is ongoing, with the latter (hopefully) decreasing as the former gradually grows. At a public university, a faculty office is a workspace indirectly owned by state government, that is, a public space. It is also a somewhat private space that can be adorned as the (temporary) resident chooses, adhering to the boundaries of a moral sensitivity and the use of "good taste." The images chosen, those of task and triumph, provide visitors to the office with a visual language of various representations of the occupant's identity. These identity representations can then be considered and responded to, or ignored if the visitor so chooses. These academic workplace images are often a part of the process of "negotiating legacies," or "learning the lessons of history by seeking to understand the contemporary and historical contexts and contributions of [one's] ancestors" (Price-Spratlen 1996, 217). Such images pierce the dialectic of oppression and the freedom of self-representation. They contribute to a visual language, conveying the ideas and ancestral idea makers of greatest importance. They respond to the demand that "what is most important to me must be spoken, made verbal and shared, even at the risk of having it bruised or misunderstood" (Lorde 1984, 40).

Ancestral images teach a great deal. They affirm courage, challenge ignorance, and provide examples of excellence that can be used as the reference points their lives provide. They serve as constant reminders of the need to resist oppressive forces, be they just outside one's door, or half a world away. As a gay scholar of African descent, I have the opportunity to negotiate legacies in a public way, including exhibiting on my office walls a set of ancestral images I value most. The relative (and often contradictory) "liberalism" within academia allows me a unique platform of visibility. True to the dialectic of oppression and the (partial) freedom of self-representation, I offer a visibility that openly presents affirming lesbian and gay images, African-descended images, working-class images, and the multiple identity intersections they combine to provide as a state employee in one of the 80 percent of states that "allow employers to fire employees simply because they are gay, lesbian, or bisexual" (Martin 1998, 7).

This platform is quite distinct from virtually any other workplace, where such visible representation of identity risks both overt and covert rejections, both individual and institutional marginalization. Consistent with the rich dialectic of academic liberalism, such risks of representation exist within academia as well. But the consequences of proactively choosing visibility are likely somewhat reduced. Acting on visibility, these ancestral images of a legacy's negotiation illustrate both singular dimensions of identity (for example, race, gender, sexuality), as well as lived identity intersections (for example, working-class lesbians of African descent). The very visibility of these lived intersections helps to challenge oppressive stigmas associated with them. Depending on what images a visitor focuses on, through the visual language of my office wall images, I can effectively use Baldwin's three gifts of language, courage, and tenderness identified by Morrison. Images of task and triumph affirm excellence. They can help (me and) my office visitors to continue striving, contributing our own individual examples of excellence to a collective achievement of broadened social justice, both in the workplace and beyond it.

The triumphant images of greatest meaning extend from each of the singular dimensions of my identity. With each individual image I hope to proactively contribute to the interplay of knowledge and ignorance, within myself and within visitors to my office as well. This interplay of knowledge and ignorance rests at the foundation of any learning environment, including that of higher education. In the academic workplace as elsewhere, images of task and triumph "can be used to teach students how knowledge is constructed and how to create their own interpretations" (Banks 1996, 340) of knowledge to be most fruitful for their own growth. These images provide diverse lessons of how knowledge, once constructed, can help others to grow and move them toward a place of valuing difference, from ignorance to awareness to tolerance and beyond. As Audre Lorde reminded us, "Difference must be not merely tolerated, but seen as a fund of necessary polarities between which our creativity can spark" (Lorde 1984, 11).

Valuing difference is a crucial aspect within my discipline of sociology. This is especially true since the two stems of the term 'sociology,' *socius* (Latin) and *logos* (Greek) literally mean the study of the processes of companionship (Abercrombie, Hill, and Turner 1988). The dynamics of transforming difference into companionship, as well as those dynamics which prevent this from occurring, can be illustrated in these images of task and triumph, these images of individual and collective excellence.

Selecting and presenting these images with care is a part of an essential task of educators: to help move students (as we move ourselves) toward what Paulo Freire (1970) calls "the practice of freedom," or the means by which people discover how to participate in the transformation of their world. Consistent with the very definition of my discipline, three such images adorning my office walls critique the dynamics of companionship and help to illustrate a few among the many possible illustrations of a sociological practice of freedom.

Nurturing Resistance

It is entitled "pre-Kindergarten Kisses." Displaying this picture recognizes the potential for affirming a queer sensibility in the mind's eye of African American and other children. In the picture two young males of African descent are embracing each other shoulder to shoulder as they smile lovingly, looking into the other's eyes. They are perhaps five or six years old and share the kinds of smiles that speak to an innocence that few, if any, persons other than children can possess. It is an innocence that lies just behind the veil of masculinities I have come to know so well.

This nurturing image is on the office wall directly in front of my desk. It hangs at eye level, so that virtually any time I look up from the task at hand it is the first image I see. The picture gives me a gentle reminder of the simple ways I can be "out" at work. It reminds me that silence will not protect me, as Audre Lorde emphasized for us all. It reminds me "that a life of resistance is at once spiritual, militantly political, and irrepressibly intimate in its sense of collective nurturing" (Browning 1993, 121). This collective nurturing can occur one picture, one image at a time.

When I sit at my desk, with "Kisses" in front of me, many other pictures hang on the wall behind me. Collectively they "got my back," as the saying goes (that is, they provide a protective sensibility, sheltering me from the hurts the academic workplace may sometimes impose). The most precious among these images behind me are two pictures at the top of the wall: of Audre Lorde and Marlon Riggs. The Audre Lorde picture is an enlarged photo of her cautious grin from the cover of *Sister Outsider* (1984). The picture of Marlon Riggs's warm, smiling face is on an advertising leaflet for California Newsreel's important film, *I Shall Not Be Removed: The Life of Marlon Riggs* (Everett 1996). These two ancestors' lives were marked by such profound excellence that I often feel unworthy of displaying them. And that feeling of unworthiness, one dimension of the process of negotiating legacies referred to earlier—coupled with the necessity to do with passion and purpose in order to affirm the powers of the legacy left by them—helps motivate my movement from one day into the next.

Taken together, these two pictures help nurture a progressive resistance within myself and within all others who might look upon them. The picture of Marlon Riggs reminds me of his spiritually centered essay "Letters to the Dead" (Riggs 1993). The "Letters," like the pictures, emphasize that the choices resting before us, the living, are a part of a continuing dialogue with our ancestors. It is an ever-present dialogue that each observer enters into. Exhibiting their pictures acknowledges the importance of urgently striving to empower myself, to connect my personal power to broader expressions of communal empowerment, and, by doing so, encourage others to do the same. The goal of empowerment, of nurturing proactive resistance, is the self-realization of each individual's own well-being and potential for changing themselves, their families, and their communities (Lorde 1984; Wilson 1996). These symbolic images of progressive change contribute to the transformative education referred to earlier, where education—including the office walls of a faculty member—becomes the "practice of freedom," the means by which men and women discover how to participate in the transformation of their world (Freire 1970).

Resting daily within what bell hooks and others have described as the power of the gaze cast by this very special pair of eyes, with Audre Lorde's picture, I again hear a crucial quote from her 1989 lecture at UCLA: "One thing I wish to leave behind when I leave this room today, is a knowledge and a sense of urgency of using who you are, in the service of what you believe. [My] poetry calls for an answer from each of you in your lives." Her picture, along with Marlon's, will forever possess the same demand. One of my responsibilities in participating in the practice of freedom that education sometimes provides is to convey this sentiment to myself and to all those who visit my office and look upon my office walls. And feeling that demand tap me on the shoulder each workday morning is an immense blessing, a pleasant reminder of the tasks within the politics of education that lie before me on any given day.

Workplace Images and "Outness"

These three pictures, "Pre-Kindergarten Kisses," Audre Lorde, and Marlon Riggs, along with the many others that adorn my walls, provide me with another means by which I can participate in "the politics of education [that includes] focusing and stimulating a desire in a potential [visitor] to learn more" (Freire 1985, 1). These images are a part of a larger process, or the praxis of "negotiating legacies [that is], learning the lessons of history by seeking to understand the contemporary and historical contexts and contributions of our ancestors" (Price-Spratlen 1996, 217). This praxis is perhaps most personal in the choices I make regarding representation of myself in my place of work and in the other environments that matter most to me. These representations are one step of that praxis of the politics of education; a step firmly rooted in ensuring that my work space affirms my life design and life desire, celebrating expressions of my best (possible) self as shown in the efforts of cherished ancestors.

Openly combining with more "moderate" images of family and loved ones, these pictures help solidify my connection to intimate representations that are a part of any substantive dialogue of living history. In other words, these pictures are historical images that say to me and all who look at them, "It is possible to act *right now*, by embracing vulnerability, embracing the demand for humility, and to continue achieving all the while. I did, and you can, too." Addressing this theme, bell hooks (hooks and West 1991, 4) has suggested that "friendship . . . makes certain forms of vulnerability possible . . . [and] vulnerability [is] one of the conditions for intimacy." "Kisses" celebrates that intimacy of friendship as being real between two young males of African descent. It connects me to the free-flowing childhood intimacies that lie within us all. Consistent with the dialectic of knowledge and ignorance, such an image openly challenges a racialized and gendered demonization, and makes "clear that the idea [many African American men] have of ourselves is drastically different from the images propagated and promoted by nineteenth-century Europe and [much of] twentieth-century America" (Wilson 1995, xii). The images of Lorde and Riggs affirm a fictive friendship and a lived intimacy that I have with them both, a connection of kindness and caring that I wish I had been blessed to share in while they were living.

In truth, I shared time with Marlon only twice, and never had the pleasure and honor of meeting Audre Lorde. But our fictive friendships remain ever-real to me, made more real each time I am blessed to look into their eyes, and to learn from their words and deeds, even if only in a picture. Visitors to my office are in a position to do the same. Although "it is very hard for academics who are often isolated to accept placing themselves in roles where they might be emotionally vulnerable" (hooks and West 1991, 4), these pictures make both my work-related, and non-work-related vulnerabilities far less caustic, far more negotiable, and bathe me in the power of the gaze.

These pictures are an attempt to show respect for the students, colleagues, and other individuals who visit me and share my office with me, if only for a few moments. The pictures may do so by potentially raising issues of representation for the visitors themselves. These issues of representation may instigate a dialogue with me in the moments of their visit, or with others in the future. Such a respect for the visitors in an educational environment can help to celebrate the dialectic unity between the words "teach" and "learn." This unity builds upon "a fundamental point of Marx in his third thesis on Feuerbach: 'The educator himself [sic] needs education' " (cited in Freire 1985, 159). I am in a position to learn and grow from every encounter, including those sparked by the pictures, as I share in the reciprocity of teaching and learning, one dialogue at a time.

These pictures are a constant affirmation of the value I place on attempting to lead a "life of resistance" (Browning 1993, 121), encouraging my office visitors to do the same, however they might define said life for themselves. Such a life extends from my desire to celebrate a reciprocity of blessing, because I know how immensely blessed I am, and how deep my sacred debt is, both to my family and to my ancestors. Blessings set duty in motion, a duty to give back more than one has been given. A duty to counter "the historical continuum of domination and servitude" (Price-Spratlen 1996, 219) that has been used to galvanize stigma and sustain abusive silences. A duty to try constantly to be spiritually and "psychologically able to experience things and each other, outside of the context of violence and exploitation" (Marcuse 1969, 25). These pictures affirm this duty, this life of resistance, because they render my office into a social space "that encourage[s] the proliferation of pleasures, desires, voices, interests, modes of individuation and democratization" (Siedman 1993, 106). This is done by visually affirming the lived intersections of race, gender, class, and sexuality, along with the other varied dimensions of both individual and collective identity. The pictures affirm these lived intersections by emphasizing the importance of, and the often dialectical link between, oppositional and affirmative representation.

Justice-Doing and the "Writings" on the Wall

Several years ago Joan Armatrading released a song entitled "Talking to the Wall." The title refers to being in a one-way dialogue "when you get no answers; just cold silence." The three pictures considered above are writings on the wall that I figuratively "speak" with on a daily basis. Pleasantly counter to the experience depicted by Armatrading, I am "talking to the wall" in a two-way dialogue: I negotiate with the written and visual legacies of Audre and Marlon, negotiate with various cultural images that constantly challenge the sustainability of intimacy between two males of African descent. These words and images provide me with affirming representations of what my best self can aspire to become as I act on "the knowledge and sense of urgency" Audre Lorde referenced in her 1989 UCLA speech, striving to contribute to empowerment and a broadened social justice in living well from one day into the next.

Any affirming representation has the potential to be in opposition to any number of things that run counter to that which is being affirmed. All three pictures, and the spiritual and intellectual dialogue they instigate for me, are an "act of resistance that is part of the decolonizing, anti-racist process" (hooks and West 1991, 5) that I attempt to contribute to using my skills and abilities. Thus, these images are at once both affirming and oppositional representations, opposing any act, notion, image, or being that exists and attempts to restrict my wholeness, my humanness, and the multiple dimensions of myself embraced by that humanness. These images are a part of the best of challenging otherness in all its forms. They are crucial links in the praxis of "justice-doing" (Goss 1993, 109) referred to earlier.

Justice-doing consists of all liberating activity that challenges human oppression and is rooted in "the resistance narrative of Jesus, His struggles, death and God's liberative practice" (Goss 1993, 110). Celebrating the legacies of sacred lesbians and gays of African descent who openly challenged invisibility and oppression contributes to "an unapologetic social space that affirms gay and lesbian experience and allows [others] to critique and critically engage the homophobia/heterosexism" (123) of the larger society.

Although these pictures are "only" visual images, they have a symbolic resonance that, however small, makes a meaningful contribution to the achievement of a broadened social justice. These images help make my office a part of that "unapologetic social space" of lesbian and gay affirmation to which Goss refers. Being bathed in the energy these images affirm is an essential part of the "decolonizing, anti-racist process" to which hooks refers. As Marlon Riggs stated in a 1990 interview, "Films don't change the world . . . but they do help [some] people understand themselves better, to help them move to take some action they might not have taken before" (Banneker 1990, 11). Hopefully, having these images on my office walls helps people understand themselves better and instigates otherwise undone actions by myself and others.

Triumphs Beyond Today

"Pre-Kindergarten Kisses." Audre Lorde. Marlon Riggs. These images are not the only images on these whispering office walls, but they are the ones I value most at the time I complete this chapter. The label "Most Valued Pictures" (MVPs) is not a constant. So were I to write this essay next year, or even next month, my MVPs likely would differ somewhat. This movement is an affirmation of blessing, a recognition of the diversity of nurturing images that can contribute to the galvanization of homeplace, a merging of safe and sacred spaces, within the environments in which I teach, write, and learn.

bell hooks (in hooks and West 1991, 16–17) has suggested that

> In our liberatory pedagogy, we must teach [students] to understand that struggle is process, that one moves from circumstances of difficulty and pain to awareness, joy, fulfillment. That struggle to be critically conscious can be that movement which takes you to another level, that lifts you up, that makes you feel better. You feel good, you feel your life has meaning and purpose.

Typically, I am in my office six days a week, doing the tasks necessary to continue my employment in academia and at my current institution. I am also striving to achieve some measure of "success" consistent with the urgency in the use of knowledge emphasized in Lorde's 1989 UCLA speech. By doing so, I hope to make my own individual contribution to the collective call to action of which hooks speaks. Unfortunately, too often I fall short of this ideal. Nonetheless, these pictures of "Pre-Kindergarten Kisses," Lorde, and Riggs remind me that awareness, outness, and success form a trinity of focused passion essential to the effective, ongoing negotiation of legacies past, present, and future.

Above all else, as bell hooks stated in paraphrasing Toni Morrison, these images "give voice to the 'unspeakable' because there are so many aspects of Black life that we talk about in private that we don't really find talked about in books or essays anywhere" (hooks and West 1991, 5). I offer this essay toward our continuing efforts to let the previously unspeakable loudly and proactively shout and, by doing so, vaporize restrictive silences. I am thankful to be one among the many who will continue growing from the gifts of a legacy; gifts of language, of courage, of tenderness. These gifts constantly inform me, as I "talk" with the wall(s) while trying to move forward, acting on the ever-present duty that my many blessings warmly, kindly, impose.

Works Cited

Abercrombie, Nicholas, Stephen Hill, and Bryan S. Turner. 1988. *The Penguin dictionary of sociology*. London: Penguin Books.

Banks, James A. 1996. Transformative knowledge, curriculum reform, and action. In *Multicultural education, transformative knowledge and action: Historical and contemporary perspectives*, edited by James A. Banks. New York: Teachers College Press.

Banneker, Revon Kyle. 1990. Marlon Riggs untied: The BLK interview. *BLK* 2, no. 4: 10–19.

Browning, Frank. 1993. *The culture of desire: Paradox and perversity in gay lives today*. New York: Crown.

Everett, Karen. (Producer, Director). 1996. *I shall not be removed: The life of Marlon Riggs* [Film]. San Francisco: California Newsreel.

Freire, Paulo. 1970. *Pedagogy of the oppressed*. New York: Seabury Press.

——— 1985. *The Politics of education: Culture, power and liberation*. South Hadley, Mass.: Bergin & Garvey.

Goss, Robert. 1993. *Jesus acted up: A gay and lesbian manifesto*. New York: HarperCollins.

hooks, bell and Cornel West. 1991. *Breaking bread: Insurgent black intellectual life*. Boston: South End Press.

Lorde, Audre. 1984. *Sister outsider*. Freedom, Calif.: The Crossing Press.

——— 1989. Speech given as a part of the 20th anniversary celebration of the Center for African American Studies, University of California at Los Angeles, March 17, 1989.

Marcuse, Herbert. 1969. *An essay on liberation*. Boston: Beacon Press.

Martin, Phil. 1998. "Out" of work: "Labor" day is a joke for gay people. *Columbus Alive* 15: 7.

Miller, Peter and Nikolas Rose. 1995. Production, identity, and democracy. *Theory and Society* 24: 427–67.

Morrison, Toni. 1989. Life in his language. In *James Baldwin: The legacy*, edited by Quincy Troupe. New York: Simon & Schuster.

Price-Spratlen, Townsand. 1996. Negotiating legacies: Audre Lorde, W. E. B. DuBois, Marlon Riggs and Me. *Harvard Educational Review* 62: 216–30.

Riggs, Marlon. 1993. Letters to the dead. In *Sojourner: Black gay voices in the age of AIDS*, edited by B. Michael Hunter. New York: Other Countries Press.

Siedman, Steven. 1993. Identity and politics in a "postmodern" gay culture: Some historical and conceptual notes. In *Fear of a queer planet: Queer politics and social theory*, edited by Michael Warner. Minneapolis: University of Minnesota Press.

Wilson, August. 1995. Foreword. In *Speak my name: Black men on masculinity and the American dream*, edited by Don Belton. Boston: Beacon Press.

Wilson, Patricia A. 1996. Empowerment: Community economic development from the inside out. *Urban Studies* 33: 617–30.

Contributors

Deborah P. Britzman is Professor of Education at York University in Toronto, cross-appointed to the graduate programs of Social and Political Thought, Women's Studies, and Psychology. Her area of interest is in psychoanalytic orientations to the study of education. She is author of *Lost Subjects, Contested Objects: Toward a Psychoanalytic Inquiry of Learning* (Albany: SUNY Press, 1998) and *Practice Makes Practice: A Critical Study of Learning to Teach* (Albany: SUNY Press, 1991).

Brent Davis is Associate Professor of Education at York University in Toronto. His primary research interests include mathematics education, cognitive studies, teacher education, and curriculum theory. He is author of *Teaching Mathematics: Toward a Sound Alternative* (1996).

Glorianne M. Leck is Professor of Education at Youngstown State University. She plants her feet through her relationship with Susan Savastuk. She moves among her identities as a political activist, a crone, a queer, a lesbian, a teacher, and a scholar. She invites e-mail interaction at f0036363@cc.ysu.edu.

Nancy Lesko teaches courses on curriculum, social theories, and gender in the Department of Curriculum and Teaching at Teacher's College, Columbia University. She is completing a genealogy of adolescence, *Act your age! Developing the modern, scientific adolescent.*

Rob Linné is an assistant professor at Adelphi University in New York. He teaches classes in secondary literacy and is director of a writing center at Adelphi's Soho Center. His research interests include adolescent literature and queer theory. His present area of focus is a saga of an ongoing attempt to purchase a co-op in Brooklyn.

Marla Morris is a Ph.D. candidate in curriculum theory at Louisiana State University. She has published in *Educational Theory, Teaching Education Journal, JCT: Journal of Curriculum Theorizing, Taboo: The Journal of Culture and Education, The Journal of Theta Alpha Kappa/National Honor Society for Religious Studies/Theology*. She is co-editor of *How We Work* (New York: Peter Lang) and *(Post)Modern Science Education*.

V. Darleen Opfer is an assistant professor in the Department of Educational Policy Studies at Georgia State University. She conducts research on interest group influence and the policy development process in education. Her book, *Who Governs Education? Educational Interest Group Influence in the U.S. Congress,* is in press.

William F. Pinar has served as the A. Lindsay O'Connor Professor of American Institutions at Colgate University and the Frank Talbott Professor at the University of Virginia. At present he serves as the St. Bernard Parish Alumni Endowed Professor at Louisiana State University. He is the author of *Autobiography, Politics and Sexuality.*

Townsand Price-Spratlen is currently living in Columbus, Ohio, where he is Assistant Professor of Sociology at The Ohio State University. He teaches and researches in urban sociology and is currently evaluating the relationships between location, community, and identity formation; local area context and individual quality of life; and African American community development and historical patterns of migration.

Eric Rofes has taught at Bowdoin College, UC Berkeley, and currently is Assistant Professor of Education at Humboldt State University in Arcata, California. He received his doctorate in social and cultural studies in education from UC Berkeley's Graduate School of Education. His research interests include school reform, charter schools, gay issues in schools, and block scheduling in middle schools.

Shirley R. Steinberg is an assistant professor at Adelphi University in New York. The author and editor of many books and articles, she is the mother of four plus one children and two dogs and the life-partner of a writer and Tennessee Vols fanatic. Her research areas include popular culture, youth culture and film, and whiteness studies. She considers herself a failed drag queen.

Dennis J. Sumara is Associate Professor of Education at York University in Toronto. His professional interests center around teacher education, curriculum studies, and English language arts education. He is author of *Private Readings in Public: Schooling the Literary Imagination* (1996) and coeditor of *Action Research as a Living Practice* (with Terrance Carson, 1997).

Susan Talburt is an assistant professor in the Department of Educational Policy Studies at Georgia State University in Atlanta. She is cross-appointed to the Women's Studies Institute and teaches courses in curriculum, social foundations, and women's studies. She is author of *Subject to Identity: Knowledge, Sexuality, and Academic Practices in Higher Education* (Albany: SUNY Press, 2000).

Index

COUNTERPOINTS

Studies in the Postmodern Theory of Education

General Editor
Shirley R. Steinberg

Counterpoints publishes the most compelling and imaginative books being written in education today. Grounded on the theoretical advances in criticalism, feminism, and postmodernism in the last two decades of the twentieth century, Counterpoints engages the meaning of these innovations in various forms of educational expression. Committed to the proposition that theoretical literature should be accessible to a variety of audiences, the series insists that its authors avoid esoteric and jargonistic languages that transform educational scholarship into an elite discourse for the initiated. Scholarly work matters only to the degree it affects consciousness and practice at multiple sites. Counterpoints' editorial policy is based on these principles and the ability of scholars to break new ground, to open new conversations, to go where educators have never gone before.

For additional information about this series or for the submission of manuscripts, please contact:

Shirley R. Steinberg
c/o Peter Lang Publishing, Inc.
29 Broadway, 18th floor
New York, New York 10006

To order other books in this series, please contact our Customer Service Department:

(800) 770-LANG (within the U.S.)
(212) 647-7706 (outside the U.S.)
(212) 647-7707 FAX

Or browse online by series:
www.peterlang.com

www.ingramcontent.com/pod-product-compliance
Lightning Source LLC
Chambersburg PA
CBHW081737270326
41932CB00020B/3310